# HIKING WASHINGTON'S
# ALPINE LAKES WILDERNESS

# Contact

## Help Us Keep This Guide Up to Date

Every effort has been made by the author and editors to make this guide as accurate and useful as possible. However, many things can change after a guide is published—trails are rerouted, regulations change, techniques evolve, facilities come under new management, etc.

We would love to hear from you concerning your experiences with this guide and how you feel it could be improved and kept up to date. While we may not be able to respond to all comments and suggestions, we'll take them to heart and we'll also make certain to share them with the author. Please send your comments and suggestions to the following address:

> The Globe Pequot Press
> Reader Response/Editorial Department
> P.O. Box 480
> Guilford, CT 06437

Or you may e-mail us at:

> editorial@globe-pequot.com

Thanks for your input, and happy travels!

# *Hiking*
# WASHINGTON'S ALPINE LAKES WILDERNESS

## Day Hikes and Easy Overnights

## Jeff Smoot

FALCON®

GUILFORD, CONNECTICUT
HELENA, MONTANA
AN IMPRINT OF THE GLOBE PEQUOT PRESS

**A FALCON GUIDE** ®

Interior photos by the author
Maps by Moore Creative Design © The Globe Pequot Press

Library of Congress Cataloging-in-Publication Data
Smoot, Jeff.
  Hiking Washington's Alpine Lakes Wilderness : day hikes and easy overnights / Jeff Smoot. — 1st ed.
    p. cm.
  Includes bibliographical references.
  ISBN 0-7627-1176-0
    1. Hiking—Washington (State)—Alpine Lakes Wilderness—Guidebooks. 2. Trails—Washington (State)—Alpine Lakes Wilderness—Guidebooks. 3. Alpine Lakes Wilderness (Wash.)—Guidebooks. I. Title.

GV199.42.W2 A467 2003
917.97—dc21
                              2002192717


Manufactured in the United States of America
First Edition/First Printing

Table of

# Contents

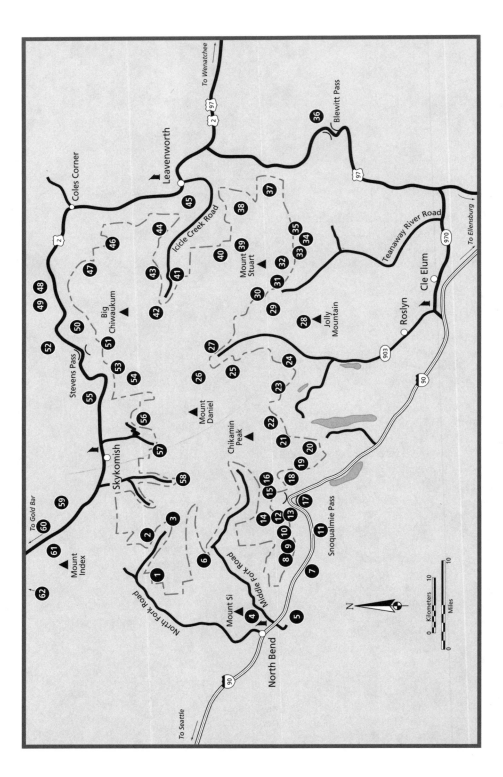

## Teanaway River Area

## Leavenworth Area

## Chiwaukum Mountains and Lake Wenatchee Area

## Stevens Pass Area

## Skykomish River Area

# Preface

When writing guidebooks, I am constantly reminded of the need for conservancy by wilderness visitors. This project was no exception. The Alpine Lakes Wilderness is one of the most accessible wilderness areas in Washington. Almost every trail listed in this guide is within one or two hours' drive of millions of people. Because of this, it is heavily used and heavily abused. Most wilderness users—hikers, climbers, skiers, and scramblers included—do take care to minimize their impact. However, with the many thousands who come to the wilderness areas each year, and the resulting overuse and abuse of many otherwise pristine areas, there is much room for improvement.

I cannot deny that guidebooks such as this one are partly responsible for the crush of visitors to our wilderness areas. But guidebooks have been around for decades and have already lured thousands of naïve visitors to the wilderness, to trample a subalpine meadow or cut a switchback. Of course, guidebooks and their authors are not solely to blame for the overuse of wilderness. With the popularity of hiking and climbing, and the influx of new residents to this state, our wilderness is shrinking at a rapid pace. In response, permit systems, quotas, and user fees are being implemented at wilderness areas throughout America. It is true what they say: we *are* loving our wilderness to death. It is my hope that this guidebook will adequately address issues of conservancy and help to educate uninitiated wilderness visitors in the ways of the "Wilderness Ethic."

It is not the guidebooks, really, that are to blame for abuses to our wilderness areas. It is people. In order to preserve our wilderness—or what is left of it—for future generations, each visitor must treat the wilderness with care, with love even. Those who love the wilderness do not cut switchbacks, discard trash, cut trees, harass wildlife, or foul streams and lakes; they come and go, in quiet appreciation, leaving no trace of their visit except a few dusty bootprints along the trail.

Although we won't likely wear our wilderness down with our boot soles, we may greatly detract from the beauty and serenity of the mountain environment unless we think and act in ways appropriate to preserving our wilderness areas.

A large part of the wilderness is discovery and exploration. In that spirit, this guide won't give away all of the surprises. This is not a fully illustrated instruction book for preassembled adventures; rather, it is a starting point for those who wish to discover and explore the trails of the Alpine Lakes Wilderness. While this guide follows the Falcon guidelines and provides more of a step-by-step description of many trails than some other guides, hopefully users of this guide will get where they are going without missing the best part of the outdoor experience—the adventure—in the process.

# Acknowledgments

I f anything is true in guidebook writing, "It's not what you know; it's who you know." Without the help of others, this guidebook would have been nearly impossible. I acknowledge those who assisted with this project, whether for providing trail information, photographs, or chapter reviews; for referring me along to someone who had information; or for chatting with me along a trail or accompanying me on a hike. Thanks to Morgan Balogh, Jim Busch, Pat Gentry, Chris and Katie Griffes, Rick Hack, Chris and Don Hanson, Darren and Ann Nelson, Michael and Kris Stanton, and Doug Weaver. Appreciation is extended to Lisa Therrell, Bill Soberoski, Lucy Schmidt, and Tom Davis of the U.S. Forest Service for providing current trail information and maintenance updates. Special thanks to Pat Gentry for driving me to distant trailheads and picking me up at others. My appreciation also to those who maintain Web sites devoted to hiking in the Cascades, which proved to be excellent sources of trail updates and information. Thanks also to the many hikers I met along the trail, who shared their experiences and told me things I never could have learned in a lifetime of hiking these trails. The list goes on and on, and I have certainly forgotten someone, whom I hope is very understanding.

Very special thanks to my wife, Karen, and daughters, Lauren and Andrea, for accompanying me on occasional hikes and for their patience and support throughout this and my many other writing projects. And as always, thanks to my parents for letting me run wild in the mountains in my youth.

# Map Legend

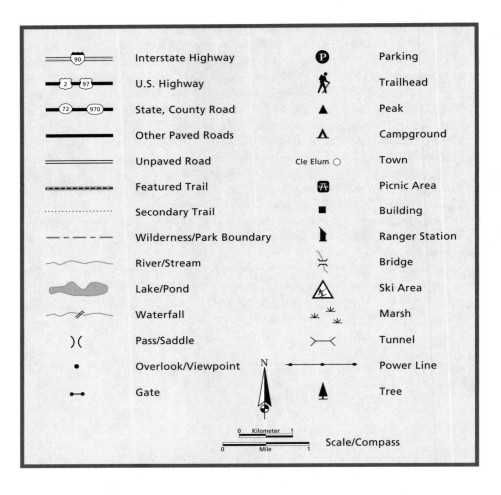

| Symbol | Label | Symbol | Label |
|---|---|---|---|
| (90) | Interstate Highway | **P** | Parking |
| (2) (97) | U.S. Highway | 🚶 | Trailhead |
| (72) (970) | State, County Road | ▲ | Peak |
| — | Other Paved Roads | ⛺ | Campground |
| — | Unpaved Road | Cle Elum ○ | Town |
| -·-·-·- | Featured Trail | ⛩ | Picnic Area |
| ........ | Secondary Trail | ■ | Building |
| – – – – | Wilderness/Park Boundary | ▌ | Ranger Station |
| ～～ | River/Stream | | Bridge |
| Lake/Pond | Lake/Pond | ⚠ | Ski Area |
| Waterfall | Waterfall | | Marsh |
| )( | Pass/Saddle | >—< | Tunnel |
| ● | Overlook/Viewpoint | •—•—• | Power Line |
| •—• | Gate | 🌲 | Tree |

N

| 0 | Kilometer | 1 |
| 0 | Mile | 1 |

Scale/Compass

# Hiking the Alpine Lakes Wilderness

The Alpine Lakes Wilderness straddles the heart of Washington's Cascade Range. It includes a majority of the rivers, streams, lakes, old-growth forest, and mountain terrain lying between Snoqualmie Pass and Stevens Pass and is roughly bordered by Washington State's two major cross-state highways, Interstate 90 and U.S. Highway 2, stretching east to west from Leavenworth to North Bend. Unlike many of the region's better-known wilderness areas, including Mount Baker, Glacier Peak, and Mount Adams, to name only a few, this 393,000-acre wilderness area has no crowning jewel such as a high volcano. Rather, its wealth of high lakes set among the region's varied landscape—from its majestic old-growth forests to its flowery subalpine meadows, from its deeply carved river valleys to its granite ridges and glaciated peaks—makes the Alpine Lakes Wilderness a very unique, very special place. Given the fact that the wilderness lies only an hour's drive away from the state's largest metropolitan and suburban area, the Alpine Lakes Wilderness is certainly one of the most-often visited wilderness areas in the western United States. People come here year-round, for recreation in all forms—hiking, backpacking, horseback riding, fishing, kayaking, climbing, skiing, and snowshoeing, to name only a few.

The uniqueness of the Alpine Lakes area was recognized by its designation as a wilderness area in 1976, although it was considered a unique place long before an Act of Congress made it official.

## Geology

The Alpine Lakes Wilderness has a complex geologic history. The wilderness lies at the southern margin of the North Cascades, which are among the most complex, varied, and rugged mountains in North America. In contrast to the gentle woodland peaks and high volcanoes of the southern Cascade Range, the North Cascades are rugged beyond compare. Actually, the range has been likened to the Swiss Alps, which, although higher in elevation, are equaled if not exceeded in sheer relief and volume of ice by the peaks of the North Cascades. Uplifted by colliding continental plates, and scoured and carved by glaciers, the mountains of the North Cascades rise abruptly from deep glacial valleys in steep cliffs terminating in sharp rocky points and crests. Rugged glaciers drape the highest peaks and hang menacingly from north-facing cirques and basins. Craggy granite escarpments lord over the deep valleys, while scattered volcanic and metamorphic peaks maintain a lower profile.

The Alpine Lakes Wilderness is one of the most rugged areas of the Cascade Range. Although in terms of sheer relief it does not quite compare with the North

Cascades, it is still a sublime region of deep, glacier-carved valleys, pristine sub-alpine meadows, and craggy peaks rising to over 9,000 feet. The wilderness is var-ied. A few geologic features typify the wilderness. Mount Stuart and the Stuart Range are the highest and most rugged of the Alpine Lakes Wilderness mountains, a granite escarpment rising thousands of feet above deep glacial valleys, reminis-cent of the Sierra Nevada. The Snoqualmie Crest peaks running from Snoqualmie Pass northward to Dutch Miller Gap are the Picket Range in miniature, a row of steep, craggy, glaciated peaks rising above wild basins and valleys. Gold Creek is a prototypical glacial valley, a broad U-shaped valley, deeply forested and flanked by steep cliffs and ridges. Mount Daniel, near the center of the wilderness, is an old volcanic remnant scoured by glaciers. The Wenatchee Mountains, extending nearly the length of the wilderness, are an old range of craggy peaks and ridges dot-ted with lakes, in wooded basins and granite cirques, weathered by snow and wind, cut deep by streams and rivers. Chiwaukum, Icicle, and Ingalls Creeks flow east-ward toward the Columbia River, down deep valleys, canyons, and gorges between high ridges and stark, granite peaks. The Snoqualmie and Skykomish Rivers flow westward into Puget Sound, down deep old-growth forest valleys, fed by rivers and streams flowing from glaciers and lakes down through quiet, narrow forest valleys, some impenetrably thick with brush. Obviously, each area of the wilderness has its own unique characteristics.

Although the mountains and valleys are important geologic features, what is unique and special about the Alpine Lakes Wilderness is the lakes. There are hun-dreds of lakes, from tiny ponds to huge reservoirs, some deep in forested valleys, some high on barren alpine plateaus. A majority of the lakes owe their existence to glaciers, which scoured the plateaus, basins, and valleys, carving out cirques that later filled with meltwater, depositing moraines that dammed the flow of streams and rivers. Nearly every trail in the wilderness leads to a tarn, pond, or lake. Some trails follow a chain of lakes higher and higher up a wilderness valley. Beyond the trails are more lakes. And more lakes.

## Flora and Fauna

Although relatively few visitors to the Alpine Lakes Wilderness come exclusively to seek out species of plants and animals—with the exception of photographers and wildflower enthusiasts, of course—the region's abundant flora and fauna is an inte-gral part of the wilderness experience. Learning to recognize different species of plants and animals in their native environment is not always easy, but it is certainly very rewarding.

The plant life in the Alpine Lakes Wilderness is varied and abundant. The low-land forests are occupied by giants: old-growth Douglas fir, western hemlock, west-ern red cedar, and occasional stands of sitka spruce. In their shade grow ferns, mosses, and a variety of herbs, shrubs, and small trees. Alder, maple, and salmonberry line old road grades outside the wilderness and fill in available space within the wilderness boundary. River bottoms and seeping slopes grow thick with mosses, ferns, and shrubs such as salmonberry, thimbleberry, and devil's club, with shade-tolerant hemlock starts and red huckleberry bushes shooting up from every nurse log and rotten stump. Slide alder, maple, and willow dominate avalanche slopes; mountain-ash, huckleberry, and white rhododendron on mid-elevation slopes. At higher elevations, the Douglas firs, hemlocks, and cedars are joined by Pacific silver fir, one of the predominant species of the wilderness forests. Above timberline, mountain-hemlock and subalpine fir predominate, with low-lying heather, juniper, and huckleberry shrubs complimenting wide-open meadows of grasses and wildflowers. Stands of larch trees grow in high lake basins in the eastern portion of the wilderness. Above treeline, gnarled mountain-hemlock and subalpine fir krummholz grow prostrate among lichen-dotted rocks. A few hardy flower species grow in high basins, meadows, and on high ridges, clinging to the barren, windswept soil.

Wildflowers are the most sought-after plants in the wilderness. The wildflower displays here are legendary: tiger lily, columbine, lupine, aster, trillium, pearly everlasting, valerian, skyrocket, shooting star, penstemon, lousewort, bog gentian, monkey flower, bead lily, glacier lily, queen's cup, monk's hood, blue bell, bell-flower, bleeding heart, Tweedy's lewissia, balsamroot, wild orchids—too many to name. If you want to see wildflowers, come from mid-July to mid-August when the flowers are usually at their peak, especially in meadows and along streambanks. In contrast to the wildflowers, the old-growth trees are equally impressive. The contrast between the second-growth forests outside the wilderness boundary and the virgin forests within the wilderness is striking and will make a lasting impression. You'll know you've reached the wilderness boundary just by the size of the trees and by the quiet sense of wonder they inspire.

On certain summer weekends, humans might seem to be the most abundant animal species in the Alpine Lakes Wilderness. With the exception of insects and birds, you will probably encounter more people on the trail than you will other wildlife. But even though you don't see them, they see you. They are everywhere. Chipmunks and ground squirrels are commonly seen scampering across the trail, as are Douglas' squirrels, rustling in the branches overhead, scolding you as you pass or nipping off seed cones that come whizzing down all around you. Hoary marmots, the "groundhogs of the west," are abundant in talus and rocky areas at higher elevations. The marmot's shrill whistle is easily recognizable, and they can often be seen scurrying through the talus. More elusive is the pika (say PEEK-a), another talus dweller commonly heard along the trail. These guinea pig–sized members of the rabbit family (sometimes called rock rabbits) have a very shrill "eek." You'll see brown rabbits on lowland trails and forest roads and may see snowshoe hares, although you are likely to see only their tracks in the snow.

Beavers used to be abundant in lowland valleys but now are a rarity, although old beaver dams may still be encountered. Porcupines are sometimes seen along the trail and are easily identified by their lumbering gait and sharp quills. They live on tree bark, leaves, and branches, like the beaver, but they climb trees instead of

*Alpine Lakes Wilderness boundary sign*

cutting them down. While you rarely need to worry about porcupine encounters, dogs frequently get a little too close and end up with a bunch of quills embedded in their snout. If you leash your dog like you're supposed to, this should not happen. What hikers should worry about is porcupines eating their boots, backpack, clothing—and certain auto parts! Porcupines crave fat and salt, and will eat anything to get it. If you see a porcupine lurking about your camp, sleep close to your boots and pack straps!

Snakes and lizards are abundant in all areas; rattlesnakes are rarely encountered but may be found in lowland areas at the eastern fringe of the wilderness. You will no doubt find frogs along many lowland trails, especially near streams and boggy areas; watch your step! The lakes are full of varieties of trout, mostly too small to be keepers but not so small as to keep anglers from bothering. There are all kinds of wild birds. You are most likely to recognize the big birds—brown and bald eagles, peregrine falcons, Cooper's and red-tail hawks, kestrels, ravens, woodpeckers, kingfishers, and owls—but the little birds are more common, especially chickadees, nuthatches, finches, jays, and juncos. Early-morning visitors to high ridges and peaks may be rewarded with close views of soaring eagles and hawks. Canadian jays, those "camp robbers" of infamy, will eat right out of your hand or your unattended bag of trail mix, if you let them.

Aside from birds, the most commonly seen animal is the black-tailed deer, abundant throughout the wilderness. Deer are most often seen early in the morning and late in the day in lowland and subalpine meadows, although a stray or small herd may be seen grazing in shady forest at midday. Elk are common in the Cascades but are only occasionally seen in the Alpine Lakes Wilderness, usually only in the Cle Elum and Teanaway regions. Mountain goats are more prevalent, especially at higher elevations east of the Cascade crest. Goats are usually wary of hikers and keep their distance, but some goats don't seem to mind. Like porcupines, mountain goats crave salt, and they don't care where they get it. For that reason, hikers are requested to urinate on rocks instead of plants or dirt in the alpine zone, so the goats don't tear up the meadows in their unabashed quest for salt.

In fall, hunters prowl the trails in and around the wilderness in search of deer, elk, goats and their predators, bears and cougars, both of which are prevalent throughout the Alpine Lakes Wilderness. Black bears are often encountered by hikers. Usually the bear will run away upon a hiker's approach, but occasionally a bear will stand its ground. When a bear stands up, it's trying to get a better look at you. Conventional wisdom says to stand your ground, make noise by talking or singing, and spread out your arms to make yourself "look big" to the bear. Bear attacks are rare around here; usually bears are after food, and hikers must take measures to protect their food—and themselves—from bears. How? For one, don't cook or clean up anywhere near where you camp, but at least 200 feet away. Then change out of the clothes you cooked in. Remove all food from your campsite and tent, and either store it in a bear-proof container or hang it from a tree. Bears are resourceful and can break into "bear-proof" food containers and knock down food bags that are improperly hung, so put a little thought into where and how you hang your food, lest you find your cache stolen the next morning. Bears seem to be the worst in the eastern half of the wilderness during summer and fall, especially in lowland areas near campgrounds and on the fringe of cities. Bears near Leavenworth are particularly pesky, raiding bakery garbage cans and campers' cars and coolers in broad daylight. The bears around here haven't learned all of the tricks of their national park brethren and are therefore more inclined to run away from you than bluff charge or stand their ground; some bears, though, seem remarkably unconcerned with hikers and continue pawing at rotten logs and snuffling for mushrooms right beside the trail, forcing hikers to make a wide detour. The presence of bears on hiking trails is another reason to keep your dog leashed, or leave it at home. The Washington Department of Fish and Wildlife publishes a brochure about black bears; it is available at Forest Service offices, a must-read for wilderness travelers. Grizzly bears are rumored to live in the North Cascades, and there have been reported sightings in the Alpine Lakes Wilderness, but no one I've talked to has seen one this far south. Perhaps the grizzlies sighted were just passing through; either that, or someone mistook a big black bear for a grizzly.

Less often seen but potentially more dangerous to hikers are cougars, or mountain lions, pumas, catamounts, or what have you. These wild cats have seen a growth in population since dog hunts were banned several years ago. Although very few hikers have been attacked by cougars, there have been an increasing number of encounters, mostly along lowland logging roads and trails. Don't worry too much. You probably will never see a cougar in the wild, let alone face one down on a trail. But if you do, experts recommend that you not turn and run, as that only encourages the cats to chase you. Instead, stand your ground, maintain eye contact, spread your arms to look big, and make noise to scare the cat away, and if the cat does not run away, back away slowly until well out of sight and then turn and walk quickly away. My instinct would be to pick up rocks and sticks and throw them at the cougar while yelling as loud as possible, and that is recommended as a last resort if the cat won't leave or gives you a menacing look or seems to be getting ready to pounce on you, fangs bared, ears back, hissing. If attacked, fight back hard to let the cat know you aren't prey. Hit it with rocks, sticks, your camera, pack, fists, whatever; grab its throat and squeeze hard. Especially keep children close, and don't try to save your dog if it happens to be attacked. There haven't been very many fatalities in cougar attacks around here. In other areas, cougars seem to have attacked solitary hikers and trail runners, especially children who have strayed too far ahead on the trail. The Washington Department of Fish and Wildlife publishes a brochure about cougars; it is available at Forest Service offices, a must-read for wilderness travelers.

To learn more about how to deal with bears and cougars or to find out about any recent sightings or problems, call or visit one of the ranger stations listed in Appendix B.

Obviously, this is a simplistic overview of plant and animal life within the Alpine Lakes Wilderness. There are so many species of plants and animals within the wilderness that to name and describe them all here would leave little room for anything else. Whole volumes have been published documenting the plant life of the Cascade mountains. Most hikers aren't interested in the minutiae of minor subspecies of moss, lichen, or rodentia, nor do they likely come only to seek out particular plant or wildlife species. Visitors interested in identifying plants should consult the list in Appendix E for topic-specific references. My favorite is *Cascade-Olympic Natural History*, an entertaining text with excellent color photos of many of the commonly seen plants and animals.

## Climate

Weather is not always poor in the Pacific Northwest, even if it seems that way. The Puget Sound region bordering the Cascades on the west is considered "rainy" by most standards but has a lower average annual cumulative rainfall than many East Coast cities. However, the Pacific Northwest's reputation for precipitation is not entirely unfounded. Washington's Olympic Peninsula has one of the highest measured cumulative annual rainfalls in the nation. The slopes of Mount Rainier, Mount Baker, and Mount Olympus have hosted record snowfalls. When it rains in the Pacific Northwest, it is usually a steady drizzle lasting several days, hence the reputation for rain. If it's not raining, rejoice—and go hiking! But don't let a little rain stop you from going hiking. Rainy-day hikes may not have the inspiring views of distant peaks and valleys, but you see a lot more when you aren't always looking off in the distance.

In a nutshell, this is how Washington mountain weather works: Warm, moist air blows in off the Pacific Ocean, squeezing moisture-laden clouds against the Olympic mountains. These clouds, like large sponges, dump excessive rain on the western slopes of the mountains until, relieved of their burden, the clouds rise over the mountains and drift eastward across Puget Sound, where the process is repeated against the Cascade foothills with similar effect, although the volume of rainfall is generally less than that which falls on the rain forests of the Olympic Peninsula. Once the clouds have dumped their load on the western slopes of the Cascades, they again drift eastward over the eastern slopes of the range, which are markedly drier and less heavily vegetated. This warm, moist marine air condenses and freezes very rapidly when it hits the cold, snowy Cascades and Olympics, which accounts for high winds and the tremendous snowfalls each year. This is a bit simplistic, but it is close enough for this guide's purposes.

*Clouds over Mount Stuart*

# Wilderness Permit Requirements

**P**ermits are required for all entry into the Alpine Lakes Wilderness, including day use and overnight visits. Self-issue permits are available at all wilderness trailheads. Sign in, attach the permit to your pack, and proceed. Your permit must be visible at all times. If you hike more than one trail during your trip, fill out a new permit for each hike. Some people don't bother, but they should. Among other things, permit data is used to monitor the number of hikers using a given trail, which is in turn used to determine the level of maintenance a trail receives.

Overnight visits to the Enchantments permit area require advance registration to limit the number of visitors to this beautiful but overused area, including Snow, Colchuck, Stuart, Eightmile, and Caroline Lakes, as well as the fabled Enchantment Lakes. Contact the Leavenworth Ranger District Office for permit details. At present, day use is still unrestricted with a trailhead day-use permit. If you get caught hiking through the Enchantments without a day-use permit or camping out in the Enchantment area without an overnight permit, you may be fined.

## Northwest Forest Passes

A trailhead parking pass (presently called a Northwest Forest Pass) is required for parking at or within 0.25 mile of most trailheads included in this guide. These passes can be obtained from Forest Service district offices and most outdoor retailers. A one-day pass is presently $5.00, an annual pass $30.00. If you do a lot of hiking in Washington or Oregon, the annual pass is well worth the money. The fee is supposed to be used in part for trail maintenance and construction, and there is evidence of this in new footbridges and trailhead improvements. Many hikers resent the imposition of yet another fee for using the wilderness, but without this money the Forest Service might have to cut back on trail maintenance, which might result in roads and trails being abandoned. Some hikers think that would be just fine, since it would reduce the number of visitors to the wilderness, allowing the wilderness to become true wilderness. Politics aside, if you don't want to get a ticket, get a pass.

## Sno-Park Passes

A separate parking pass—the Sno-Park Pass—is required at winter recreation trailheads. Sno-Park Pass fees are used to clear and maintain access to ski and snowshoe trailheads. Hikers planning a winter or spring hike may need to get a Sno-Park Pass.

## Wilderness Regulations

In addition to permit requirements, Alpine Lakes Wilderness use is subject to certain regulations. These regulations are posted at most trailheads and are summarized on the back of your permit. They include the following:

- Maximum group size is twelve, including all people and stock. In the Enchantment Lakes, maximum group size is eight. The Forest Service refers to this as the "heartbeat rule"; count the number of heartbeats in your group, not legs. Include your dog in the count.
- No motorized or mechanized equipment is allowed. That means no motorbikes, bicycles, chainsaws, carts, or aircraft allowed within the wilderness boundary.
- Many areas have camping restrictions such as setbacks from lakes or designated sites, usually at least 200 feet from lakes and certain meadows.
- No campfires above 5,000 feet elevation or at popular lakes and meadows. Signs usually warn you of entry into a no-campfire area.
- Cutting switchbacks is not allowed. Stay on established trails.
- Caching of supplies for longer than forty-eight hours is prohibited.
- Do not cut trees, snags, or boughs. Do not walk or camp in areas closed for restoration.
- Pack out all litter.
- Bury human waste and pet waste well away from camps and water sources. Dispose of wash water well away from water sources.

# How to Use This Guide

This is a guide to day hikes and short overnight hikes, those hikes that are short and accessible enough that most hikers can drive to the trailhead, complete the hike, and return home the same day, or camp out at their option. Originally intended to cover only trails in the Alpine Lakes Wilderness, this guide was expanded to include trails outside of the wilderness, including many of the popular hikes across the highway. Those who enjoy hiking in the Alpine Lakes Wilderness region will hopefully appreciate the inclusion of these other hikes and the fact that they do not have to buy three separate guidebooks to read about them. However, inclusion of trails outside of the wilderness came at a price, namely the exclusion of many of the longer hikes in the Alpine Lakes Wilderness. Day hiking is certainly the most popular wilderness activity, but a hiking guide to the Alpine Lakes that doesn't include Tuck and Robin Lakes, the Pacific Crest Trail, or the Enchantment Lakes? Heresy, you might say. Indeed. So a second volume of this guide is forthcoming, devoted solely to backpacking the longer trails of the Alpine Lakes Wilderness. This guide hints at what lies beyond "trail's end" for day hikers. True wilderness hikers will venture forth without a guidebook, trail or no trail.

This guide is intended to assist hikers and wilderness visitors in locating and following the many, varied hiking trails in the Alpine Lakes Wilderness. To that end, each chapter of this guide includes written descriptions with driving directions, trailhead and permit information, mileage and elevation charts, a description of the hike including scenic highlights, and a map showing the approximate route of the trail. Trail descriptions and maps are deemed accurate, based on in-field observations and other information, but may vary from season to season and year to year. Maps are approximate only and should not be relied upon except to the extent that they will help get you to your chosen hike and on the right trail. Although these descriptions and maps will be helpful in choosing and following a given trail, they are not exact and cannot substitute for wilderness experience. Use your best judgment on each hike, based on what you see when you arrive, regardless of the written descriptions, illustrations, and photographs contained in hiking guides. Basically, this guide will show you what's there and approximately where to go; from there it's up to you.

All route descriptions and directions assume you are facing your objective or your direction of travel, unless otherwise stated. Whenever there is apparent confusion in the directions given, an approximate compass direction will be provided for clarity. All distances, including road and trail mileages, elevation gain and loss figures, and elevations of points along the trail, are approximate only.

Each hike chapter begins with a list of particulars about the hike, including a description, mileage, a difficulty rating, elevation gain, maps, and so on, following the Falcon guidelines.

## Overview

The hike description begins with an overview, a one sentence summary of where you're going and how you're going to get there. It will let you know whether you are going to a lake or summit, whether the trail loops, and so on.

## Distance

The mileage given for each hike is for a round-trip from the trailhead to the primary destination and back or for the loop hike, where applicable. Mileage listed for some hikes will differ slightly from the "official" mileage published by the Forest Service or other sources. Since nearly every source of information lists a different mileage and the author did not take a measuring wheel to each trail, mileage given is approximate only. Your actual mileage may vary.

## Difficulty

Each hike's overall difficulty is given as Easy, Moderate, or Strenuous. No particular formula was used to determine a hike's difficulty. Elevation gain and distance factored in, but were not necessarily determinative. For instance, a 10-mile hike with little elevation gain could be called Easy, while a 10-mile hike with steady elevation gain might be Moderate, and a 10-mile hike with 9 miles of level hiking and 1 mile of steep hiking could be Strenuous. Likewise, a short hike with lots of elevation gain might be Strenuous. In general, if the hike gains less than 500 feet per mile average, it will be Easy or Moderate. If the hike gains between 500 and 1,000 feet per mile, it will be Moderate or Strenuous. And if the hike gains 1,000 feet per mile or more, or has any segment where elevation gain is over 1,000 feet in a mile, it will most likely be Strenuous or possibly Very Strenuous. This is a subjective rating, which really just depends on the hike. Your fitness level will also play a large part in determining whether a hike seems easy or strenuous on a given day.

Some hikes are also described as Difficult, which usually means those hikes follow trails that are either unmaintained or difficult to follow due to overgrowth, fallen trees, washouts, rocky tread, risky stream crossings, and the like.

## Best Season

The best season for hiking in the Alpine Lakes Wilderness is early summer through early fall. Some of the lower elevation trails are snow-free almost all year, but many high-elevation trails are impassable to a majority of hikers until August or even September, depending on the previous winter's snowpack. Some years you can hike in the high country until early November; other years, it starts snowing in late September. Some hikers are willing to brave snow-covered trails; some even prefer it. Conditions vary from year to year, so the "best season" given in this guide may not be the best season if the winter snowpack is deep or the spring was unusually rainy. It is always best to check trail conditions before your hike, so you aren't disappointed to find your trail buried under feet of snow or the access road washed out. When hiking in early season, carry an ice ax and know how to use it to self-arrest, since you will probably be crossing snowfields as you venture into the high country.

## Traffic

All trails are open for foot traffic. Some are open for stock (horses, llamas, and the like). A few are open to mountain bikes, at least to a certain point. No hike in this guide is open for motorbike use, except for two that are outside the Alpine Lakes Wilderness—Jolly Mountain Trail and the last 6 miles of Nason Ridge Trail, which can be bypassed. All allowed trail uses will be noted in the introduction to each hike.

The volume of traffic on each trail is described as Light, Moderate, or Heavy. Again, this is not based on any set formula but was based on typical weekend volume, which is when a majority of us go hiking. Light traffic means you are likely to encounter only a few other hikers on the trail during a summer weekend. Moderate traffic means you may encounter several hikers and groups of hikers on the trail. Heavy traffic means you'll be running into hikers and their dogs all along the trail. If you want some solitude, come on a weekday when the trails are much less crowded.

Dogs are not allowed on any trails in the Enchantment Lakes area, including Snow Lakes, Colchuck and Stuart Lakes, and Eightmile and Caroline Lakes, nor at Ingalls Lake. For the most part, dogs are allowed on other trails in the wilderness, except as noted in particular hike chapters. Some hikers are annoyed by dogs and get angry about them being on the trail. Most hikers don't mind a dog or two on a hike, as long as they are leashed and under control.

## High Point

An approximate high point of each hike is provided because most hikers like to know how high the trail leads. In some cases, the high point is estimated and rounded to the nearest 100 feet. When the high point is a summit, an official elevation is given.

## Maps

USGS (United States Geological Survey) and Green Trails maps are listed for each hike. The USGS maps tend to be outdated; Green Trails maps include trail mileage and elevation data and are popular with hikers. A good but somewhat dated topographic map of the entire Alpine Lakes Wilderness is published by the Alpine Lakes Protection Society. Other maps covering the Alpine Lakes Wilderness are listed in Appendix C, along with several outdoor retailers who carry them. Please note that none of these maps is entirely accurate, so check with the Forest Service before setting out on a hike, especially a long hike, in case trails have been rerouted, closed, or abandoned.

## Elevation Profiles

All hike descriptions include elevation profiles. Use these charts to get a general picture of how much elevation gain and loss a hike entails. The charts are not meant to be a detailed foot-by-foot account of the route but serve as a quick glimpse of the overall elevation change.

## For More Information

Because road and trail conditions change throughout the season, it is highly recommended that you check road and trail conditions and current regulations regarding trail use, camping setbacks, and other information before each hike by calling the local Forest Service office or other agency managing the trail listed for each hike. Phone numbers and addresses are listed in Appendix B.

## Dogs and Stock Animals

Dogs are allowed on most hikes included in this guide but must be leashed on all hikes off Interstate 90 west of Rachel Lake Trail and off U.S. Highway 2 west of Stevens Pass. Although dogs are not required to be leashed on all trails, as a matter of trail etiquette it is suggested that dogs be leashed so they don't scare off wildlife, spook horses, attack other dogs, or annoy hikers. Some hikers are offended by dogs on the trail, leashed or not, but most hikers are at least tolerant of dogs as long as the dogs and their owners are not a nuisance. Dogs are not permitted in the Enchantments permit area including Nada and Snow Lakes, the Enchantments, Colchuck and Stuart Lakes, and Eightmile and Caroline Lakes, or at Ingalls Lake.

Stock, including horses, llamas, and other pack animals, are permitted on many trails in the Alpine Lakes Wilderness. Hikes open for stock animals are noted in each hike chapter. Stock must be contained at least 200 feet from all lakes. If hobbled, stock can be tied to trees larger than 6 inches in diameter for up to four hours. When using highlines, hobble stock standing within 8 feet of trees. Use only processed stock feed to avoid introducing exotic grasses and other plants into the wilderness. This is not a guide to horse packing or stock trails; for specific information about where and how to hike with stock, contact the Forest Service.

When encountering horses and other stock animals along the trail, hikers should yield the right of way. Step off the trail on the downhill side. Horses tend to shy away from hikers, and their riders get mad when you stand uphill, since the horses get close to the trail's edge and have occasionally stumbled, dumping their riders and provisions.

# Backcountry Safety and Hazards

## Hiking Safely

All things considered, hiking on trails is probably the safest mode of wilderness travel, where usually only weather and your own or others' actions are reasons for concern. But hiking, like other modes of wilderness travel, has numerous objective dangers, and the hikes described in this guide are no exception. Hikers venturing into the wilderness subject themselves to numerous hazards. Some trails become treacherous after dark or during poor weather; losing the trail after dark is a leading cause of hiking accidents, well justifying packing a flashlight, especially given the frequency with which many overly ambitious hikers find themselves hiking out in the dark. High rainfall and snowmelt cause flooding, which can erode or undermine trails. In certain glacier-fed stream valleys, outburst floods are an infrequent but potentially serious hazard. More often, it is high streams and rivers during early-season snowmelt that cause problems; high water can wash out footlogs and bridges, making for difficult and potentially dangerous stream crossings. Falling trees and rocks have killed unfortunate hikers; these hazards are more prevalent in areas burned over by recent fires. Loose rock and gravel on trails can cause slips, falls, and sprained ankles or worse. Snow, ice, and mud on trails can be treacherous. A slip on snow, ice, wet rocks or roots, or mud can cause broken wrists and more. Snow bridges over streams easily collapse. Footlogs may be slippery; fording streams can be tricky; a plunge into an ice-cold stream can quickly lead to hypothermia. Brush covering the trail can hide rocks, roots, and holes, and can trip you up. An unseen branch can cut and scar or put an eye out. An untied bootlace can lead to a broken leg or worse. Lightning can strike anywhere but is especially frequent on the high eastern ridges and peaks during the summer months. Bears and cougars lurk in the mountains, and although animal attacks are rare, they do occur. Rattlesnakes are present in some areas on the eastern fringe of the wilderness. Insects, including bees, wasps, yellow jackets, and ticks, can cause problems for hikers, especially those with allergies. There is also the human element to consider; although rare, hikers are sometimes assaulted by other hikers.

Despite all of the obvious potential dangers, thousands of hikers make it into and out of the wilderness each year without incident or injury. However, we shouldn't be too smug about this. There are no guarantees of safety in the mountains, so proceed with caution and at your own risk. This guide will make an effort to point out obvious objective hazards. Warnings in this guide are intended to let users know of dangers that are frequently encountered on given trails. However, no guide can accurately or completely foresee every conceivable accident waiting to happen, nor point out every latent hazard along the trail. Proceed with due regard for your own safety no matter what this or any guidebook says.

This guide does not presume to know every feature of every trail or road mentioned within its pages. Mountain environments change from day to day, week to week, season to season, and from year to year. Rockfalls, avalanches, floods, storms, and other occasional and seasonal changes will continue to alter the nature, course, and safety of roads and trails. Trails erode, streams and rivers flood, bridges are washed out, trees fall or are blown down, rocks freeze and thaw and tumble down, and so on. Trails may be relocated or closed. Because wilderness features can change from day to day and season to season, hiking trails may vary accordingly. A feature identified in a trail description may have changed or even disappeared between now and the time you are looking for it. Changes can and do occur overnight. Be prepared!

You should check weather conditions before each trip. Make sure you and your entire party have adequate food, water, clothing, and experience for your chosen hike. Don't be afraid to turn back if weather or trail conditions make proceeding unwise. There are plenty of days to go hiking in the future and plenty of other trails to follow.

This guide occasionally suggests a cross-country route or scramble as an option. No off-trail route is recommended for any but those with proven route-finding ability and experience. No scrambling or climbing route is recommended for any but those with proper equipment and experience in alpine scrambling and climbing. When you venture off the trail, you subject yourself to greater risks. Leave the trail with caution, exercising good judgment, at your own risk.

Safety rules for driving to the mountains are not included in this guide, since it is assumed that all drivers on our state's highways are duly licensed to drive and therefore understand the elementary principles of auto safety. Still, there are occasional auto accidents in the mountains, usually due to inattention or unfamiliarity with driving on mountain roads. Slow down, keep your eyes on the road, and your hands on the wheel. If you wish to view the scenery, pull off into a scenic turnout and then look about. Don't speed up forest roads; it is too easy to slide off the road in loose gravel, crash into oncoming traffic or wildlife crossing the road (or hikers walking up the road), or get forced off the road to avoid a collision. Most of all, pay attention to your driving!

Some may find the numerous safety suggestions and warnings in this guide to be a bit much. However, each year many inexperienced and ill-equipped visitors set off into the backcountry armed only with a water bottle and a bag of trail mix, and some wilderness visitors seem not to know any better than to walk off the edge of a cliff unless somebody tells them not to do so. Those who don't already know enough to stay out of harm's way are requested to heed this guide's warnings and to exercise a good measure of caution when traveling in the wilderness.

## Mountain Weather

Of all considerations of mountain travel in Washington's mountains, weather should be among the foremost to hikers. Many a day has began calm and clear only

*Keekwulee Falls, Denny Creek Trail*

to end in a storm. Effects of weather lead to more hiking fatalities (from hypothermia) than any other cause. The Cascade Range experiences severe storms each year, and these storms cannot always be predicted. Storms often come without any warning, sometimes with fatal consequences to unprepared hikers. But it doesn't take a big storm to create hazardous conditions. Prepare yourself for the worst, including wind, rain, and snow, no matter what the weatherman says.

Check the weather forecast and snow conditions before any hike. Although the weatherman is not always right about good weather, when it comes to poor weather—considering your life may be at stake—you should give him or her the benefit of the doubt. Weather resources, including on-line weather reports, are listed in Appendix D.

## Clothing and Equipment

Alpine Lakes Wilderness hikers should make clothing a primary consideration. It has been suggested that the only clothing modern hikers need is Gore-Tex. However, as a practical and economic matter, wool clothing is still recommended in the rainy Cascades and Olympics, as it retains some body heat even when wet. Cotton clothing is certainly more comfortable than wool, but when wet, cotton is worthless and can be deadly because it retains absolutely no body heat. Modern synthetics (e.g., polypropylene) have heat-retaining qualities similar to wool, with the comfort of cotton, making them a popular substitute for the heavy, scratchy wool garments us old-timers remember, provided rain-tight outer garments are worn in poor weather. However, these can also be expensive. Whatever you choose to wear, make sure you have warm, dry clothing available in case what you're wearing gets wet. And if you are hiking in the Alpine Lakes Wilderness, it *will* get wet!

Rain and wind-proof outer garments are a must for any mountain travel. Gore-Tex and other "waterproof" fabrics are excellent at repelling water and wind but are very expensive. A plastic poncho or less-expensive, all-weather parka may suffice for those who can't afford more high-tech, high-priced clothing. Hikers should have several light layers of clothing, which may be shed or donned as the temperature rises or falls or the wind comes up. Remember that your body temperature will rise and fall more often than the ambient temperature, depending on your level of exertion and the steepness of the trail, sun exposure, wind, and so on. A t-shirt, light wool sweater, polypro vest, and hooded Gore-Tex parka should cover you in almost every situation short of a full-on arctic blast. If all you have is a t-shirt and a jacket, you'll sweat or freeze all the way up the trail and never be comfortable.

Lug-soled, watertight boots are also recommended for all wilderness hikers, although modern lightweight boots and trail shoes are becoming more popular. A lightweight, multipurpose boot will do, but make sure your boots are waterproof or at least strongly water resistant unless you enjoy wet, shriveled, or frozen feet. Waterproofing is a must for whatever your footwear. Even on sunny days, you may end up with wet feet from wading through miles of dew-drenched underbrush. (Hint: Bring rain gear and an extra pair of socks even if the weatherman promises sunny skies!)

Lug-soled boots provide good traction and better protection against the pounding you will receive from rocks and roots on many hikes included in this guide.

Mittens or gloves and a warm hat are important accessories for all wilderness travel, particularly if you are hiking on snow or at high elevations. Always bring sunglasses to keep out harmful light rays during any snow or high-elevation travel. Gaiters are recommended for any snow and scree travel and for wading through wet underbrush. Sunscreen is often overlooked but is as important for your skin as sunglasses are for your eyes, particularly for extended snow and high-elevation travel.

The point of bringing proper clothing is to keep warm and dry in a hostile mountain environment. While it may be possible and enjoyable to hike these trails in shorts and a t-shirt on perfect, warm, windless days, there have been many hypothermia deaths and close calls attributed to wilderness hikers wearing casual clothing. Dress properly and prepare for the worst; your very life may depend on it.

Anyone venturing onto steep snow should carry and know how to use an ice ax. Many trails have dangerous snow crossings through early summer. Crampons may be helpful on snowy trails in winter and spring. Small instep crampons are preferred by winter hikers. While a climbing rope might seem like a bit much for a mere hike, when hiking some trails in early season, you never know when you might want to belay across an avalanche gully. For most of us, though, the prospect of such a crossing is sufficient incentive to turn back and try again later in the summer, when the snow is long gone. Don't climb or cross a snow slope lacking a safe runout. Even a short slide on snow can be dangerous if there are rocks, trees, or water at the bottom of the slope.

Some of the trails included in this guide pass through or enter old railroad tunnels, where a powerful headlamp, lantern, or flashlight is a necessity, and extra batteries are strongly recommended. Remember, it gets cold in tunnels and caves, so have warm clothes packed along so you don't freeze. If signs warn against entering a tunnel or cave, stay out!

## Ten Essentials

Everyone hiking in the Cascades should know the "ten essentials" by heart, but if not, here they are:

1. Map (in a waterproof cover)
2. Compass
3. Flashlight (with extra bulb and batteries)
4. Extra food (at least enough for an extra day)
5. Extra clothing (in a waterproof container)
6. Matches (in a waterproof container)
7. Candle or other fire starter
8. Knife
9. Sunglasses
10. First-aid kit

These items have, through time and experience, proven to be lifesavers when things go bad, even on short hikes. Of course, water, a water filter, and sunblock are very important to bring along, too. On long day hikes, a bivouac sac or plastic tarp could be a lifesaver in the event of a forced bivouac in the rain or wind. Some hikers eschew the ten essentials, or at least some of them. But then, a map carried in a waterproof container can do double duty as fire starter if an emergency arises. Each individual hiker will have his or her preferences as to what is really necessary and what is optional. Don't limit yourself only to these ten items.

## Hypothermia

Hypothermia is a genuine risk for all backcountry travelers, especially hikers in the Cascade Mountains. This often fatal lowering of the body temperature is brought on by continued exposure to low temperatures, winds, and rain soaking, usually a combination of all three. Hikers venturing too far from the safety and comfort of shelter with inadequate clothing risk hypothermia. Wool clothing and some synthetics, such as polypropylene, insulate even when wet and are recommended. However, without a weather-resistant shell, any insulating clothing has limitations. It doesn't have to be cold, wet, and miserable for hypothermia to set in. At high elevation, even a sunny day can be cool and breezy enough to bring on hypothermia. Do everything possible to stay warm and dry, particularly during rain and windy conditions. Heed the wind even on sunny summer days. At high elevations, a prevailing cold breeze may blow all day, lowering your body temperature little by little. Have a sweater handy, and put it on whenever you feel a chill.

Hypothermia's symptoms include fatigue, awkwardness, chills, lethargy, irritability, clumsiness, uncontrolled shivering, and slurred speech. Most victims don't realize they are hypothermic and will deny it up to the end. Act quickly to save them. Stop, find or make shelter, get the victim's wet clothes off, and get him or her into a sleeping bag (with somebody undressed and warm if they appear to be seriously hypothermic, although decency permits wearing underwear for you modest would-be rescuers). If you can't stop where you are, get down the trail fast! Warm liquids should be given to conscious victims but not to comatose victims. If the victim does not appear to recover, send someone for help immediately. The faster the victim's body temperature is raised, the better his or her chance of survival.

Like altitude sickness, prevention of hypothermia is easier than the cure. If you suspect you or one of your partners is becoming hypothermic, don't delay—get to shelter quickly and get the victim warm and dry. Don't hesitate to call for emergency assistance.

## Altitude Sickness

Altitude sickness is not an uncommon malady in the mountains. Although it is usually suffered by climbers on the Cascade volcanoes and other high peaks, people have died from its symptoms at modest elevations. Trails in this guide lead up to more than 7,000 feet elevation, high enough to suffer altitude sickness. Hikers who rush into the mountains from sea level and hit the high trails may suffer some symptoms of altitude sickness, including headache, dizziness, nausea, vomiting, weakness, shortness of breath, blueness of lips, chills, insomnia, increased pulse and respiration, blurred vision, confusion, and disorientation. If you or any of your party experience or exhibit any of these symptoms, descend immediately, slow down to reduce demand for oxygen, and breathe deeper and faster (which may cause nausea and dizziness, but keep at it). Usually, all you will notice is a bad headache, which is common enough on sunny summer days, especially when hiking on snow or in high granite basins. If the headache doesn't go away, you may want to consider heading down soon. The sooner you get to lower elevation, the faster you will recover from mountain sickness.

Like almost any other mountain hazard, prevention is easier than treatment: acclimatize, increase fluid intake and carbohydrate consumption, decrease fats in your diet, avoid alcohol prior to your hike, and don't smoke, drink carbonated beverages, or take antidepressants.

## Preparation

Although even the most sedentary among us can manage some of the hikes in this guide, hikers should be in good physical condition when hiking a majority of these trails. Fatigue is a leading cause of accidents on the trail; if your legs are tired, you are more likely to trip or stumble over rocks and roots. Tired legs cramp easily. Repetitive strain injuries are easier to suffer if your legs are weak. Although you don't need to train like a marathon runner to go hiking, it's a good idea to stay active during the "off season," taking walks whenever possible and visiting lowland trails through the winter so you're ready to go when spring and summer hikes open up.

## Winter and Spring Hiking

Despite inherent hazards, winter and spring hiking are popular. Winter hikes can sometimes be made under perfect conditions with little more risk than a late spring or late fall hike. With snowshoes, you can plod right along atop the snow. With instep crampons, you can walk along slippery trails with impunity. Ice and hard snow on trails is a hazard; ask anyone who has slipped on a winter trail and broken their wrist or tailbone.

The major considerations for winter hiking are weather and snow conditions. Cascade weather is unpredictable enough during the summer; during the winter, storms lasting several days at a time are common. Rain, snowfall, and high winds mean trouble for hikers. Whiteout conditions are frequent, particularly above timberline. Winter hikers have become lost or pinned down for days by storms, unable find their way out or unable to move because of severe avalanche risk caused by several feet of new, wet snow.

Although foul weather is the major hazard for winter hikers, avalanches are more feared. This is not a snow hiking guide, so an extensive discussion of avalanche safety is not included. If you're going to venture into the mountains during winter and spring, you should have training and experience with spotting and avoiding dangerous avalanche conditions and with avalanche rescue techniques. Avoiding potential avalanche slopes is the best way to avoid getting caught in an avalanche.

Frostbite is also a risk during winter hikes. Keeping your extremities warm, dry, and unconstricted is important. Overly tight boots (which reduce circulation) are a leading cause of frostbite.

This guide, being a hiking guide, cannot provide a thorough lesson on avalanche safety, snow travel, navigation, or winter safety and survival strategies. Winter and spring hikers should learn about preventing frostbite, hypothermia, and avalanche prediction and rescue and should know how to prepare for winter travel before they find themselves lost in a blizzard or sunk in up to their necks (or worse) in wet snow.

## No-Trace Ethics

Because of the popularity of the Alpine Lakes Wilderness, many popular trails, campsites, and high routes are showing signs of overuse. No-trace use of the wilderness areas of the Cascade Range is urged by the Forest Service. Here are some simple suggestions to help minimize your impact on the mountain environment:

- Travel in small groups to do less damage to meadows and campsites.
- Stay on trails, even when muddy, to avoid sidecutting or erosion; do not take shortcuts or cut switchbacks.
- Tread gently if you stray off the trail to avoid trampling fragile vegetation.
- Use a stove for cooking, and bring a tent rather than rely on scarce natural resources. Do not cut trees or boughs for any reason.
- Use existing campsites rather than create new ones.
- Choose stable sites for camps and rest stops, not areas with fragile vegetation.
- Don't construct rock windbreaks or clear bare-ground areas of rocks or vegetation for any reason.
- Camp on snow instead of bare ground whenever possible.
- Avoid having leftover food, so as not to attract wildlife to your camp.
- Use pit toilets or practice accepted human waste disposal practices (such as not eliminating waste near water sources, burying your waste at least 200 feet from water sources, or packing it out in plastic bags).
- Don't bring your pets with you. If you do bring them with you, keep them under control or leashed and clean up after them.
- Pack out your trash and any other trash you find.
- Plan your actions so as to make the least impact on the environment.

## Water

Long gone are the days when hikers could dip their tin Sierra cups into a stream or lake and drink freely. These days, many streams and lakes are contaminated with bacteria and microorganisms that can make a hiker quite ill. Hikers must now bring water from home or the grocery store on day hikes and either filter or purify drinking water in the wild. Boiling is the best way to purify water; boil for five minutes to be safe. Most hikers bring a filter, which weighs less than a stove and fuel. Check with the experts to find out which filter is right for you. Some filters filter out everything but are very expensive. Since your health is on the line, though, maybe money isn't the most important thing to consider.

## Camping

Although the hikes included in this volume are day hikes that can be done in a day without the necessity of camping, many of the hikes are popular as overnight or weekend backpacks. Nearly all of the trails in this guide have campsites. The longer the trail, the more campsites—at trail junctions, in meadows, and beside rivers and lakes. A few considerations for those who will be camping out: Many areas are overused and often crowded; please limit your use to day visits to avoid further impacts to already abused areas. If camping at a popular lake, don't just drop your pack and set up camp at the first bare-ground site you come to. Take the time to explore first, to find the designated camps, or a camp away from the lake. Always camp at least 200 feet away from a lake, unless a designated campsite is closer to the water or camping farther away is impossible due to terrain. Use existing sites only; don't clear rocks, logs, or vegetation to create a new campsite or stack rocks or logs to create a windbreak. Camp on snow, rock, or gravel when possible to avoid adverse impacts. Don't dig trenches or create new fire pits. Spread out to do less damage. If an existing path to the water source exists, use it so a new path isn't created. Be sure to do your cooking and cleaning well away from your tent, to avoid attracting bears, and don't wash up in the lake. Try not to camp right next to the trail, for your sake and the sake of other hikers on the trail; nobody likes tripping over your tent lines or backpack any more than you'll like the invasion of privacy. No campfires above 4,000 feet elevation west of the crest, above 5,000 feet elevation east of the crest, or at any of the "popular" lakes. Don't cut live trees for firewood; find deadfall in the woods well away from camp. Police your campsite before you leave to make sure you've left nothing behind. Protect your food from bears and other wildlife in a bear-resistant container or by properly hanging it from a tree. Don't keep any food in your tent.

## Human Waste Disposal

Litter and human waste disposal are major problems on many Alpine Lakes Wilderness trails. Use pit toilets and trash containers where available or else pack it out, particularly in high-use areas. Pit toilets are available at many lakes and high-country campsites; side trails leading to toilets are usually well marked. In and above the subalpine zone, do your business well away from lakes and streams, and don't dig "cat holes" in fragile meadows and tundra. For a thorough discourse on proper human waste disposal in the wilderness, please read *How to Shit in the Woods* (see Appendix E).

## In Case of Emergency

To report a hiking accident, or any other life-threatening emergency, dial 911. If the situation is less critical or you don't feel it is an emergency worthy of dialing 911, contact the nearest Park Service or forest district office, campground ranger or host, or the local sheriff or police department. See Appendix B for a list of Forest Service phone numbers. Also, consider carrying a cellular phone, just in case of an emergency. A cellular phone can aid rescue personnel in locating your exact position if you are lost or injured. Just make sure your battery is fully charged before you leave home. And when you get through, be sure to state your location and the nature of your emergency right away in case you lose the connection and can't get it back. Also, don't expect to get cellular service everywhere in the wilderness. Your phone may get a signal from a high ridge, but in most valleys and basins service is spotty to nonexistent. Even with a cell phone, you still have to rely on yourself.

# North Fork
# SNOQUALMIE RIVER

# 1

# Sunday Lake

**Overview:** *An unmarked, hard-to-follow trail to tranquil Sunday Lake.*

**Distance:** 6.4 miles round-trip.
**Difficulty:** Moderate.
**Best season:** Early summer through early winter.
**Traffic:** Foot and mountain bike traffic to Sunday Creek, foot traffic only beyond; light use.

**High point:** 1,950 feet.
**Maps:** USGS Mount Phelps; Green Trails No. 174 (Mount Si).
**For more information:** USDA Forest Service, North Bend Ranger District Office.

**Finding the trailhead:** Sunday Lake Trail 1000 is approached from North Bend via North Fork Road. To get there, drive I–90 to North Bend, exit 31, and head north on Bendigo Boulevard South, past the outlet mall and across the railroad tracks to SE North Bend Way, the main intersection in town. Turn right and go two blocks east, then turn left on Ballarat Avenue. Follow Ballarat northward; it soon curves westward and becomes 428th Avenue SE, which meanders through pastures across the river from the rocky buttress of Mount Si. Just over 4 miles from town the road forks. Take the left fork, which goes steeply uphill and passes a gate just after the pavement ends. Follow the unpaved logging road 14.1 miles to Weyerhaeuser Gate 30, on the right. Park here, being careful not to block either the gate or the main road. A Northwest Forest Pass is not presently required.

## Key points:

**0.1** Trail register.
**1.0** A fork in the road.
**1.5** Sunday Creek crossing.
**2.2** Alpine Lakes Wilderness boundary.
**2.9** Lower Sunday Lake.
**3.2** Upper Sunday Lake.

**The hike:** Sunday Lake Trail is the westernmost trail in the Alpine Lakes Wilderness and among the least traveled. The trail is unmarked and not well maintained, requires walking 1.5 miles on a logging road and fording a creek, and is sometimes downright unpleasant. Yet for all that, it still has one thing that many wilderness visitors seek but few trails provide—solitude. Small wonder, since few people know there is a trail here, or even that Sunday Lake exists. In that sense, this is a wonderful wilderness hike—once you cross into the Alpine Lakes Wilderness, at least.

The hike begins from Weyerhaeuser Gate 30, just over 14 miles up North Fork Road. No signs advertise the hike, and even the trail register, though stocked with

# Sunday Lake

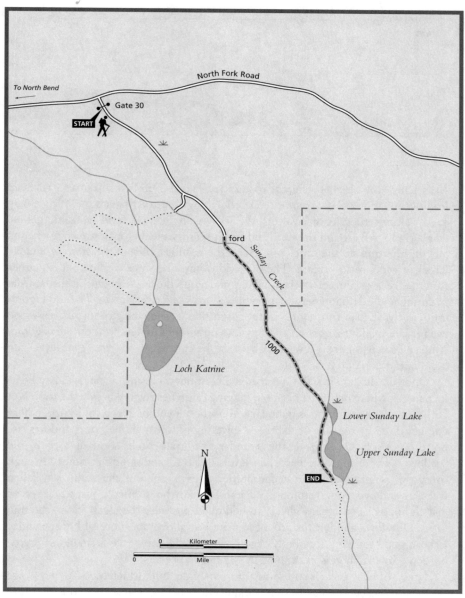

registration cards, was unmarked at last check. Register anyway and proceed. The first mile leads down an old logging road, passing through swampland that has invaded a stretch of the road, creating a large pond, home to frogs, snakes, and other water creatures, and forcing a detour over logs and high ground on the left.

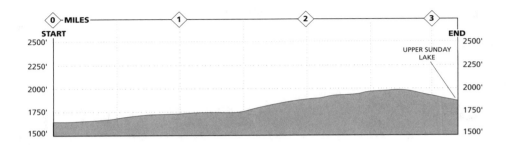

Eventually, after about 1 mile, the road forks. Take the left fork, up a rocky roadbed leading into the woods. Another 0.3 mile along, the road passes a cliff of mossy meta-volcanic rock. At a clearing, the trail seems to end amid landslide debris. Angle rightward around the trees and stumps, cross a wide rocky stream wash, and pick up the trail on the other side. Soon the roadbed ends at the edge of Sunday Creek, a wide, rocky stream. The old bridge has long since washed out, so either ford the creek or hop across the boulders and climb the eroded bank on the far side. In spring and early summer, the stream is more like a river and may be too high to cross easily. It may run higher in the afternoon as snowmelt runoff increases, so even if you made it across on the way in, you might fare less well on the way out. A hiker drowned here a few years back, so be careful. If you aren't sure you can cross safely, don't do it.

Once on the far side, the old roadbed continues, passing through mossy hemlock forest, where debris from an old logging camp lies rusting beside the trail. Not far beyond is the wilderness boundary. You can tell you're in the wilderness before you get there by the size of the trees; towering old-growth hemlocks and firs rise up to greet you. Once inside the boundary, the trail climbs some up a rocky old roadbed, away from the creek, then levels off. It's tough going at times, through overgrown salmonberry and hedge-nettle, across numerous snags and windfallen trees, up and over rotten stumps, and across muddy bogs. Finally, just when you've lost all hope of getting anywhere, an odd quiet pervades the forest. Soon the trail forks. Dip down the left fork to a campsite just above the shore of lower Sunday Lake, a good rest stop if nobody's camped out. The lower lake is small but pretty, bordered by marsh grasses, framed by big firs and cedars.

Upper Sunday Lake is still some 0.3 mile up the trail, which seems to get worse the farther you go. Sunday Lake is tranquil and inviting, but access to the lakeshore is difficult. There is a small campsite a couple hundred yards up the shore, with room enough for a small tent, and that's about it. Otherwise, there is scarcely a good spot to even sit and enjoy the scenery.

**Options:** A diminishing trail continues along Sunday Creek another few miles to Mowitch Lake and Honey Lake, but only the hardiest hikers and most determined anglers willing to endure miles of poor trail would keep going.

If you go down the right fork at 1 mile, you can find a trail leading to Loch Katrine, a larger lake nestled in a basin high above the valley floor. You have to ford Sunday Creek and find a faint trail on the opposite bank leading along an old, overgrown roadbed. The trail is flagged but is very brushy and not easy to follow.

# Bare Mountain

**Overview:** *A strenuous hike to a former lookout site atop Bare Mountain.*

**Distance:** 10.0 miles round-trip.
**Difficulty:** Strenuous.
**Best season:** Summer through fall.
**Traffic:** Foot traffic only; moderate use.
**High point:** 5,353 feet.

**Maps:** USGS Mount Phelps; Green Trails No. 175 (Skykomish).
**For more information:** USDA Forest Service, North Bend Ranger District Office.

**Finding the trailhead:** Bare Mountain Trail 1037 is approached from North Bend via North Fork Road, which becomes Forest Service Road 57 after crossing into the national forest. To get there, drive I–90 to North Bend, exit 31, and head north on Bendigo Boulevard South, past the outlet mall and across the railroad tracks to SE North Bend Way, the main intersection in town. Turn right and go two blocks east, then turn left on Ballarat Avenue. Follow Ballarat northward; it soon curves westward and becomes 428th Avenue SE, which meanders through pastures across the river from the rocky buttress of Mount Si. Just over 4 miles from town the road forks. Take the left fork, which goes steeply uphill and passes a gate just after the pavement ends. Follow the unpaved logging road 15.4 bumpy miles from the gate to a fork. Turn left and cross Lennox Creek, then take the first right on FS Road 57 and continue 3.2 miles to the Bare Mountain trailhead, on the

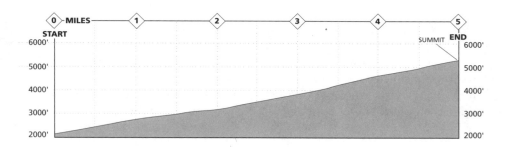

# Bare Mountain

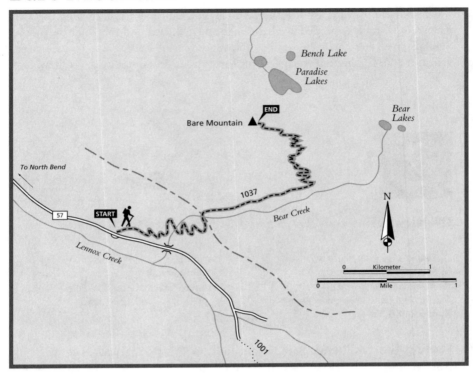

left. There is a small turnout with room for a few cars. Be nice and leave room for others. A Northwest Forest Pass is required.

## Key points:
**0.7** First crossing of Bear Creek.
**1.2** Second crossing of Bear Creek at Alpine Lakes Wilderness boundary.
**2.5** Switchbacks begin.
**3.4** Talus slide halfway to summit ridge.
**4.5** Summit ridge and views of Paradise and Bench Lakes.
**5.0** Bare Mountain summit.

**The hike:** Bare Mountain Trail leads up Bear Creek to a former lookout site atop Bare Mountain, elevation 5,353 feet. You might think the name is misspelled. After all, the first half of the hike follows Bear Creek. It's Bear Mountain, right? But once you reach the mountain's upper slopes, you'll know how it got its name. Yet it still seems a misnomer. Although mostly devoid of trees, the mountain is not at all bare. Wildflowers bloom profusely during the early summer, after the snow has melted away. However, if you are hiking here on a hot summer day, the mountain may seem bare, as the trail is fully exposed to the sun, with very little shade.

The trail begins on an old roadbed. Typical of old roadbeds in the western Cascades, the path is over loose cobble, like hiking up a shallow streambed. The road meanders upward and soon passes near a noisy waterfall cascading down a long, narrow granite slab. At 0.7 mile the trail crosses Bear Creek just below a higher slabby waterfall. The old bridge is washed out, but you can get to the other side via footlogs and boulder hopping, unless the water is running high. Once on the other side, the rocky roadbed continues, climbing a gradual curve above the creek before leveling off at 1.2 miles, crossing a footbridge over Bear Creek and entering the Alpine Lakes Wilderness.

Once inside the wilderness boundary, the trail traverses open slopes above the creek, through lush bracken fern, salmonberry, and thimbleberry brush, with tiger lilies, columbine, aster, bleeding heart, fireweed, and spirea adding color. If the brush hasn't been cut back by trail crews, it may be difficult to see the trail underfoot. Go slow and watch your step; hidden rocks, logs, and holes lurk beneath the brush, and bent-over bracken stems can trip you up. (I only barely jest in recommending that you bring a machete for this section of the trail, a walking stick at least to whack the worst of the underbrush.) If you come in the early morning before the sun has dried things out, expect to get drenched by dew dripping off the brush; later in the day expect hot, muggy going.

The trail switches back for the first time just over a mile from the boundary marker and scarcely stops for the next 2 miles. At first, the switchbacks climb tightly through a swath of curved cedars, with tiger lily, columbine, and paintbrush lining the trail. The cedars offer intermittent shade, much welcome on a sunny summer day. About a mile up the slope, the trail passes a talus slide, where some flat boulders offer a place to sit, enjoy a snack, take in the view, and rest up for the remaining climb to the summit ridge. From here, it's more of the same—relentless switchbacks up an increasingly subalpine slope. The change in plant life is notable above the talus. Cascades blueberry and fool's huckleberry replace the bracken and salmonberry, penstemon dots the rocky soil, and heather and lupine make their debut. Birds flit among the trees; pika shriek from the talus. Views expand.

As you climb higher, the switchbacks tighten and the trail ascends more steeply, yet the ridge crest seems eternally just up the next switchback. Finally, the trail reaches the crest, where a short side trail leads to a rocky viewpoint overlooking Paradise Lakes and Bench Lake. The trail continues up the ridge crest, traversing and switching back up steep meadows. The meadows seem to hang on the mountainside, falling away to the verdant valley below. Lupine, aster, spirea, bistort, and heather bloom here among blueberry and juniper scrub and diminutive cedars, subalpine firs, and mountain-hemlock. There are still a few more switchbacks, but at long last, a final rocky step leads to the summit. Mount Rainier looms to the south, Glacier Peak to the north, and lesser peaks rise up all around. The summit is rocky

*Upper Bare Mountain Trail*

and flat, with cables and other debris from the former lookout cabin that occupied Bare Mountain.

This is not a good choice for an overnight hike unless you plan on a summit bivouac. The summit is flat but rocky, with some broken glass and other debris, and provides a memorable night out for those willing to haul overnight gear up the mountain. You can see city lights in the distance and stars everywhere above.

**Options:** Old maps show a trail leading up Bear Creek to Bear Lakes. This trail has long since been abandoned and is difficult to find, let alone follow. A scramble down to Paradise Lakes and Bench Lake also is a possibility. There's no easy route down to the lakes, at least not from the trail. Getting to the lakes will put your route-finding skills to the test. Most will wisely stick to the trail.

# Lennox Creek–Anderson Lake

**Overview:** *A high subalpine meadow traverse to little Anderson Lake.*

**Distance:** 7.6 miles round-trip from trailhead; 10.6 miles round-trip from bridge.
**Difficulty:** Moderate.
**Best season:** Summer through fall; snow may linger into August.
**Traffic:** Foot traffic only; light to moderate use.

**High point:** About 4,620 feet.
**Maps:** USGS Mount Phelps; Green Trails No. 175 (Skykomish).
**For more information:** USDA Forest Service, North Bend Ranger District Office.

**Finding the trailhead:** Lennox Creek Trail 1001 begins near the end of Forest Service Road 57, about 1 mile past the Bare Mountain trailhead. Follow the directions listed for Bare Mountain Trail (Hike 2) and continue just over 1 mile on FS 57 to the Lennox Creek trailhead. At present, the bridge just past Bare Mountain trailhead is damaged and not scheduled to be repaired anytime soon, so park at Bare Mountain trailhead and start hiking from there. A Northwest Forest Pass is required.

## Key points:

**0.4** Alpine Lakes Wilderness boundary.
**2.4** Heather meadow traverse above Lennox Falls.
**3.4** Anderson Lake saddle.
**3.8** Anderson Lake.

# Lennox Creek–Anderson Lake

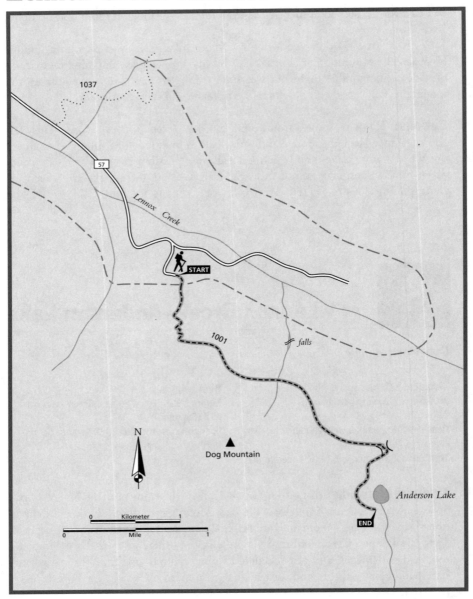

**The hike:** This was my first Alpine Lakes Wilderness hike, when I was twelve years old, long before the Alpine Lakes Wilderness was officially designated. I remember the hike fondly—except for getting thoroughly soaked by overnight rain, suffering incessant cold rain on the hike out, and slipping and falling off a

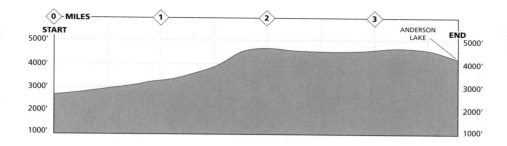

footlog into the mud. But memories of traversing high alpine meadows below craggy peaks and down to a small, quiet lake still linger. Such is the stuff of Alpine Lakes Wilderness hiking. The trail isn't much different today; muddy in the woods, magnificent in the meadows, and far enough up North Fork Road that relatively few people hike here, allowing some solitude for such a short hike.

Assuming the bridge is not repaired, get a permit at the Bare Mountain trailhead, then hike or mountain bike 1.5 miles up the road to the trailhead. From the trailhead, Lennox Creek Trail climbs gradually through silver fir and hemlock forest, soon entering the Alpine Lakes Wilderness. The first part of the trail is muddy in places, over slippery roots and rocks, like a streambed—at times complete with running water. Not much maintenance work is done here since the bridge washed out; not especially pleasant going. Several switchbacks follow as the trail climbs a forested ridge, then swings eastward across a broad avalanche slope and around a shoulder of Dog Mountain, about 2.4 miles from the trailhead. The next section of the trail is a joy to hike, traversing a broad, rocky heather basin a short mile—with views of nearby peaks to the north—to a 4,620-foot saddle in the craggy ridge dividing Lennox Creek and Anderson Lake basin. As you hike across the heather meadows, you can hear but never quite see a waterfall below. (If you want a view of Lennox Falls, your best bet is to hike from the trailhead up an abandoned road on the north side of the creek.)

From the saddle, the trail descends 0.4 mile to Anderson Lake, elevation 4,180 feet. The trail is a boot track traversing the steep basin headwall that may be hard to follow in places. There are campsites at the lake, near the outlet stream.

The upper meadows are snow-free by July of most years but can remain snowy into August. If you come early, bring an ice ax and be prepared to camp on snow.

**Options:** A scramble up 5,406-foot Dog Mountain is relatively easy for experienced off-trail travelers. There are several possible routes; the most direct leaves the trail just after crossing the avalanche slope and ascends a forested ridge about 0.5 mile to the top. Beware of cliffs, especially on the south and east sides.

# Middle Fork
# SNOQUALMIE RIVER

# Mount Si

**Overview:** *A steep, very popular hike to Haystack Ridge.*

**Distance:** 8.0 miles round-trip.
**Difficulty:** Strenuous.
**Best season:** Accessible all year; best spring through early winter.
**Traffic:** Foot traffic only; very heavy use.

**High point:** About 3,900 feet.
**Maps:** Green Trails No. 174 (Mount Si).
**For more information:** Washington Department of Natural Resources.

**Finding the trailhead:** Mount Si Trail is approached from North Bend via SE Mount Si Road. Drive I–90 to North Bend, exit 32, and follow SE 432nd Street north about 0.5 mile to SE North Bend Way. Turn left and drive 0.3 mile, then turn right on SE Mount Si Road and continue 2.4 miles to the Mount Si trailhead, on the left. The parking lot is huge but not always big enough for all of the hikers who park here on sunny weekends and summer evenings. Beware of car prowlers who are often loitering in the parking lot; leave nothing of value in your car. A Northwest Forest Pass is not presently required.

## Key points:

**0.1** Mount Si Trail leaves the creek loop.
**0.5** An intermittent stream and mileage marker.
**1.0** A rocky ledge, which offers a glimpse of the valley.
**1.8** Snag Flats.
**3.0** A milepost, near the end of the steepest switchbacks.
**3.8** The first real viewpoint, looking east up the Snoqualmie River valley.
**4.0** Trail's end at a signpost on the rocky summit shoulder.

**The hike:** Mount Si is the craggy peak rising to the northeast of the town of North Bend. It is one of Washington's most recognizable and most often climbed mountains, at least among those without a summit trail, due to its proximity to the suburban sprawl of the Puget Sound region and because a popular trail leads to within a few hundred feet of its summit. It also made a cameo appearance in the opening credits of the cult classic TV show, *Twin Peaks*. Mount Si offers unsurpassed views of the Snoqualmie River valley and the western front of the Cascade Range, with the Olympic Mountains spread out in the distance to the west and Mount Rainier looming to the south. The views attract an endless stream of hikers, as many as 50,000 per year by one estimate, who variously plod, walk, and run up the trail to the rocky shoulder just below the summit. Others hike the trail in winter and spring as training for bigger peaks. Thus, you will likely encounter at least one lone hiker

# Mount Si

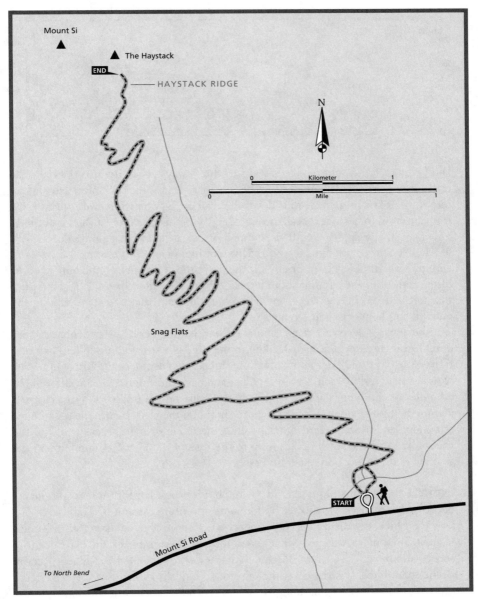

or group trudging wearily up the trail under the weight of a fully loaded expedition pack, in stark contrast to the majority of hikers dressed in shorts, T-shirts, and sneakers, carrying no backpack at all.

The trail begins on a short, flat loop around the picnic area. After a scant 0.1 mile, the Mount Si Trail leaves the loop and begins climbing up through maple, fir,

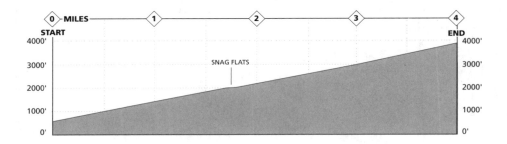

and hemlock forest, not too steeply at first, but always up. In the first 0.5 mile, the trail gains over 500 feet, and it keeps on like that most of the way. After crossing an intermittent stream (which runs down the trail during the winter and spring), the trail climbs in long switchbacks through deepening hemlock forest. Just past the 1-mile mark is a rock ledge, with just enough of a clearing to get a glimpse of the valley. Don't bother, though; the real views are higher up. After some 1.8 miles of climbing, the trail levels off briefly for the first time at Snag Flats, the only flat area of the trail until the summit shoulder. An exhibit here describes a 1910 forest fire that left several charred trees, and some big old snags that still stand among the taller, living hemlocks and Douglas firs.

Above Snag Flats, the trail climbs an unrelenting series of switchbacks up a quiet forest ridge, occasionally leading to the edge of a stream gully. There is a section of the old trail here that is sometimes hiked by old-timers and lost souls. Stick with the new trail, which is more gradual and easier to follow. Finally, after about 3.8 miles of climbing, the trees suddenly thin out and the trail comes to a clearing and the first good views. After a bit more climbing, the trail reaches the rocky summit shoulder. After the trail officially ends, scramble over the rocks and find the trail on the other side, which leads up to the base of the Haystack summit and the best views this side of Snoqualmie Pass.

**Options:** Hiking the old trail is an option, but it is best left for those who remember it from way back or who are up for some adventure. Mount Si Trail is a popular winter hike, but the trail is very slippery when snow covered. Bring ski poles and instep crampons, if you know what's good for you. A scramble up the Haystack (the actual summit of 4,167-foot Mount Si) is not recommended for hikers lacking alpine scrambling experience. Although not technically difficult, it involves steep, exposed, Class 3 rock scrambling on sometimes loose rock, where a slip could be fatal. Refer to *Climbing Washington's Mountains* (see Appendix E) for additional information about this and other nearby scrambles and summit trails.

Another option is to hike the 3-mile trail to the 1,759-foot summit of Little Si, a craggy knoll at the base of Mount Si, which provides good views of the Snoqualmie River valley and the town of North Bend. The trailhead is on the left as you drive up Mount Si Road. Little Si is a popular rock climbing area, so the parking lot can get crowded on sunny days.

# 5

# Twin Falls

**Overview:** *A popular hike up Snoqualmie River to a 150-foot waterfall.*

**Distance:** 3.0 miles round-trip.
**Difficulty:** Easy.
**Best season:** All year.
**Traffic:** Foot traffic only; heavy use.

**High point:** About 1,000 feet.
**Maps:** Green Trails No. 206 (Bandera).
**For more information:** Washington State Parks.

**Finding the trailhead:** Twin Falls Trail is approached from North Bend via 468th Avenue SE. Drive I-90 to Edgwick Road/468th, exit 34. From the exit, drive south on 468th Avenue SE nearly a mile, then turn left on the well-signed road leading to Twin Falls Natural Area and the Twin Falls trailhead at road's end. A Washington State Parks parking pass ($5.00 a day) is required.

## Key points:
**0.3** The trail passes a cluster of mossy maples alongside the river.
**0.7** A bench overlooking the river and waterfalls.
**0.9** A giant Douglas fir tree.
**1.4** Trail junction to lower falls overlook.
**1.5** Footbridge overlooking falls.

**The hike:** If you like waterfalls, you'll love this hike, unless you like solitude, and then you may have mixed feelings unless you come on a rainy winter weekday morning, when you are likely to have the trail all to yourself. The waterfalls are spectacular, especially the lower falls, which cascades in a mare's-tail ribbon down a slabby cliff, then free-falls into a deep pool below. The trail allows hikers a close-up look and feel of the waterfalls, both from above and below, although the view might be a little too close for hikers with a fear of heights or steep drop-offs. If you

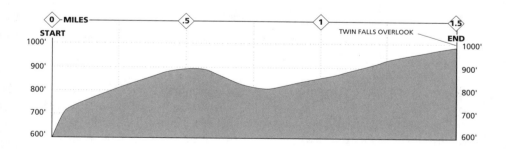

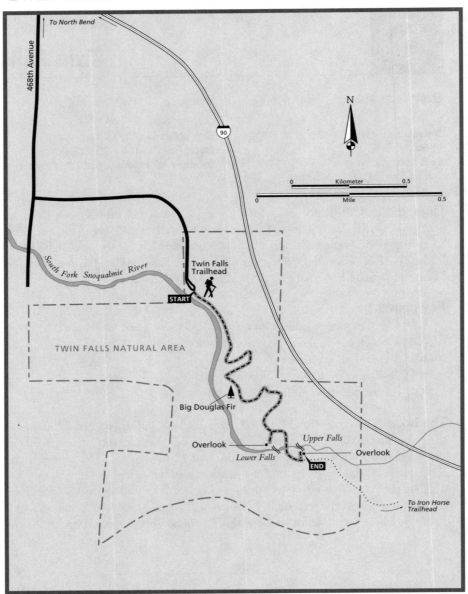

want the best photos, bring an array of lenses, including your widest wide-angle lens.

The trail begins gradually, traversing along the bank of the South Fork Snoqualmie River, soon passing through a grove of bigleaf maples festooned with hanging mosses. The trail leaves the river shortly, climbing to a shelf out of sight

*Twin Falls Trail*

but not out of sound of the river, then switching back up a steep slope. Careless or indifferent hikers have eroded the slope here by shortcutting the switchback; restoration efforts might help restore this blight, but the best thing to do is stay on the trail. The trail crests at a ridge overlooking the river and at last offers a view of the falls, enticement enough for hikers who found that last bit of climbing a bit steep. There's a bench here, allowing a rest stop for those with the patience to sit and wait. The trail descends briefly and passes a giant old-growth Douglas fir tree that, according to the signs, is the largest specimen found in King County, Washington. Whether this is true or not, it is still a remarkable specimen. The tree is fenced off for its protection, not yours; please look but do not disturb the tree. A side trail leads to the river here.

Once past the big Douglas fir, the trail starts climbing again, away from the river, then curves back toward the river. If you think you hear traffic, you probably do; the freeway is just up and over the hill above you. Soon enough the falls will drown out the freeway noise. At 1.4 miles, a side trail leads down a series of wooden steps to a platform perched over the canyon walls, within a stone's throw of the lower falls. Farther up the trail, a bridge spans the canyon just above the lower falls. Most hikers stop at the bridge, but for the best view of the upper falls, continue another few minutes up the trail to a higher viewing platform.

Twin Falls is within Olallie State Park. Park hours are from 6:30 A.M. to dusk; winter hours are from 8:00 A.M. to dusk. Day use only.

**Options:** The trail continues above the falls, eventually leveling out and following an old railroad grade another 1.2 miles to a trailhead just off exit 38. If you prefer, you can hike in this way, although it's longer and has just as much climbing (on the way out) as the lower trail. The upper trail has some interesting features a bit farther up the valley, including a high trestle crossing and close-up encounters with rock climbers on the cliffs above the trail. With arranged transportation, you can make this a one-way hike that is nearly all downhill. Have someone drop you off at the Iron Horse trailhead and drive down to the Twin Falls trailhead to hike up and meet you at the falls.

# 6

# Taylor River

**Overview:** *An abandoned road leading through forest along Taylor River.*

**Distance:** 10.0 miles round-trip to Big Creek.
**Difficulty:** Easy.
**Best season:** All year for most of lower trail.
**Traffic:** Foot and bike traffic on lower trail; heavy use.
**High point:** About 1,800 feet.

**Maps:** USGS Lake Philippa and Snoqualmie Lake; Green Trails No. 174 (Mount Si) and 175 (Skykomish).
**For more information:** USDA Forest Service, North Bend Ranger District Office.

**Finding the trailhead:** Taylor River Trail 1002 is approached from North Bend via Middle Fork Road. Drive I–90 to North Bend, exit 34 (Edgwick Road/468th). Head north from the exit on 468th Avenue SE, past the truck stops, 0.6 mile to SE Middle Fork Road. Turn right and continue 0.9 mile to a fork. Stay right, taking the high road (the sign says LAKE DOROTHY ROAD), and continue another 1.6 miles to pavement's end, where the road becomes Forest Service Road 56. Continue on FS 56 another 9.5 miles, past the Middle Fork trailhead and across a bridge over Taylor River to a junction. Stay left, along the river, and proceed 0.2 mile to the trailhead parking lot at road's end. The trailhead used to be several miles up the road, but a bridge washout many years ago closed the road, forcing hikers to start here. Park your car at the gate or back at the river if the parking lot is full, and start hiking. A Northwest Forest Pass is required.

## Key points:

**2.8** Marten Creek crossing.
**4.4** Otter Falls and Lipsy Lake.
**5.0** Big Creek bridge.

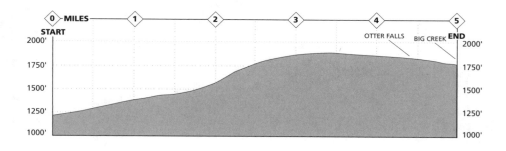

# Taylor River

**The hike:** Taylor River Trail follows an abandoned road grade along Taylor River, a tributary of the Middle Fork Snoqualmie River. Being an old road grade, the hike is mostly flat and easy, through shady forest, passing several waterfalls, including the spectacular Otter Falls. Due to its relatively low elevation, this trail is passable much of the year and is a good hike for early winter, after snow has buried the high trails.

Get your permit and start hiking up the old road grade. A short distance along, a side trail leads down and left to cross the river. If you miss it, you'll end up at the old washed out bridge. Once across the river, the trail climbs up to rejoin the old road grade; stay right at a road fork in another 0.2 mile. The trail leads along the road on the western side of the river, through deep, mossy forest, barely gaining elevation, crossing several creeks. At 2.8 miles is Marten Creek and a small water-fall. The path is flat and wide this far, making it popular not only with hikers but mountain bikers as well. Crossing Marten Creek is easy but unnerving, as the bridge seems about ready to collapse. Tread lightly across the bridge and continue up the trail, which becomes more trail-like, narrowing down and weaving in and out of forest and talus, and across several streams, which can be difficult to cross during early season, especially after winters with high snowfall.

At 4.3 miles is Otter Creek. Otter Falls, a 700-foot-high waterfall, is 0.1 mile north and 100 feet above the road, reached via a short unmarked trail. A path leads down to Lipsy Lake. At 5 miles is Big Creek, which is crossed on an oversized con-crete bridge left over from the days when you could drive this far. The hike to Big Creek has only about 600 feet elevation gain, making it a popular winter and spring warm-up.

Middle Fork Road may someday be paved from North Bend to Taylor River. That project may take awhile, and while paving is being completed, the road may be closed. After paving, count on more hiker traffic on the trails.

**Options:** At 2 miles up from the trailhead is an old, abandoned trail that leads about 1.5 miles to Marten Lake, a small lake set in a swampy basin at 2,958 feet ele-vation. The trail isn't too hard to find or follow but is a bit brushy and is best left to experienced wilderness hikers.

Taylor River Trail continues past Big Creek, climbing to Snoqualmie, Deer, and Bear Lakes, then over a divide and down to Lake Dorothy (Hike 58), a 15-mile, one-way hike.

# Snoqualmie
# PASS AREA

# 7

# McClellan Butte

**Overview:** *A strenuous hike to the summit ridge of 5,162-foot McClellan Butte.*

**Distance:** 9.4 miles round-trip.
**Difficulty:** Strenuous.
**Best season:** Summer through fall.
**Traffic:** Foot traffic only; heavy use.
**High point:** About 5,100 feet.

**Maps:** USGS Bandera; Green Trails No. 206 (Bandera).
**For more information:** USDA Forest Service, North Bend Ranger District Office.

**Finding the trailhead:** McClellan Butte Trail 1015 begins from Tinkham Road, about 11 miles east of North Bend. Drive I–90 to Tinkham, exit 42, and turn south on Tinkham Road 0.2 mile to the trailhead turnoff, on the right, just where the road curves eastward. This is a high car-prowl trailhead, so park and lock your car and leave nothing of value inside. A Northwest Forest Pass is required.

## Key points:

**0.5** Iron Horse Trail junction.
**1.3** Logging road crossing.
**1.8** Switchbacks.
**2.8** Avalanche gullies.
**4.2** Tarn.
**4.7** Trail's end on summit ridge.

**The hike:** McClellan Butte is the prominent forested horn rising dramatically from the South Fork Snoqualmie River valley a few miles east of North Bend, easily seen as you drive past on I–90. A popular hiking trail climbs to the summit ridge, from where a short scramble leads to the summit. Although hiking guidebooks routinely advise hikers to leave the summit for experienced climbers, hikers routinely ignore such advice and scramble on up to the top. The summit view is a sufficient lure, apparently, despite the fact that much of the view is of clearcut slopes to the south. Fortunately, Mount Rainier rises magnificently above and beyond the carnage, and the peaks of the Alpine Lakes Wilderness dominate the northeastern skyline. On a clear day, you may see the skyscrapers of downtown Seattle and the Olympic Mountains farther west.

From the trailhead, traverse brushy clearcut slopes, in and out of forest and beneath power lines into quiet second-growth silver fir and hemlock forest, eventually joining the Iron Horse Trail after about 0.5 mile of mostly unappealing trail. Take a right and follow this wide gravel grade westward about 0.3 mile, past a large, modern toilet facility. At the old trail crossing, rejoin Trail 1015 on the left and

# McClellan Butte

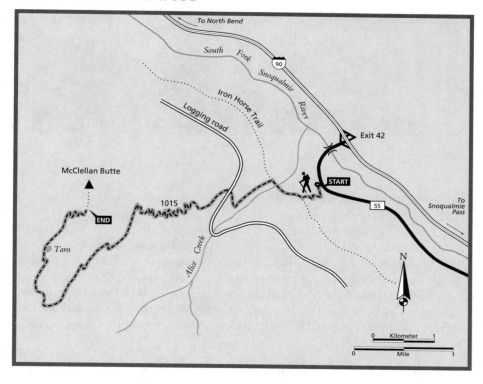

ascend another 0.5 uneventful mile through an old clearcut to a logging road. Cross the road and continue up the trail, which angles up through older growth forest slopes to a broad shelf thick with towering hemlocks and Douglas firs. The trail meanders through these old-growth giants, weaving around and over windfallen trees, right up to the edge of a brushy clearcut. Now the trail starts climbing in earnest, ascending switchbacks and more switchbacks for nearly a mile up a shady forested slope, gaining a quick 1,000 feet elevation. As abruptly as they started, the switchbacks end and the trail contours around and crosses the east slope of McClellan Butte, crossing several avalanche gullies. These slopes are wide open, allowing some views eastward, mostly of logging roads and clearcuts and the freeway far below, and of the craggy north face of Mount Kent. About halfway across the east slope, the trail passes a large spruce tree, seemingly out of place among the smaller firs and hemlocks.

Once across the eastern slope, the trail turns a corner and crosses the southern slope, gaining significant elevation as it climbs through brushy fir forest. In the fall, huckleberries may slow you down a bit here. Glimpses of Alice Lakes can be seen through the trees. Before long, the trail rounds another ridgeline and contours northward, now along the western slope, descending to a lovely but abused sub-

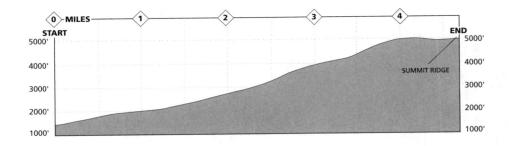

alpine bench and tarn, soon climbing again up rocky switchbacks that lead to trail's end at the crest of the summit ridge.

A word of caution about the gully crossings: They are easy by mid-summer, after the snow melts, but are dangerous in spring and early summer due to avalanche danger and exposure. More than one hiker has met his demise as a result of a slip on steep snow while attempting to cross these gullies. When the gullies are snow covered, hikers are advised to turn back. If you decide to risk it, at least carry an ice ax and know how to self-arrest, and consider bringing a rope and belaying across the steepest gullies. Or just be patient and do the hike later in the summer when the snow is gone.

**Options:** A scramble to the 5,162-foot summit of McClellan Butte is pretty much obligatory. It's a short, rocky scramble up a slabby ridge. Every guidebook cautions that the summit scramble is not recommended for hikers, but nearly every hiker who suffers the trail to the summit ridge heads up the rocks to the summit anyway. It's climbing, not hiking, but if you climb carefully and avoid loose rock, you should have no trouble. Remember that the rocks are slippery when wet or snow/ice covered and that it's easier on the way up than on the way down. For safety's sake, don't try it unless you have some scrambling experience.

# 8

# Mason Lake

**Overview:** *A strenuous hike to Mason Lake.*

**Distance:** About 9.0 miles round-trip.
**Difficulty:** Strenuous.
**Best season:** Early summer through fall.
**Traffic:** Foot traffic only; heavy use.
**High point:** About 4,200 feet.

**Maps:** USGS Bandera; Green Trails No. 206 (Bandera).
**For more information:** USDA Forest Service, North Bend Ranger District Office.

**Finding the trailhead:** Mason Lake Trail 1038 begins just north of I–90 about 12 miles east of North Bend. Drive I–90 to Forest Service Road 9030, exit 45. Turn north and follow FS 9030 about 0.8 mile to a fork. Stay left and follow Forest Service Road 9031 another 3 miles to the Mason Lake trailhead at road's end. A Northwest Forest Pass is required.

## Key points:
**0.8** Mason Creek.
**3.7** Bandera Mountain fork.
**4.5** Mason Lake.

**The hike:** Mason Lake is a small lake tucked into a talus basin high on the west flank of Bandera Mountain. Mason Lake is only the starting point for high ridge, lake, and meadow wandering. This is a popular hike, mostly because the trail is easily accessible and leads to a quiet lake. The existing trail is scheduled to be closed during the 2002 hiking season and possibly through the summer of 2003 while the trail is rerouted. According to the Forest Service, the Mason Lake and Bandera Mountain Trails will be improved, with more of the Mason Lake Trail traversing the slopes of Bandera Mountain via switchbacks, with a final traverse across the western slopes of Bandera Mountain down to Mason Lake. The trail described below and the mileage points listed above are based on the Forest Service descrip-

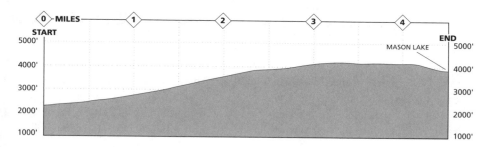

# Mason Lake

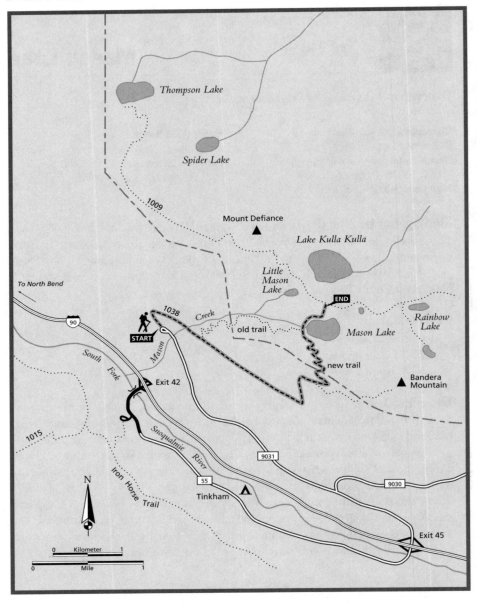

tion of where the rerouted trail *will* go, and may not be entirely accurate once the actual trail is completed.

Get your permit at the trailhead register and start hiking. The trail follows a grassy road grade first westward, then eastward, climbing gradually through fir,

54

*Mason Lake*

hemlock, and alder forest, with the steady drone of freeway traffic rising from the valley below. In about 0.2 mile, the trail curves back to the east. In another 0.6 mile the trail crosses Mason Creek at a noisy waterfall. Another couple of hundred yards of hiking through shady alder and hemlock forest is the old Mason Lake Trail junction. Stay on the road grade, which traverses eastward across the lower slopes of Bandera Mountain. The trail traverses past the old Bandera Mountain "trail" then switches back a few times as it climbs the mountain slopes, which were burned by a 1960s forest fire. Beargrass, lupine, tiger lily, and columbine are among the wildflowers here. At about 3,800 feet, the trail forks. The right fork leads up talus slopes to the summit of Bandera Mountain. The left fork contours westward, ascending over the western ridge slopes of Bandera Mountain, then descending briefly to Mason Lake.

Some boulders off to the right of the outlet stream offer a good place to sit and enjoy the scenery. There are many overused campsites at Mason Lake, mostly along the western shore. Please camp in designated campsites only; no campfires are allowed at Mason Lake or elsewhere above the lake.

**Options:** The trail to the summit of 5,241-foot Bandera Mountain is steep and strenuous—but not too far from the fork—and is a recommended side trip. The trail, when rerouted (as described earlier), will make this summit a popular destination, easily combined with the hike to Mason Lake.

Mount Defiance Trail 1009 leads off to the east through a meadow bench dotted with talus and pretty lakes and off to the west to within a few dozen yards of the summit of 5,584-foot Mount Defiance.

Those in a hurry to get to Mason Lake may attempt to hike the old trail, if they know where it goes. It is shorter but is steep and muddy, with windfallen trees to duck under and a brushy talus slope to climb. This route is not recommended, and the Forest Service prefers that you not use it.

# 9

# Talapus Lake

**Overview:** *A short, very popular hike to Talapus Lake.*

**Distance:** 3.2 miles round-trip.
**Difficulty:** Moderate.
**Best season:** Summer through fall.
**Traffic:** Foot traffic only; very heavy use.
**High point:** About 3,250 feet.

**Maps:** USGS Bandera; Green Trails No. 206 (Bandera).
**For more information:** USDA Forest Service, North Bend Ranger District Office.

**Finding the trailhead:** Talapus Lake Trail 1039 begins just north of I–90, about 12 miles east of North Bend. Drive I–90 to Forest Service Road 9030, exit 45. Turn north and follow FS 9030 about 0.8 mile to a fork. Stay right and continue another 2.3 miles up FS 9030 to the Talapus Lake trailhead at road's end. This is a very popular trail, and consequently the parking lot is often overflowing. Please do not block the road or other vehicles. A Northwest Forest Pass is required.

## Key points:
**1.1** Talapus Creek.
**1.6** Talapus Lake.

**The hike:** Talapus Lake is a small, heart-shaped lake set in a talus-lined basin between Pratt and Bandera Mountains. Talapus Lake Trail is a popular hike, mostly because it provides the shortest hike to lake country in the western half of the Alpine Lakes Wilderness. It is a fast and easy introduction to wilderness hiking, a little steep but not too strenuous, although a bit too crowded for some.

From the trailhead, the trail climbs gradually up a rocky road grade through typical second-growth hemlock and silver fir forest, switching back a few times in the first 0.5 mile before crossing bridge work at a boggy area and becoming a real trail. Switchbacks follow as the trail climbs the wooded slope; salal, Oregon grape, bead lily, and tiarella line the trail. These are lazy switchbacks, long and gradual, up

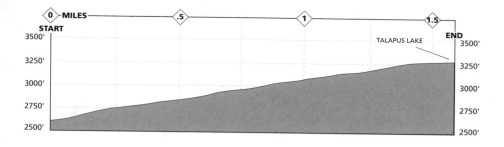

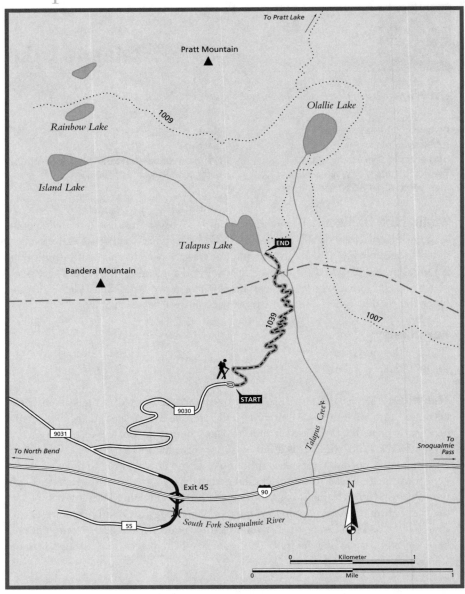

a boulder-lined trail that comes tantalizingly near Talapus Creek but always turns away at the last moment. The freeway noise is gradually supplanted by the chatter of the creek and the many other hikers. After an unusually long traversing section without a switchback, the trail crosses a brief talus slope and leads to the edge of

Talapus Creek. More switchbacks follow, a little tighter than before but barely steep, leading away from then coming back to the creek. After a few more switchbacks, the trail levels out and crosses a flat area with some old-growth cedars, announcing your entry into the Alpine Lakes Wilderness. Meander through a marshy area with big skunk cabbage, cross the several branches of the creek via footbridges, then meander more through flat woods, more bead lily and twisted stalk underfoot. In a short distance there is a side trail leading down to Talapus Lake, elevation 3,250 feet. The trail leads through some old campsites (no camping allowed; the lakeshore is presently being restored) to the outlet stream logjam. The logs provide a good place to sit and enjoy the scenery, if you don't mind company.

**Options:** The trail continues beyond Talapus Lake, switching back up the slope and around a ridge to a trail junction just across the outlet stream of Olallie Lake about 1.3 miles past Talapus Lake. The left fork leads shortly to Olallie Lake, only a little less crowded than Talapus Lake; the right fork 0.1 mile to the Pratt Lake Trail (1007) junction.

Day hikers can continue another 2.5 miles to Pratt Lake for a 10-mile round-trip. From Olallie Lake, backtrack to Pratt Lake Trail 1007, then ascend a wide arc above the lake to a divide and junction with Mount Defiance Trail 1009. Continue over the divide and down the other side another 2 miles through old-growth forest to Pratt Lake. Or follow Mount Defiance Trail 1.5 miles to Rainbow Lake and lovely talus-strewn meadows, from where you can scramble up talus blocks to the summit of 5,099-foot Pratt Mountain.

# 10

# Granite Mountain

**Overview:** *Climb to a lookout cabin atop 5,629-foot Granite Mountain.*

**Distance:** 9.0 miles round-trip.
**Difficulty:** Strenuous.
**Best season:** Summer through fall.
**Traffic:** Foot traffic only; heavy use.
**High point:** 5,629 feet.

**Maps:** USGS Snoqualmie Pass; Green Trails
No. 207 (Snoqualmie Pass).
**For more information:** USDA Forest Service,
North Bend Ranger District Office.

**Finding the trailhead:** Granite Mountain Trail 1016 begins from the Pratt Lake trailhead just west of Snoqualmie Pass. Drive I–90 to Denny Creek/Asahel Curtis, exit 47. Head north to a junction, turn left, and follow the paved road about 0.3 mile to the Pratt Lake trailhead. The parking lot is often very crowded on sunny weekends. Come early to find a parking space. This is a high car-prowl trailhead, so lock up and leave no valuables behind. A Northwest Forest Pass is required.

## Key points:
**0.9**  Granite Mountain Trail junction.
**2.7**  Avalanche gully traverse.
**3.7**  Tarn in boulder basin.
**4.0**  Cross ridge into upper basin.
**4.5**  Granite Mountain summit.

**The hike:** Granite Mountain is one of the most popular summit hikes in the Alpine Lakes Wilderness, mostly because the trail is easily accessible and the summit views are wide and wonderful. It's a fairly rugged trail, though, climbing relentlessly from the valley floor to the summit lookout, but the views are worth the effort. Granite Mountain offers a panoramic view of the Cascade Range, with Mount Rainier rising in stark relief to the south and Glacier Peak, Mount Stuart, and the interior Cascades jutting up in rugged profile to the north.

Begin on Pratt Lake Trail 1007, which heads eastward at first, then reverses course, climbing gradually through shady second-growth forest. In just under 1 mile is the junction with Granite Mountain Trail 1016. From here, Trail 1016 climbs steeply, over rocks and roots, and keeps going that way, switching back up and up through thinning silver fir and hemlock forest, eventually reaching the western edge of a broad avalanche gully. The trail crosses the gully a bit higher up, at about 3,900 feet elevation. In winter and spring, the gully presents a major avalanche hazard to hikers, who are advised to stay away until summer. By late June the trail is usually snow-free this far. (If you come in early season, bring an ice ax

# Granite Mountain

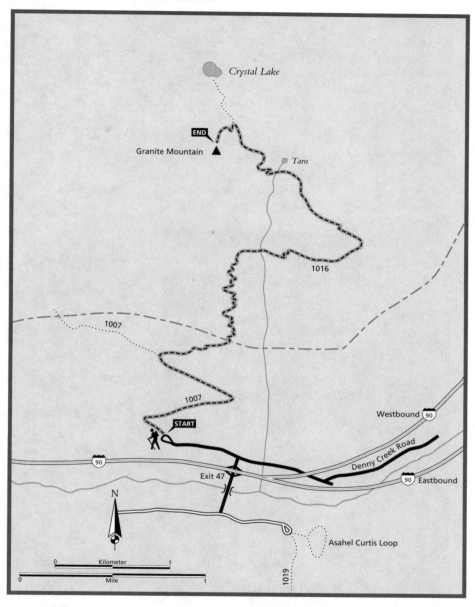

just in case.) Once across the gully, the trail traverses eastward through heather, kinnickinick, and juniper scrub meadows, which burst alive with lupine, tiger lily, Indian paintbrush, and beargrass by midsummer. Eventually the trail curves back to the west, where the summit lookout cabin comes into distant view. After crossing a noisy outlet stream or taking a deserved break beside a boulder-lined tarn, the

*Granite Mountain lookout*

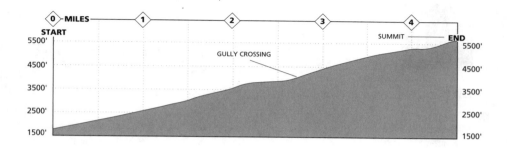

trail climbs more steeply to the foot of a rocky ridge. Drop over the ridge and continue through a rocky basin just east of the summit. In early season, the basin is snow filled, so come prepared for snow travel. As the snow melts, the trail becomes muddy.

Once across the basin, the trail climbs briefly to the summit. Views are fantastic! Mount Rainier dominates to the south, while dozens of peaks rise dramatically to the north and east, including nearby Kaleetan Peak and The Tooth, with Mounts Thompson and Stuart farther off, and Glacier Peak and Mount Baker in the distance. The lookout is no longer used to spot fires but is often occupied during summer months by volunteers who help maintain this and other trails in the Alpine Lakes Wilderness.

**Options:** A popular variation is to ascend the final rocky ridge westward to the summit. It involves easy scrambling over big, granite blocks. A few loose blocks and some steep drop-offs make this a potentially dangerous route for the inexperienced. Definitely stay off of snow patches on the ridge, because there's no safe runout; if you slip and fall, you'll wipe out on the boulders for sure.

During late spring, when snow makes crossing the gully a risky proposition, you can go cross-country up the southwest ridge, a bit more strenuous but pleasant enough. Much of the way is on big, granite blocks, easy enough by scrambling standards, but a few loose blocks will be encountered here and there, so be careful both going up and down.

# 11

# Annette Lake

**Overview:** *A strenuous forest hike up Humpback Creek to Annette Lake.*

**Distance:** 7.2 miles round-trip.
**Difficulty:** Moderate.
**Best season:** Summer through fall.
**Traffic:** Foot traffic only; heavy use.
**High point:** About 3,700 feet.

**Maps:** USGS Snoqualmie Pass and Lost Lake;
Green Trails No. 207 (Snoqualmie Pass).
**For more information:** USDA Forest Service,
North Bend Ranger District Office.

**Finding the trailhead:** Annette Lake Trail 1019 begins from the Asahel Curtis trailhead, just off I–90. Drive I–90 to Denny Creek/Asahel Curtis, exit 47. Turn south and after a hundred yards or so come to a junction with Forest Service Road 5590. Turn left and follow unpaved FS 5590 about 0.4 mile to the trailhead parking lot. The Annette Lake trailhead is on the southeast side of the parking lot, just right of the kiosk. This is a high car-prowl trailhead, so park and lock your car and leave nothing of value inside. A Northwest Forest Pass is required.

## Key points:
**0.3** Humpback Creek.
**0.5** Power lines.
**1.0** Iron Horse Trail junction.
**1.4** Footbridge.
**1.6** The first of many switchbacks.
**2.5** A couple more switchbacks.
**2.6** Steep gully crossing.
**3.6** Annette Lake.

**The hike:** Annette Lake is a small, secluded lake set in a talus and silver fir–lined basin at the foot of Silver and Abiel Peaks, just south of I–90 near Snoqualmie Pass. It is not within the Alpine Lakes Wilderness but is a popular hike, perhaps too popular for its own good, as the lake and trail are suffering from years of unmitigated abuse.

From the parking lot, find the trailhead just past the gated road right of the bulletin board. The trail register is a few steps up the trail, on the left. The first 0.5 mile of the trail climbs steadily through logged-over forest. The trees have grown back, but the slopes are mostly devoid of undergrowth except near the creek, which thankfully drowns out some of the traffic noise from the interstate. In 0.3 mile, a footbridge crosses Humpback Creek at a pretty spot where the creek cascades over boulders. The trail soon intersects a couple of old road grades, then just past 0.5

# Annette Lake

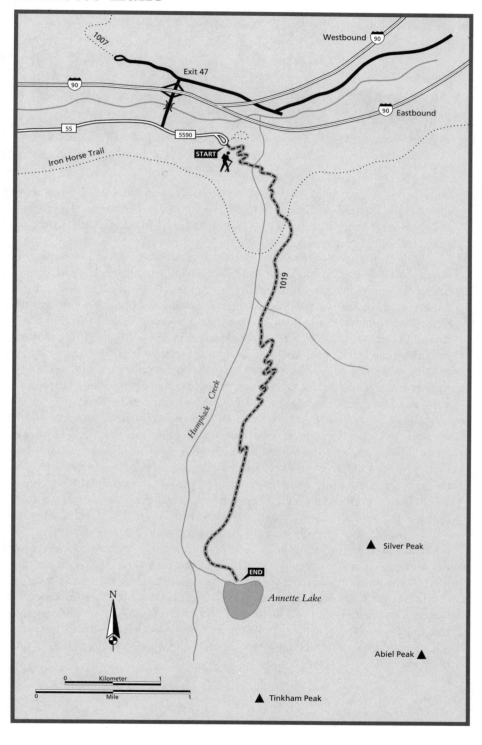

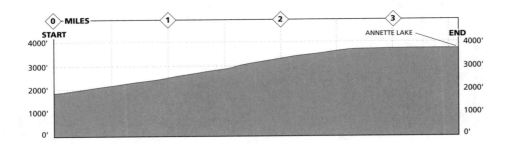

MILES 0 1 2 3
START ANNETTE LAKE END
4000' 4000'
3000' 3000'
2000' 2000'
1000' 1000'
0' 0'

mile, it crosses a clearing, where crackling power lines hang overhead. Once across the clearing, the trail continues climbing, now through open forest. Big cedars—somehow spared the lumberman's ax—dominate this shady slope, with slender silver firs shooting up everywhere.

About 1 mile up the trail is Iron Horse Trail, a flat, gravel grade. Look both ways before crossing, so you aren't flattened by mountain bikers. The trail continues on the other side, crossing a footbridge, then starts climbing. In a few minutes, footbridges lead across a marshy area thick with ferns and devil's club. A stream is crossed a few minutes farther on. Soon, the trail starts up switchbacks, eventually flattening out after gaining 500 feet of elevation in just 0.5 mile. A pair of quick switchbacks and some steep trail lead another 0.5 mile and 400 feet up to a stream crossing in a steep gully. The worst is over; the trail levels out, even loses a little elevation, traversing several talus slides, some overgrown with slide alder, maple, ferns, and lilies, some just bare rocks falling away to the canyon floor.

About 0.5 mile before the lake, the slope levels out. Hike across the forest floor, up, over, and around tree roots worn bare by the passing of thousands of pairs of boots. Finally, you arrive at Annette Lake, elevation 3,700 feet, a modest alpine lake framed by talus and silver fir, with a small waterfall spilling over a rocky outcrop on the far shore. Trails lead part of the way around the lake, providing access to a proliferation of overused campsites. There are several places where you can get down to the water, although the lakeshore is thick with alder, ash, huckleberry, and rhododendron shrubs, especially near the outlet stream. Beargrass and white rhododendron bloom on the rocky slopes here, beneath a canopy of hemlocks and silver firs. Chipmunks and camp robbers, adapted to human visitors, will eat from your hand, if you let them, although you're not doing them a favor by feeding them.

If you want to be alone at Annette Lake, come on a rainy fall day, the wetter the better. A good, hard rain will discourage all but the most stubborn hikers from trudging up the muddy, slippery trail. You probably won't have the lake all to yourself, though; even on the rainiest days, a handful of soggy hikers are sure to find their way here.

**Options:** The Asahel Curtis Nature Trail begins just left of the Annette Lake trailhead. This 0.5-mile interpretive loop leads through old-growth fir and hemlock forest. The Snoqualmie Tunnel (Hike 17) is easily reached by hiking east on Iron Horse Trail from the junction; it's flat going for about 1.5 miles to the tunnel, a worthwhile side trip if you have time to spare before heading home.

# 12

# Denny Creek–Melakwa Lakes

**Overview:** *A popular hike up Denny Creek and over Hemlock Pass to Melakwa Lakes.*

**Distance:** 9.2 miles round-trip.
**Difficulty:** Moderate.
**Best season:** Summer through fall.
**Traffic:** Foot traffic only; heavy use.
**High point:** About 4,620 feet.

**Maps:** USGS Snoqualmie Pass; Green Trails No. 207 (Snoqualmie Pass).
**For more information:** USDA Forest Service, North Bend Ranger District Office.

**Finding the trailhead:** Denny Creek Trail 1014 begins near Denny Creek Campground, about 3 miles west of Snoqualmie Pass. Drive I–90 to Denny Creek/Asahel Curtis (Tinkham Road), exit 47. Go north briefly to a junction and turn right, following the paved road 0.2 mile under the freeway overpass to a fork. Turn left up Denny Creek Road (Forest Service Road 58) and follow it another 2.1 miles to Denny Creek Campground. Continue 0.3 mile past the campground entrance to Forest Service Road 5830, then turn left and follow FS 5830 to the Denny Creek/Melakwa Lakes trailhead parking lot. Alternatively, get off at Snoqualmie Pass West Summit, exit 52 and go north, briefly following Alpental Road 0.1 mile, then take a left on Denny Creek Road and follow 2.4 miles down to the FS 5830 turnoff. This is a very popular trail, so the parking lot is usually overflowing on summer weekends. This is also a high car-prowl trailhead, so park and lock your car and leave nothing of value behind. A Northwest Forest Pass is required.

## Key points:
**0.5** The trail passes under the westbound lanes of I–90.
**1.2** Denny Creek crossing.
**2.0** Keekwulee Falls.
**2.8** The trail crosses Denny Creek above Snowshoe Falls.
**4.2** Hemlock Pass.
**4.6** Lower Melakwa Lake.

# Denny Creek–Melakwa Lakes

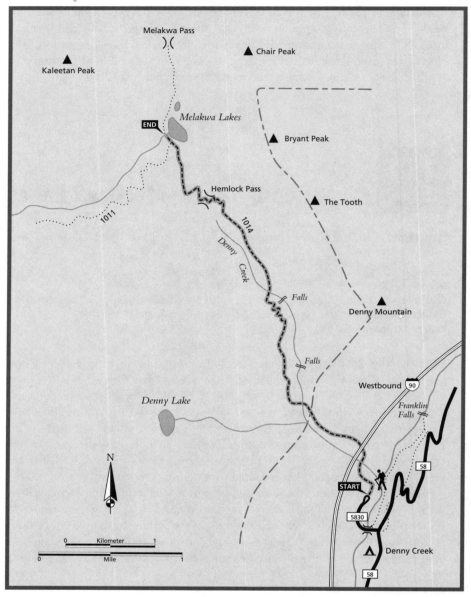

Melakwa Pass

▲ Chair Peak

▲ Kaleetan Peak

*Melakwa Lakes*

END

▲ Bryant Peak

Hemlock Pass

▲ The Tooth

1011

1014

*Denny Creek*

*Falls*

▲ Denny Mountain

*Falls*

Westbound 90

*Franklin Falls*

*Denny Lake*

N

58

START

5830

0  Kilometer  1
0  Mile  1

△ Denny Creek

58

**The hike:** Denny Creek Trail is a popular hike near Snoqualmie Pass, leading 4.6 miles over Hemlock Pass to Melakwa Lakes, two beautiful alpine lakes set in a rocky, talus-rimmed basin between Kaleetan and Chair Peaks. *Melakwa* means "mosquito" in the Chinook jargon; the lakes are a little buggy in early summer, but

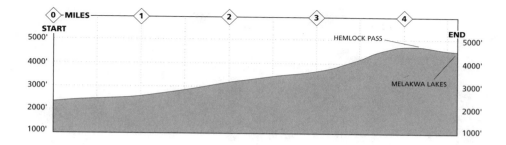

that doesn't seem to stop anyone from visiting. This is one of the most crowded hikes in the area on sunny summer weekends, but there is room to spread out once you reach the lakes.

Get your permit and start hiking. The trail begins climbing gradually from the trailhead, through fir and hemlock forest, crossing under the mammoth concrete freeway bridge in 0.5 mile. Easy hiking through old fir and hemlock forest leads to Denny Creek, which is crossed by a sturdy footbridge. The creek flows down granite slabs here, making this a popular spot for hikers and their kids, who like to sunbathe and splash in the water. Some treat the slabs as a water slide, a bad idea, since sliding too far could land you in rocks and trees.

Once across the creek, the trail starts climbing, first contouring lush talus slopes opposite Keekwulee Falls, through bracken ferns, thimbleberry, and wildflowers—columbine, paintbrush, and tiger lily among them. Steep switchbacks follow, climbing along the edge of a steep canyon. You can sneak a peak at the creek, and Snowshoe Falls just up the canyon, but the cliffs are steep and dangerous. Be careful here, especially when hiking in the dark; hikers have walked right off the edge, with predictable results.

The trail levels out and crosses Denny Creek once again, just above Snowshoe Falls. You can find a side trail here, leading downstream for a look at the falls. The trail eventually levels out in a broad basin overgrown with hemlocks and huckleberries, with views of The Tooth, a craggy, canine tooth–shaped peak popular with rock climbers. All too soon the trail starts climbing again in a series of open switchbacks that finally reach the high point of the hike, Hemlock Pass, elevation 4,620 feet. From the pass, the trail drops quickly to the larger of the two Melakwa Lakes, elevation 4,500 feet. This final stretch of trail is muddy in early season and after a good rain. Once at the lakes, find a quiet spot near the shore to rest and snack, or a campsite if you are spending the night. There are several campsites at the lakes; they fill up fast on summer weekends. No campfires are allowed. There is a privy up a side trail near the outlet stream. Be warned: The popular scrambling route up Kaleetan Peak begins via the privy trail, so don't be surprised if a party of climbers comes trudging by.

**Options:** A "mandatory" side trip is to continue hiking up the basin above the lakes, through big talus, to Melakwa Pass, the 5,400-foot divide between Kaleetan

*Lower Melakwa Lake*

and Chair Peaks. Cairns may mark the way, which is pretty easy as "off-trail" hikes go. Be careful in early season to avoid plunging through a snow patch into a hole between the rocks, and of shifting talus. Very experienced off-trail travelers can follow a high route over Melakwa Pass and down to Snow Lake; there is no trail, and it's steep and difficult going, definitely not recommended for any but the most experienced.

Overnight options include a 2.5-mile hike down to Tuscohatchie Lakes or another 3.5 miles to Kaleetan Lake. There are several options here for two- and three-day backpacks.

# 13

# Franklin Falls

**Overview:** *A short hike along South Fork Snoqualmie River to a waterfall.*

**Distance:** 0.2 mile round-trip from upper trailhead or 2.0 mile loop.
**Difficulty:** Easy.
**Best season:** Early summer through fall.
**Traffic:** Very heavy.

**High point:** About 2,700 feet.
**Maps:** USGS Snoqualmie Pass; Green Trails No. 207 (Snoqualmie Pass).
**For more information:** USDA Forest Service, North Bend Ranger District Office.

**Finding the trailhead:** Franklin Falls Trail begins just north of Denny Creek Campground near Snoqualmie Pass. Drive I–90 to Denny Creek/Asahel Curtis (Tinkham Road), exit 47. Go north briefly to a junction and turn right, following the paved road 0.2 mile under the freeway overpass to a fork. Turn left up Denny Creek Road (Forest Service Road 58) and follow it another 2.1 miles to Denny Creek Campground. For the loop hike, park near the bridge on the spur road leading up to Denny Creek trailhead. For the shortcut trail, continue 0.4 mile up the road from the turnoff to Denny Creek trailhead. The trail begins on the northwest side of the road, next to a section of split-rail fence. There are usually several cars parked here. A Northwest Forest Pass is not required at the upper trailhead but is required at the lower trailhead.

## Key points:
**0.9** Shortcut trail junction.
**1.0** Franklin Falls.
**1.6** First road crossing.
**1.8** Second road crossing.

# Franklin Falls

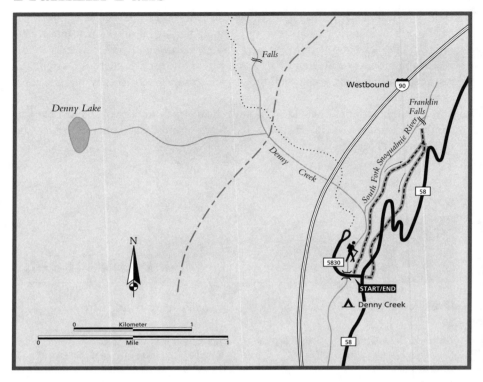

**1.9** Third road crossing.
**2.0** End of wagon road loop.

**The hike:** Franklin Falls is a pretty waterfall located about 0.5 mile upriver from Denny Creek Campground. The falls can be reached via a very short downhill trail from Denny Creek Road, making it a very popular hike. The last little bit of trail is a scramble down a slabby rock, making this hike a bit difficult for some, but most manage to get up close and personal with the falls despite this obstacle. The best way to do this hike is as a loop from the trailhead on the east side of the Denny Creek bridge.

Find the trail on the east side of the bridge and start hiking northward up alongside the South Fork Snoqualmie River, not much more than a wide creek here. The trail passes several private cabins; stay on the trail. The trail goes in and out of trees, always close to the creek. Just short of a mile, the trail climbs up to a junction with the shortcut trail. Continue down the trail to the creek just short of the falls, visible just upstream. Scramble down a slabby rock to the gravel bar at the base of the falls. Not much to it. Just be careful not to slip and hurt yourself on the last bit to the falls.

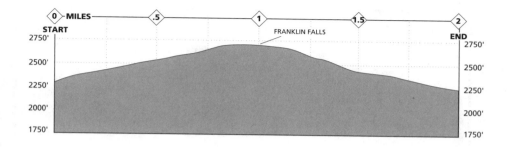

On the return trip, take the shortcut trail up to the road and cross, then hike through shady hemlock forest back to the trailhead. This portion of the trail follows a segment of an old wagon road, which followed an old Indian trail across Snoqualmie Pass. It's mostly quiet forest hiking here, away from the crowds at the falls. The trail crosses the road a few times and comes out just across the road from Denny Creek Campground.

**Options:** Those in a hurry can hike the shortcut trail, which drops down from the road briefly to join the trail leading up from Denny Creek, then turns right and continues down to the falls, a hike of maybe 0.2 mile round-trip.

# 14

# Snow Lake

**Overview:** *The most popular hike in the Snoqualmie Pass area.*

**Distance:** 6.6 miles round-trip.
**Difficulty:** Easy to moderate.
**Best season:** Midsummer to fall.
**Traffic:** Foot traffic only; very heavy use.
**High point:** About 4,380 feet.

**Maps:** USGS Snoqualmie Pass; Green Trails No. 207 (Snoqualmie Pass).
**For more information:** USDA Forest Service, North Bend Ranger District Office.

**Finding the trailhead:** Snow Lake Trail 1013 begins from the Alpental Ski Area parking lot just northwest of Snoqualmie Pass. Drive I–90 to Snoqualmie Pass West Summit, exit 52. Head north and follow Alpental Road some 1.3 miles to the ski area parking lot. The Snow Lake trailhead is on the northwest side of the parking lot, up a short service road. A Northwest Forest Pass is required even though this is a private parking lot.

# Snow Lake

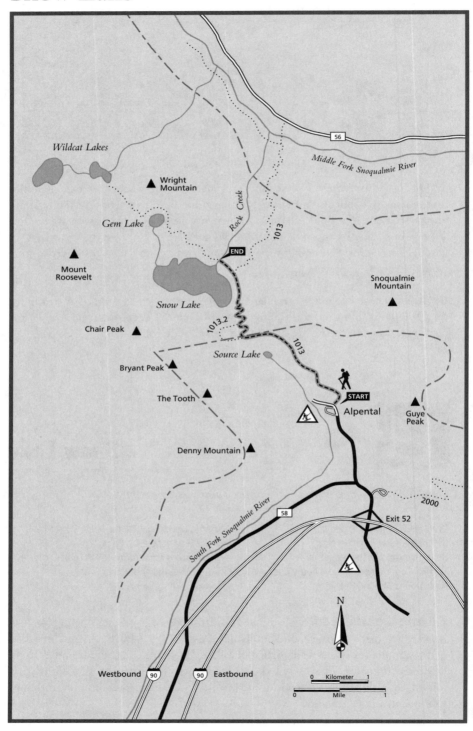

## Key points:
**1.8** Source Lake Overlook junction.
**2.3** Snow Lake divide.
**3.3** Rock Creek Trail junction at Snow Lake.

**The hike:** Snow Lake Trail is one of the most popular hikes in the Alpine Lakes Wilderness. It is a relatively short hike on a wide, accessible trail with gradual elevation gain and great views. The problem with this hike is that it is so popular—too popular for some, who avoid it and the crowds of hikers it attracts, especially on summer weekends. If you dislike crowded hikes, come on a rainy weekday. You'll miss the views, but at least you'll have the trail mostly to yourself.

The trail begins just up a service road from the Alpental parking lot. Get your permit and start up the trail, which contours up the northern slope of the South Fork Snoqualmie River valley, through hemlock and silver fir forest, crossing several small streams and, soon, the wilderness boundary. At about 1 mile, the trail breaks into the open, crossing a brushy talus slide, with views across the valley of The Tooth, Bryant Peak, and Chair Peak, views which get better as you continue up the trail. At about 1.8 miles, the trail reaches a junction with Source Lake Overlook Trail 1013.2, an old climbers' trail leading off toward The Tooth, providing views down the valley to Source Lake, source of the Snoqualmie River. The trail switches back a couple of times as it climbs a rocky 0.5 mile to the Snow Lake divide, the high point of the hike at 4,380 feet elevation. Views here extend down to Snow Lake and up to the mountains, including Chair Peak and across the North Fork Snoqualmie River to Big Snow Mountain, and look back to Guye Peak and down the South Fork Snoqualmie River to the pass. You may find snow on the north side of the divide until midsummer, even as late as August some years. If so, unless you have an ice ax and snow hiking experience, turn back. Hikers who continue on steep snow without an ice ax risk injury or worse.

From the divide, the trail descends a series of switchbacks that drop quickly into the Snow Lake basin. You get glimpses of the lake as you descend, which may make you impatient, but resist the urge to cut switchbacks. The trail soon levels out and meanders above the northeastern shore of Snow Lake, through heather meadows, mountain-hemlock, subalpine and silver fir, mountain-ash, and huckleberries. At 3.3 miles, the trail reaches the junction with Rock Creek Trail, the turnaround point for most hikers, who find a spot to sit, eat lunch, and soak in the views of the

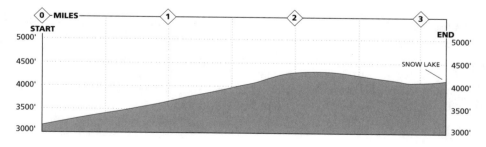

craggy north face of Chair Peak rising directly up from the lake waters. The lakeshore has been heavily abused over the years, and there are areas where restoration efforts are in progress. Try to find an established path to the water's edge instead of tromping over the meadows and flowers and creating another path. Stay out of restoration areas, please.

The lakeshore is designated day use only. There are a few designated campsites, spread out and hidden in the trees away from the lakeshore. Those wanting to camp out at Snow Lake should take some time to find a designated campsite instead of just dropping their packs at the first bare spot. Better to continue on to Gem Lake or Wildcat Lakes to get away from the crowds.

**Options:** If Snow Lake isn't far enough, or if you want to escape the crowds, the trail continues another 1.5 miles to Gem Lake, elevation 4,860 feet, a small lake tucked in a hemlock-lined basin just northwest of Snow Lake, then up and over a divide and down another 1.4 miles to Lower Wildcat Lake, elevation 3,900 feet, 6.2 miles from the trailhead. The views on the hike up to Gem Lake are the best on the entire trail, although many hikers scramble up to the summit of Wright Mountain, a 5,430-foot talus hump rising just north of Gem Lake, which offers the best views around. This scramble isn't recommended for casual hikers, but then, most of the casual hikers turned back at Snow Lake.

# 15 Commonwealth Basin

**Overview:** *A hike through Commonwealth Basin to a saddle below Red Mountain.*

**Distance:** 9.4 miles round-trip.
**Difficulty:** Strenuous.
**Best season:** Summer through fall.
**Traffic:** Foot traffic only; moderate use.
**High point:** About 5,300 feet.

**Maps:** USGS Snoqualmie Pass; Green Trails No. 207 (Snoqualmie Pass).
**For more information:** USDA Forest Service, North Bend Ranger District Office.

**Finding the trailhead:** Commonwealth Basin Trail 1033 begins from the Pacific Crest Trail (PCT) north trailhead at Snoqualmie Pass. Drive I–90 to Snoqualmie Pass West Summit, exit 52. Turn north and drive a scant 0.1 mile to the PCT parking lot turnoff. The hikers' trailhead is on the right; the stock trailhead is on the left. This is a high car-prowl trailhead, so lock your car and leave nothing of value behind. A Northwest Forest Pass is required.

# Commonwealth Basin

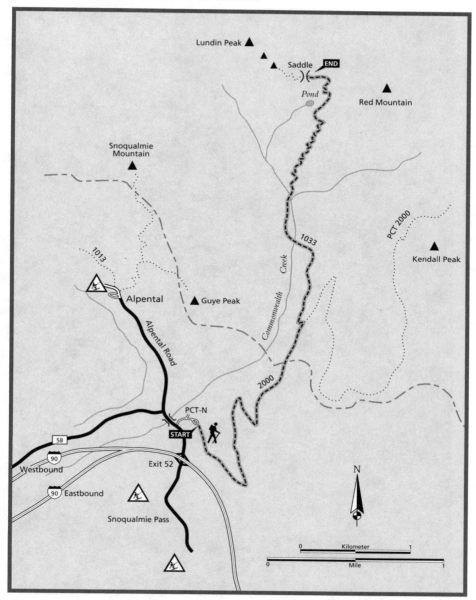

## Key points:

**2.4** Commonwealth Trail junction.

**2.9** Boulder hop across or ford Commonwealth Creek.

**3.1** Cross a small stream, which flows down part of the trail; switchbacks begin.

*Meadow in Commonwealth Basin*

**4.0** The switchbacks end abruptly at a basin below Red Mountain.

**4.7** Trail's end at Red Mountain saddle.

**The hike:** Commonwealth Basin Trail 1033 is an old segment of the Cascade Crest Trail that hardly anybody used because of a dangerous snow gully on the north side of Red Mountain saddle. The trail beyond the saddle has been abandoned, but the trail leading through Commonwealth Basin and up to the saddle has not. It is not the most popular trail in the Snoqualmie Pass area, but is hardly forgotten.

Get your permit and start hiking. Since the old trail is abandoned and unmarked, the first 2.4 miles of the hike now officially follow the PCT segment leading north from Snoqualmie Pass (see Kendall Catwalk, Hike 16). The trail starts out traversing eastward through marshy woods, then switches back northward, then again, climbing steadily through silver fir and hemlock forest, gaining about 900 feet in the first 2 miles. Soon the trail crosses a broad talus slide, entering the Alpine Lakes Wilderness and descending briefly past big boulders and curious marmots. At the far side of the talus slope is a noisy stream splashing over the rocks and across the trail; soon the trail reenters the woods, and a few minutes farther, at 2.4 miles, is the Commonwealth Trail junction.

From the PCT, the trail drops down briefly and passes a junction with the old trail, which was abandoned after the PCT was rerouted. The trail turns upstream and soon flattens out, winding through old-growth fir and hemlock, huckleberry, and mountain-ash. The transition between new trail and old is abrupt; the old trail is over exposed roots and rocks, well eroded by snowmelt runoff and decades of beating by hikers' boots. In about 0.5 mile, the trail crosses Commonwealth Creek; there's no bridge, so just hop across the rocks or get your feet wet. There are a few abused campsites near the crossing, a harsh contrast to the lush green meadows fringing the creek. A few minutes farther is another stream crossing; here the stream has invaded the trail, but you can still get across without getting wet if you are careful. Once across this stream, the trail starts up a wooded ridge, and keeps going that way, switchback after switchback, gaining some 800 feet in less than a mile, but rewarding you with increasing views. Western hemlock is gradually supplanted by mountain-hemlock, and silver firs tend to subalpine as you climb higher; Indian paintbrush and tiger lily make their appearance amid the ubiquitous lupine.

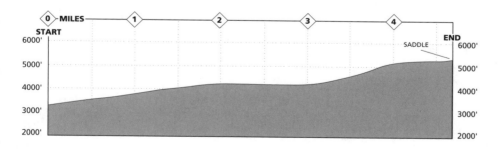

Finally, the switchbacks end and the trail drops briefly into a basin below Red Mountain. A side trail leads down to a large pond; there are a few campsites here, good snow camping in early season.

On the uphill side of the basin, pick up the trail and traverse rust-colored talus slopes toward the saddle, amid phlox, bistort, valerian and spirea, curvy hemlocks, and low-lying mountain-ash. Listen for marmots whistling in the near distance as you climb the last switchbacks to the ridge crest. The views are tremendous—Big Snow Mountain, Mount Thompson, Chimney Rock, and Summit Chief Mountain, to name only a few. It's a long way down on the north side, so stay back from the edge.

The trail traverses the ridge crest some, then drops down to the saddle. This is trail's end, as far as most hikers venture.

**Options:** You can see the old, abandoned trail leading down the other side of the ridge, but don't risk it unless it is snow-free and you are sure of your ability to follow a long-abandoned trail. Better is to continue up the climbers' trail leading west from the saddle to a 5,700-foot false summit of Lundin Peak. This is really the best part of the hike. The going is a bit steep and rocky but easy enough, up white granite blocks and through heather and juniper meadows, with fantastic views. You can see south to Mount Rainier and Mount Adams, east to Mount Stuart and Mount Thompson, and all directions to myriad other peaks. The climbers' trail ends abruptly at a rocky peak. Don't stray too close to the edge; there are steep cliffs about. Find a nice spot, enjoy the view, then head back down the trail.

Signs along the trail point the way to Red Mountain, and consequently some hikers come thinking they will find a trail to the summit of 5,890-foot Red Mountain. There is no trail. There is a scrambling route, but it isn't recommended for hikers. For details, refer to *Climbing Washington's Mountains* (see Appendix E).

# 16

# Kendall Catwalk

**Overview:** *A popular segment of the Pacific Crest Trail north of Snoqualmie Pass.*

**Distance:** 11.0 miles round-trip.
**Difficulty:** Strenuous.
**Best season:** Midsummer through fall.
**Traffic:** Foot and stock traffic; heavy use.
**High point:** About 5,400 feet.

**Maps:** USGS Snoqualmie Pass, Chikamin Peak; Green Trails No. 207 (Snoqualmie Pass).
**For more information:** USDA Forest Service, North Bend Ranger District Office.

**Finding the trailhead:** The hike to Kendall Catwalk follows a segment of the Pacific Crest Trail (PCT) 2000 north from Snoqualmie Pass. Drive I-90 to Snoqualmie Pass West Summit, exit 52. Turn north and drive a scant 0.1 mile to the PCT parking lot turnoff. Stay right to the hikers' trailhead. This is a high car-prowl trailhead, so lock your car and leave nothing of value behind. A Northwest Forest Pass is required.

## Key points:

**1.9** Alpine Lakes Wilderness boundary and talus slide.
**2.4** Commonwealth Trail junction.
**2.8** A sharp switchback below Red Mountain.
**3.3** A stream, the last reliable water source before the lakes.
**4.0** Kendall Flats.
**5.3** Kendall Peak saddle.
**5.5** Kendall Catwalk.

**The hike:** The Kendall Catwalk is a segment of the PCT traversing a narrow shelf blasted out of slabby cliffs, one of the most airy and exposed sections of trail in the Alpine Lakes Wilderness. Hiking as far as the catwalk and back is a popular day hike of about 11 miles.

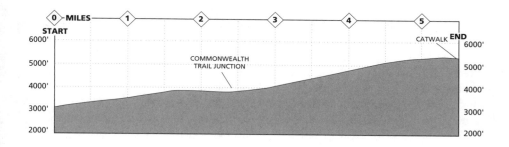

# Kendall Catwalk

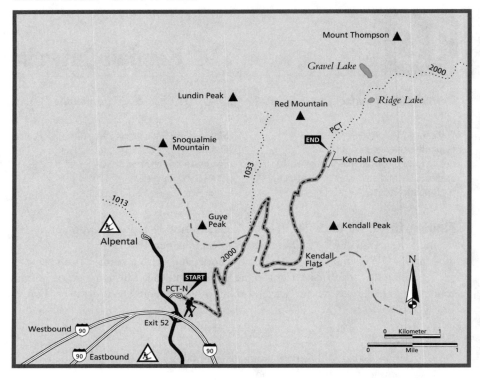

Begin from the PCT-N trailhead at Snoqualime Pass. The PCT starts out traversing eastward through marshy woods, then switches back northward, then twice more, climbing steadily through old-growth silver fir and hemlock forest, the forest floor dotted with bead lily, tiarella, vanilla leaf, and bunchberry, with columbine and monkshood amid the ferns and salmonberry swaths. The trail gains about 900 feet in the first 2 miles, never steep but always climbing ever gradually away from the freeway noise. Soon the trail crosses a broad talus slide, descending slightly past big boulders and curious marmots, and enters the Alpine Lakes Wilderness. There are great views of surrounding peaks as you cross the talus. At the far side of the talus slope is a noisy stream splashing over the rocks and across the trail; soon the trail reenters the woods, and in a few minutes reaches the Commonwealth Trail junction (Hike 15).

The PCT continues northward another 0.5 mile, opening up to offer views of Red Mountain, Lundin Peak, and Guye Peak, before switching back again and reentering the forest. In another 0.5 mile is a stream splashing over a rock ledge and across the trail; this is the last reliable water source until the lakes. Just past the stream, the trail suddenly comes into a clearing created by a massive avalanche that, as you will see, snapped big trees like matchsticks. Once past the carnage, the trail

*Alta Mountain from Kendall Catwalk*

reenters the woods and switches back again, then traverses a wooded slope. Soon the trail gains Kendall Flats, a wooded ridge crest at a flat area with a few campsites. The trail crosses the ridge crest, then back over, and curves gradually northward. Trees give way to open talus slopes, exposed to the afternoon sun, but also to increasing views. The trail switches back twice more, then curves around the north side of Kendall Peak to a 5,400-foot-high gap in the rocky ridge dividing Commonwealth and Silver Creek drainages. Take a break and enjoy the view, then continue on the trail, which soon crosses the Kendall Catwalk, a narrow shelf blasted out of a slabby cliff that drops away hundreds of feet into Silver Creek basin. Watch your step! If there is snow on the catwalk, it is best to call it a day and head back. A slip here could be fatal.

**Options:** For most, the catwalk is far enough, but another 1.5 miles of hiking lead to Ridge and Gravel Lakes, a 14-mile round-trip that makes for a good overnight hike.

An ascent of Kendall Peak is an obvious diversion, as a scrambling route plainly leads up the ridge crest directly from the gap. However, the route has loose rock and is very exposed in places and is not recommended for any but experienced alpine scramblers. There is an easier route, but it isn't as obvious as the ridge route. If you try it, be very careful not to knock off loose rock on unsuspecting hikers on the trail below. Refer to *Climbing Washington's Mountains* (see Appendix E) for information about climbing this and other nearby peaks.

# 17 Snoqualmie Tunnel

**Overview:** *A spooky hike through an abandoned railroad tunnel.*

**Distance:** 5.4 miles round-trip.
**Difficulty:** Easy.
**Best season:** May 1 to October 31.
**Traffic:** Foot and bike traffic; very heavy use.

**High point:** About 2,600 feet.
**Maps:** USGS Snoqualmie Pass; Green Trails No. 207 (Snoqualmie Pass).
**For more information:** Washington State Parks.

**Finding the trailhead:** The Snoqualmie Tunnel's east portal is located about 2 miles east of Snoqualmie Pass. Drive I–90 to Hyak/Gold Creek, exit 54. Turn south to a stop sign and turn left onto the Washington Highway 906 West spur. Follow about 0.5 mile and turn right to enter the trailhead parking lot. A trailhead parking pass is not presently required. Park hours are from 6:15 A.M. to dusk.

## Key points:
**0.4**  The tunnel's east portal.
**2.7**  The tunnel's west portal at Portal Creek.

Snoqualmie Tunnel

**The hike:** This hike follows a segment of Iron Horse Trail, an old railroad grade converted to a multiuse trail that extends over 100 miles from Cedar Falls near North Bend across the Cascade Range to the Columbia River. The most popular segment of the trail is through the Snoqualmie Tunnel. The tunnel is not so much a hike as an experience. The hike description is as easy as they come: Enter the tunnel, hike straight ahead until you come out the other side, then turn around and hike back through. But there's more to the hike than just that. It's a long, spooky walk in the dark that's just plain fun.

From the trailhead parking lot, hike or bike 0.4 mile to the east portal. Enter the tunnel, passing the old wooden doors that used to be closed in winter to prevent a cold wind from blowing through the tunnel, forming dangerous icicles. The tunnel is closed in winter now because of that very same risk. As you enter, your eyes will take a few minutes to adjust to the darkness, but you don't need your flashlight just yet. You can see the west portal in the distance and can usually see a line of flashlight and headlamp beams coming toward you. Walk straight ahead into the darkness, occasionally past or through a water drip or puddle. It takes about forty-five minutes for most hikers to hike from one end of the tunnel to the other.

The tunnel is chilly, usually about 50 degrees Fahrenheit, a little cooler if a breeze is blowing through or you are riding a mountain bike. Put on a sweater or a windbreaker. The tunnel is not lighted, so you'll need flashlights, and you would be wise to bring extra batteries. Although you might be able to hike through relatively safely without flashlights, bike riders and other hikers in the tunnel might not be able to see you.

Keep in mind that if nature calls while you're in the tunnel, you can't just go wherever—like in the woods. Just try to hold on; there's a toilet at each end of the tunnel. The tunnel is barrier free, so you may see a person in a wheelchair go whizzing past every now and then.

Iron Horse Park is designated for day use only. Summer hours are from 6:30 A.M. to 9:00 P.M.; winter hours are from 8:00 A.M. to 5:00 P.M. However, the tunnel is closed from November 1 through May 1 because big icicles form in the tunnel during winter, creating a safety concern.

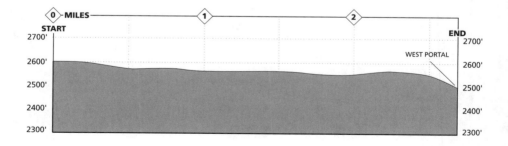

**Options:** You can approach the tunnel from the west via Annette Lake Trail 1019 (Hike 11), which intersects Iron Horse Trail just 1.5 miles west of the west portal. If you can arrange transportation, this is a good one-way hike of about 4.8 miles, in either direction. The Annette Lake Trail junction is 3.8 miles west from the east portal trailhead.

# Gold Creek–Alaska Lake

**Overview:** *An old, less-traveled path leading up Gold Creek to Alaska Lake.*

**Distance:** 11.0 miles round-trip.
**Difficulty:** Moderate.
**Best season:** Summer through fall.
**Traffic:** Stock and foot traffic; moderate to heavy use.

**High point:** About 4,230 feet.
**Maps:** USGS Snoqualmie Pass and Chikamin Peak; Green Trails No. 207 (Snoqualmie Pass).
**For more information:** USDA Forest Service, North Bend Ranger District Office.

**Finding the trailhead:** Gold Creek Trail 1314 begins a few miles east of Snoqualmie Pass. Drive I–90 to Hyak/Gold Creek, exit 54, about 2 miles east of Snoqualmie Summit. Turn north and proceed to the frontage road marked Gold Creek (Forest Service Road 4832), then follow the paved road 1 mile to the Gold Creek turnoff. Proceed up the road 0.4 mile to a fork. Stay right on the gravel road; if you end up on the paved picnic area loop, you went the wrong way. From the picnic area fork, continue 0.8 mile, staying on the main line until you reach the trailhead kiosk beside a gate. Park along the road, being careful not to block the road or other vehicles. A Northwest Forest Pass is not presently required.

## Key points:
**0.5** The old trailhead at road's end.
**1.9** Alpine Lakes Wilderness boundary marker.
**3.5** Gold Creek crossing.
**3.8** Silver Creek crossing.
**4.3** Alaska Creek crossing.
**4.5** Alaska and Joe Lakes junction.
**5.5** Alaska Lake.

**The hike:** Gold Creek Trail is an old trail leading up a broad glacial valley northeast of Snoqualmie Pass. It is a quiet valley hike through old-growth forest, with

# Gold Creek–Alaska Lake

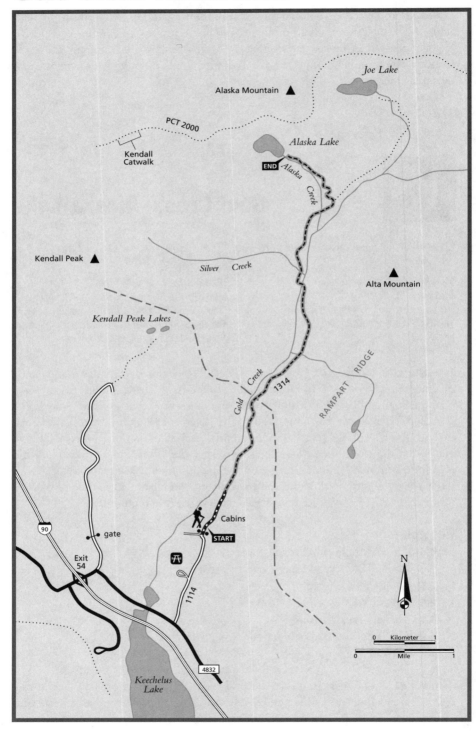

Joe Lake

Alaska Mountain ▲

PCT 2000

Kendall
Catwalk

*Alaska Lake*

END *Alaska Creek*

Kendall Peak ▲

*Silver Creek*

▲ Alta Mountain

*Kendall Peak Lakes*

*Gold Creek*

1314

RAMPART RIDGE

90

gate

Cabins

START

Exit
54

1114

N

4832

*Keechelus Lake*

0  Kilometer  1

0  Mile  1

limited views but a bit more solitude than many of the shorter, more scenic lake hikes in this area. The farther you hike on this trail, the fewer people you are likely to see. Just don't expect solitude at Alaska Lake, which lies just below the Pacific Crest Trail (PCT).

**The hike** begins from the unmarked kiosk and follows a gravel road through private cabins. Walk up the main road, going pretty much straight ahead and ignoring all of the spur roads and loops leading to the cabins. In just over 0.5 mile is the old trailhead. The unsigned trail continues along a mossy old road grade about 0.2 mile to a log bridge, then leaves the road grade behind and becomes a real trail. Wildflowers line the trail this far, including columbine, paintbrush, monkshood, and thistle. The trail curves up toward the slope of Rampart Ridge, climbing gradually through overgrown talus slopes with occasional views up the valley to the ridges at the head of Gold Creek, then through quiet hemlock and silver fir forest. The talus slopes are brushy in early season; expect to do some wading before the trail crews brush them out. As the trail nears the creek, it passes through old-growth forest, with some impressive big hemlocks, cedars, and firs. The trail is marshy in places, crossing intermittent streams, muddy in early season. At just under 2 miles the trail passes the Alpine Lakes Wilderness boundary marker.

Typical wilderness forest trail continues up the valley. Hemlock needles carpet the trail bed; a variety of ferns, trillium and vanilla leaf, bead lily, and bunchberry sprout up everywhere. Devil's club runs riot in the muddy stream gullies. Gold Creek chatters off in the distance here, then closer, louder, until you are right above it. The trail curves back into the woods, up over roots and logs, then back to the creek, rock-hopping across intermittent streams. After passing a buggy marsh, the trail breaks out into the open on a gravel bar for a view up the valley and a narrow ribbon waterfall cascading down the cliffs of Rampart Ridge. After coming right up to the edge of Gold Creek, the trail climbs viciously for about 100 feet, then levels out again. Another overgrown talus slope follows, then the trail leads down to the creek again to a not-very-private campsite. The trail seems to vanish here. If lost, hike up the gravel bar along the creek about 100 yards and find another campsite, from where the trail continues into the woods. In a few minutes, the trail leads through another campsite and back to the river's edge, where a footlog invites you across. Most hikers stop here.

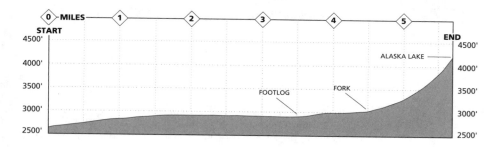

*Footlog across Gold Creek*

If you choose to continue, cross Gold Creek by using the footlog or by fording it, which can be difficult and even dangerous during high water. Pick up the trail on the other side, following a gravel bed a short distance, then cutting up a steep ramp, and dropping down to Silver Creek. Across Silver Creek, the trail traverses a rocky slope, much drier than the other side of the valley due to a local rainshadow provided by Kendall Peak, then drops again and crosses another creek, and meanders through brushy wooded flats. Alaska Creek is soon crossed; there is a small campsite beside the creek, just off the trail. Beyond the creek, the trail briefly leads through quiet forest to a fork. This is the end of the maintained trail but it's not the usual turnaround point. Take the left fork and climb a steep mile to Alaska Lake, a popular destination for those who didn't turn back at the footlog. From there, you're only a short climb away from the Pacific Crest Trail.

**Options:** At the fork at "trail's end," the right fork leads to Joe Lake. This trail is unmaintained and is woefully brushy and hard to follow. It is only used by anglers and climbers, and even they usually opt for a different way. If you try it, be prepared for some real bushwhacking. Perhaps a better route would be to hike up to Alaska Lake and continue up to the PCT, hike the PCT to near Ptarmigan Park, and descend to Joe Lake.

# 19 Lake Lillian/Mount Margaret

**Overview:** *A moderate hike to Lake Lillian, with side trails to the summit of Mount Margaret, alpine lakes, and high ridge explorations.*

**Distance:** 8.2 miles round-trip to Lake Lillian.
**Difficulty:** Moderate.
**Best season:** Early summer through fall.
**Traffic:** Foot traffic only; heavy use.
**High point:** 5,200 feet.

**Maps:** USGS Chikamin Peak; Green Trails No. 207 (Snoqualmie Pass).
**For more information:** USDA Forest Service, North Bend Ranger District Office.

**Finding the trailhead:** Lake Lillian Trail 1332 is located a few miles east of Snoqualmie Pass. Drive I–90 to Hyak/Gold Creek, exit 54, about 2 miles east of Snoqualmie Summit. Turn north and proceed to the frontage road marked Gold Creek (Forest Service Road 4832) on the north side of the interstate. Turn right and follow the road (first paved but later gravel) 3.6 miles to a fork, where a sign points left to Lake Lillian Trail. Stay on the main road and continue briefly to the next fork, where a sign points to Mount Margaret Trail. Stay right, following the signs, onto Forest Service Road 4934, and continue 0.4 mile to the trailhead parking lot on the left. If you stay on the main road, watching the signs and ignoring less-traveled spurs, you should have no difficulty. A Northwest Forest Pass is required.

# Lake Lillian/Mount Margaret

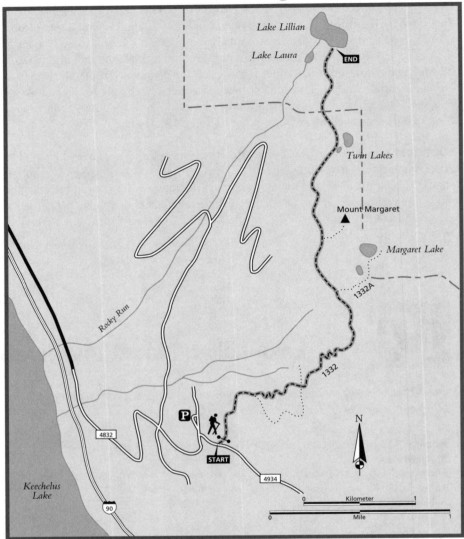

## Key points:

**0.6** Old trail junction.

**0.9** Upper road crossing.

**2.0** Margaret Lake Trail junction.

**2.3** Mount Margaret summit trail junction.

**3.3** Twin Lakes.

**4.1** Lake Lillian.

**The hike:** Lake Lillian Trail is popularly known as Mount Margaret Trail, since Mount Margaret's 5,539-foot summit is the usual destination of the many who hike this trail. However, the official trail does not lead to Mount Margaret's summit but to Lake Lillian and the several other lakes in this lovely little corner of the Alpine Lakes Wilderness.

Get your permit and start hiking. Walk a short distance up the road to a gate on the left. The gate may or may not prevent autos and motorbikes from passing; although this is a hiker-only trail, be on the lookout for renegade bikers and motorists. Hike up the road, which climbs for 0.6 mile through replanted forest and brush, to where the old trail begins. This trail segment may or may not be signed; it also may not show up on some maps. It leads up through an old clearcut, oddly reminiscent of subalpine slopes with all the diminutive silver and subalpine firs and surprisingly little brush. After a steep 0.3 mile the trail crosses the logging road and climbs the opposite bank, then climbs some more through the clearcut, with some wildflowers in season and increasing views to the south, including Silver Peak and Mount Rainier. Finally the trail leaves the clearcut and enters cool old-growth hemlock forest. The trail still climbs, now in lazy switchbacks, all the way to the ridge crest, where it levels out and traverses to a big patch of bare ground, marking the junction with Margaret Lake Trail 1332A.

To get to Lake Lillian, stay left and continue along the ridge. Stay left at a confusing little fork a few yards beyond; the right fork leads to views only. The trail soon leaves the crest and traverses the west slope of Mount Margaret, through subalpine forest, crossing heather meadows and talus slopes, then descends more abruptly down the opposite ridge and into a basin. Shortly along are Twin Lakes, just within the Alpine Lakes Wilderness boundary. The trail continues on through the basin, soon crossing the outlet stream and traversing wooded slopes and climbing overgrown talus slides another 0.8 mile to Lake Lillian. There are a few campsites at Twin Lakes and Lake Lillian, but not many.

**Options:** The trail down to Margaret Lake is steep, narrow, and not well maintained. The first "lake" you come to is Yvonne Lake, a mere pond. Margaret Lake is another 0.2 mile beyond. This lake is often crowded, sometimes with hikers who took a shortcut via logging roads from Lake Kachess. There are other lakes and ponds nearby.

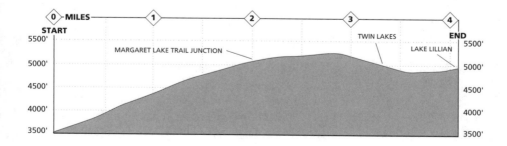

The summit of Mount Margaret is a short, steep hike from the Lake Lillian Trail. From the Margaret Lake Trail (1332A) junction, continue about 0.4 mile toward Lake Lillian. After crossing the first talus slope, look for a rough trail leading up through the trees. It leads steeply up the wooded slope to the ridge crest, then up the ridge and flowery meadows to the summit. It's worth the extra effort for the views of Rampart Ridge and surrounding lakes, meadows, and mountains, including Mounts Rainier, Stuart, and Thompson, Chimney Rock, and many others.

There are many high routes on Rampart Ridge. From Lake Lillian, you can scramble up to one of the high points for views, or find a cross-country route leading north to Rampart Lakes (Hike 20) and Alta Mountain.

# 20 Rachel Lake–Rampart Ridge

**Overview:** *A day hike to Rachel Lake and more lakes nestled on Rampart Ridge.*

**Distance:** 11.4 miles round-trip to Rampart Lakes.
**Difficulty:** Strenuous.
**Best season:** Summer through fall.
**Traffic:** Foot traffic only; heavy use.

**High point:** About 5,120 feet.
**Maps:** USGS Chikamin Peak; Green Trails No. 207 (Snoqualmie Pass).
**For more information:** USDA Forest Service, Cle Elum Ranger District Office.

**Finding the trailhead:** Rachel Lake Trail 1313 is approached from I–90 via Lake Kachess Road. Drive I–90 to Lake Kachess, exit 62. Turn north on Lake Kachess Road (Forest Service Road 49) and follow about 6 miles to Lake Kachess and Kachess Campground. Turn left on Forest Service Road 4930 and follow about 4 miles to a junction. Turn left on a spur road that leads 0.2 mile to the Rachel Lake trailhead parking lot. A Northwest Forest Pass is required.

## Key points:
**4.8** Rachel Lake.
**5.2** Rampart Ridge junction.
**5.7** Rampart Lakes.

**The hike:** Rampart Ridge is the craggy ridge rising up on the east side of Gold Creek valley, just a few miles east of Snoqualmie Pass. Lake Lillian Trail (Hike 19) flirts with the southern end of Rampart Ridge, but the ridge continues northward to its climax at the summit of Alta Mountain. In between are several high lakes dotting subalpine meadow basins famed for their fall colors. These lakes and the high ridge

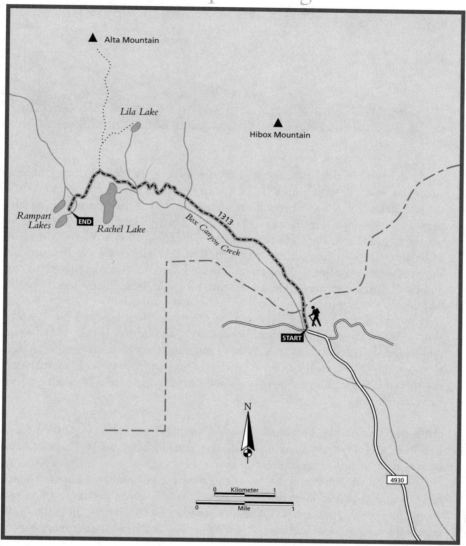

trail are popular and have been loved to death in places. Because of past abuse, hikers are encouraged to treat this as a day hike to avoid further adverse impacts.

From the trailhead, the trail contours through dense fir and hemlock forest, soon crossing a creek and entering the Alpine Lakes Wilderness. The trail climbs gradually along Box Canyon Creek for the first mile, then levels out, gaining barely 100 feet elevation in the second mile. The creek babbles along, with little rapids and falls punctuated by quiet pools. As you hike farther along the creek, you get views up to Hibox Mountain and, unfortunately, encounter a couple of brushy sections that will drench you if you come on a dewy summer morning.

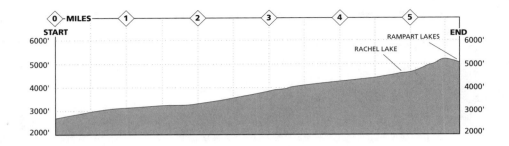

At the head of the basin, the trail crosses a buggy creek and starts climbing, steeply at first, but easing up a bit as it traverses an increasingly subalpine shelf, through heather and huckleberry shrubs, aster, and lupine, passing a little waterfall partway up the slope, a recommended rest stop. The trail climbs some more, strenuously, but soon levels out at Rachel Lake, elevation 4,640 feet. Rachel Lake used to be a pretty, deep lake set in a steep, rocky basin, but the lake is overused and shows it. There is a lot of bare ground around the lake, bearing witness to past abuses. If you camp here, find an existing campsite at least 200 feet from the lakeshore. No campfires are allowed at Rachel Lake or beyond.

Continuing from Rachel Lake, a must since you have come this far, ascend a short 0.5 mile up subalpine meadow slopes to a trail junction at the crest of Rampart Ridge. To reach Rampart Lakes, head south another 0.5 mile. Rampart Lakes, elevation 5,040 feet, are a cluster of little lakes set in a meadow basin on the western side of Rampart Ridge. There are a few campsites here, usually taken early on summer weekends.

**Options:** The trail leading north from Rampart Ridge junction leads 0.9 mile to Lila Lake, elevation 5,100 feet, a secluded lake set in a basin below Alta Mountain. Don't expect solitude here, either.

For views, you can wander to one of the many high points along Rampart Ridge from the various lakes. Most of these summits are easy scrambles; if the going gets rocky and exposed, perhaps you should reconsider. Alta Mountain, elevation 6,250 feet, is the high point of Rampart Ridge. A climbers' trail leads to the summit from the Lila Lake spur trail. The trail isn't technically difficult, just long and strenuous, climbing over endless ridge points. Alta Mountain offers supreme views of the surrounding peaks and valleys, including Kendall Peak, Mount Thompson, Chikamin and Lemah Peaks, Three Queens and Hi Box Mountains, and Mounts Stuart to the east and Rainier to the south.

Experienced off-trail hikers and scramblers can explore the high meadows and ponds on the southeast shoulder of Alta Mountain and traverse the ridge northward to Alta Pass and down to Park Lakes (Hike 21), or to Chikamin Pass. There is also a high route leading south from Rampart Lakes over a pass to Lake Lillian (Hike 19) and vice versa.

# Cle Elum
# RIVER AREA

# 21 Mineral Creek–Park Lakes

**Overview:** *A hike up Mineral Creek to Park Lakes.*

**Distance:** 9.6 miles round-trip.
**Difficulty:** Moderate.
**Best season:** Summer through fall.
**Traffic:** Foot and stock traffic; moderate to heavy use.

**High point:** About 4,650 feet.
**Maps:** USGS Chikamin Peak; Green Trails No. 207 (Snoqualmie Pass).
**For more information:** USDA Forest Service, Cle Elum Ranger District Office.

**Finding the trailhead:** Mineral Creek Trail 1331 is approached from Roslyn via Cooper Lake Road. Drive I–90 to Roslyn/Salmon la Sac, exit 80. Drive north 2.8 miles to the State Route 903 junction. Turn left and follow SR 903 through the towns of Roslyn and Ronald and along the east shore of Cle Elum Lake to Cooper Lake Road (Forest Service Road 46). Follow FS 46 past Cooper Lake and over Cooper Pass to the Mineral Creek trailhead at road's end, about 3 miles down from the pass. Parking is limited; please do your best to leave room for other vehicles. A Northwest Forest Pass is required.

## Key points:
- **0.1** Kachess River crossing.
- **0.4** Kachess Lake Trail junction.
- **1.5** Mining camp ruins.
- **1.8** Alpine Lakes Wilderness boundary.
- **2.0** Mineral Creek crossing.
- **3.9** Lower Park Lake creek crossing.
- **4.8** Upper Park Lake.

**The hike:** Park Lakes are two lovely alpine lakes set at the head of Mineral Creek basin, just east of Chikamin Pass. They are reached via a 4.8-mile trail leading up Mineral Creek from the east or a short descent from the Pacific Crest Trail (PCT). Although the hike is steep, rocky, and brushy, the trail is popular, and the lakes are swarmed nearly every weekend. The hike is a reasonable day hike, but often done as an overnight trip to permit exploring of Mineral Park and Chikamin Ridge.

Get your permit at the trailhead register, then start hiking. From the trailhead, the trail descends briefly and crosses Kachess River, then climbs through hemlock and fir forest to a junction with Kachess Lake Trail. Until the logging road went in over Cooper Pass, this hike began some 4.5 miles down the shore of Kachess Lake, making it an almost mandatory overnight trip. The lakeshore trail is still accessible but not often traveled; most hikers take the "shortcut" for easier access to the high country.

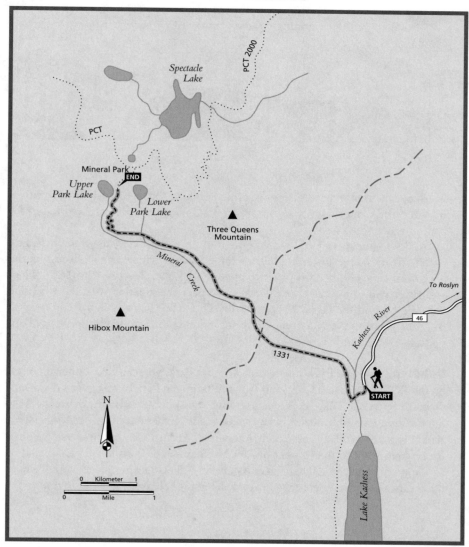

From the junction, stay right on Mineral Creek Trail, which contours the wooded slope, then curves westward above Mineral Creek, following an old road grade through deep fir and hemlock forest. The trail passes an old mining camp in 1.5 miles, then continues upstream, traversing rocky avalanche slopes thick with brush. At 2 miles, just after crossing the wilderness boundary, the trail crosses Mineral Creek via a footbridge, then continues up the opposite bank, climbing steadily but not too steeply across more avalanche swaths. If you come before the trail crews

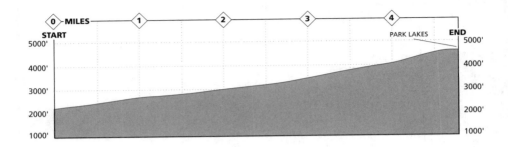

brush out the trail, expect sections of difficult hiking through brush. In early morning, wet brush can soak you as thoroughly as a rainstorm. Be prepared to get wet and to whack some weeds.

At 3.9 miles, about two hours up the trail for most hikers, the trail crosses the outlet stream of the lower of the two Park Lakes, then swings westward, curves back north, and climbs a final mile to upper Park Lake, elevation 4,650 feet. There are designated campsites near the lakes and near the junction with the PCT, just 0.6 mile beyond the lakes. No campfires. The upper basin is shortly up the trail from the lakes; spend some time exploring, wading through wildflowers, or hiking up to the ridgetops for views.

**Options:** From the PCT junction at Mineral Park, you can hike either direction on the PCT, west across Chikamin Pass to Ptarmigan Park or east over a divide and down to Spectacle Lake. If you can arrange transportation, one-way backpacks to Snoqualmie Pass or Cooper Lake can be made. Experienced off-trail hikers and scramblers can make a cross-country traverse to Alta Pass, then traverse Rampart Ridge southward to the summit of Alta Mountain and down to Lila Lake, and on to Rampart Lakes or Rachel Lake. As always, hikers lacking off-trail and scrambling experience are discouraged from leaving the relative safety of the trail.

# 22

# Pete Lake

**Overview:** *A relatively flat, easy hike to Pete Lake.*

**Distance:** About 8.2 miles round-trip.
**Difficulty:** Easy.
**Best season:** Early summer through late fall.
**Traffic:** Foot and stock traffic; very heavy use.
**High point:** About 3,000 feet.

**Maps:** USGS Polallie Ridge; Green Trails No. 208 (Kachess Lake).
**For more information:** USDA Forest Service, Cle Elum Ranger District Office.

**Finding the trailhead:** Pete Lake Trail 1323 begins from the western end of Cooper Lake. Drive I–90 to Roslyn/Salmon la Sac, exit 80. Drive north 2.8 miles to the State Route 903 junction. Turn left and follow SR 903 through the towns of Roslyn and Ronald and along the east shore of Cle Elum Lake to Cooper Lake Road (Forest Service Road 46). Turn left and follow Cooper Lake Road 4.6 paved miles to the Cooper Lake turnoff, then turn right on Forest Service Road 4616 and follow the gravel road 1.6 miles down across the river and up along the lakeshore to the Pete Lake Trail turnoff. A spur road leads 0.2 mile down to the trailhead. A Northwest Forest Pass is required.

## Key points:
**1.2** Tired Creek Trail junction.
**2.1** Cutoff trail junction.
**2.6** Alpine Lakes Wilderness boundary.
**3.5** Cooper River crossing.
**3.8** Escondido Creek crossing.
**4.1** Pete Lake.

**The hike:** Pete Lake is a small, low-elevation lake lying near the head of Cooper River, a tributary of Cle Elum River. It is reached via a flat, easy, 4-mile segment of Cooper River Trail 1323, popular with hikers and horseback riders. The trail leads

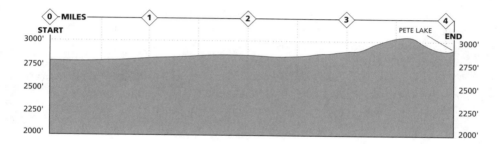

# Pete Lake

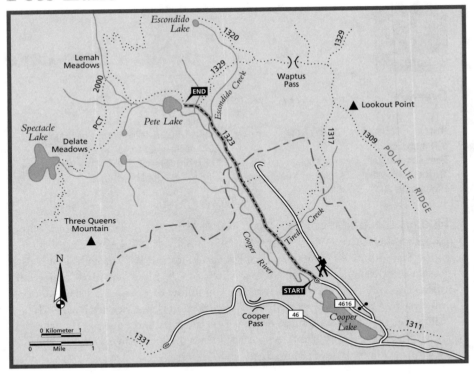

through shady old-growth pine and fir forest along the river, crossing several streams. If you don't mind sharing the trail with dozens of hikers and horses, you will enjoy this hike. If you prefer solitude, there are many more-lonesome trails in this area; the farther you hike, the farther away from the crowds you get.

The trail begins flat and easy, hiking directly up the Cooper River valley from the northwest shore of Cooper Lake, through deep old-growth forest. Just past the 1-mile mark, the trail crosses Tired Creek and just beyond the creek reaches the Tired Creek Trail (1317) junction (Hike 23). The trail continues straight ahead along the river bottom, crossing another creek and reaching another trail junction at 2.1 miles. Continue upriver; in another 0.5 mile the trail crosses the Alpine Lakes Wilderness boundary at the first of three streams. The next mile is much the same—flat forest hiking along the river bottom with occasional stream crossings. At 3.5 miles, the trail crosses Cooper River and then a tributary of Lemah Creek in another 0.3 mile. Pete Lake is reached in another 0.3 mile.

There are several campsites at Pete Lake, although the lake is often over-crowded on summer weekends. It is best treated as a day hike, unless you don't mind camping out with a lot of hikers and horse packers.

**Options:** Several trails lead off from the vicinity of Pete Lake. A 4.8-mile loop can be made through Delate and Lemah Meadows via a segment of the Pacific Crest Trail (PCT). Longer loops via Tired Creek, Waptus Pass, and the PCT can be made. From the Delate Meadows junction, you can follow the PCT southward to Spectacle Lake, a strenuous 5-mile hike from Pete Lake.

# Tired Creek

**Overview:** *A steep hike up Tired Creek to Polallie Ridge.*

**Distance:** About 10.8 miles round-trip.
**Difficulty:** Strenuous.
**Best season:** Summer through fall.
**Traffic:** Foot and stock traffic; moderate use.
**High point:** About 5,500 feet.

**Maps:** USGS Polallie Ridge; Green Trails No. 208 (Kachess Lake).
**For more information:** USDA Forest Service, Cle Elum Ranger District Office.

**Finding the trailhead:** Tired Creek Trail 1317 begins from the Pete Lake trailhead. Drive I–90 to Roslyn/Salmon la Sac, exit 80 Drive north 2.8 miles to the State Route 903 junction. Turn left and follow SR 903 through the towns of Roslyn and Ronald and along the east shore of Cle Elum Lake to Cooper Lake Road (Forest Service Road 46). Turn left and follow Cooper Lake Road 4.6 paved miles to the Cooper Lake turnoff, then turn right on Forest Service Road 4616 and follow the gravel road 1.6 miles down across the river and up along the lakeshore to the Pete Lake Trail turnoff. A spur road leads 0.2 mile down to the trailhead. A Northwest Forest Pass is required.

## Key points:
    **1.2** Tired Creek Trail junction.
    **1.7** Road crossing.
    **3.5** Tired Creek basin.
    **5.0** Polallie Ridge Trail junction.
    **5.4** Polallie Ridge viewpoint.

**The hike:** Tired Creek Trail is a steep trail leading 3.8 miles up from the Cooper River bottom to near the crest of Polallie Ridge. This is a shortcut to Polallie Ridge viewpoint, shaving 3 miles each way from Polallie Ridge Trail proper, but it is not

*Polallie Ridge*

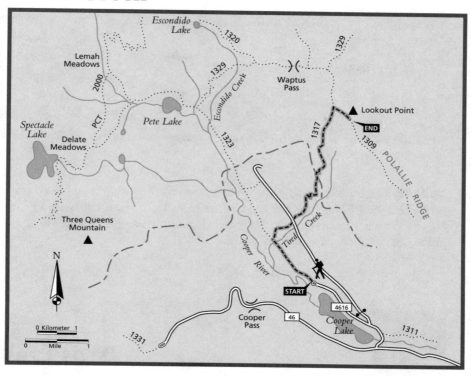

a popular hike. The trail is dry, strenuous, and downright demanding. But oh, the views!

This hike begins via Pete Lake Trail 1323 (Hike 22), through deep old-growth forest for about 1.2 miles, crossing Tired Creek and soon reaching the Tired Creek Trail (1317) junction. From the junction, the trail leads gradually uphill through fir and pine forest about 0.5 mile to an old road grade. Turn right and follow the road grade about 100 yards or so and pick up the trail, which climbs more steeply up the dusty slope, at first along Tired Creek but soon switching back up a rib and into hot, open forest slopes away from the creek. This section of the hike is the steepest and is a miserable, sweaty hike in the heat of a summer's day. Much of the trail is loose and rocky, tilled up by horses and making for tiresome hiking. Once the switchbacks end, the trail contours an open, rocky meadow slope to the head of Tired Creek basin, then climbs a final 0.5 mile to the Polallie Ridge Trail (1309) junction. There is a campsite near the junction, but no reliable water source by midsummer.

From the junction, the Polallie Ridge lookout site is only 0.4 mile up Trail 1309. This is one of the supreme scenic viewpoints of the Alpine Lakes Wilderness, not to be missed.

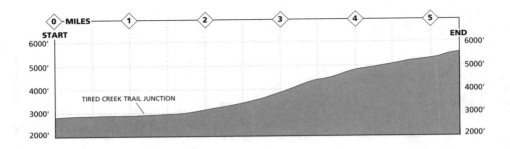

**Options:** There are several loop hike possibilities that begin via Tired Creek, cross over or around Waptus Pass, and end via Pete Lake Trail. The meadows and ridges around Waptus Pass are not heavily traveled, allowing much solitude. There are places here where you can literally get lost.

# 24

# Davis Peak

**Overview:** *A steep hike to a former lookout site atop Davis Peak.*

**Distance:** 11.8 miles round-trip.
**Difficulty:** Very strenuous.
**Best season:** Summer through fall.
**Traffic:** Foot and stock traffic; light use.
**High point:** 6,426 feet.

**Maps:** USGS Davis Peak; Green Trails No. 208 (Kachess Lake).
**For more information:** USDA Forest Service, Cle Elum Ranger District Office.

**Finding the trailhead:** Davis Peak Trail 1324 is approached from Roslyn via Cle Elum River Road. To get there, drive I-90 to Roslyn/Salmon la Sac, exit 80, then drive north 2.8 miles to the State Route 903 junction. Turn left and follow SR 903 through Roslyn and Ronald and up Cle Elum Lake's shore, 16.5 miles to pavement's end. The road forks here; take the right fork and continue another 1.6 miles up Forest Service Road 4330 and across Paris Creek to the Davis Peak trailhead on the left. A Northwest Forest Pass is required.

## Key points:
**0.4** Footbridge over Cle Elum River.
**0.9** The switchbacks begin.
**3.6** Alpine Lakes Wilderness boundary.

# Davis Peak

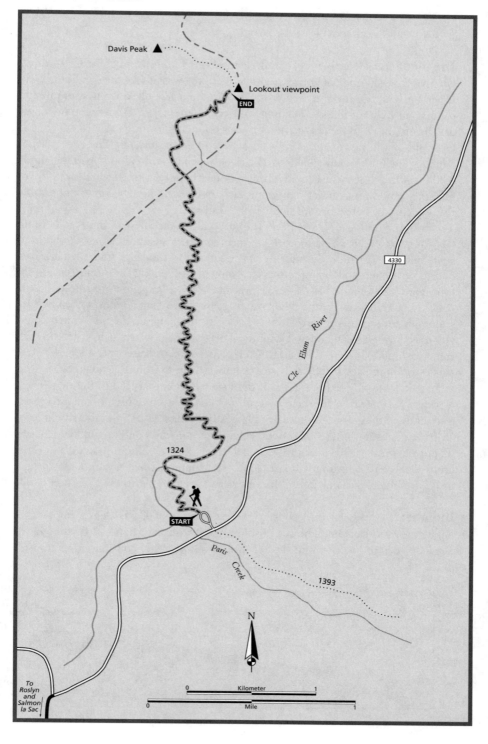

**4.6** The trail crests a high ridge.

**5.9** Davis Peak lookout site.

**The hike:** Davis Peak is a rocky peak rising at the southern end of the Goat Mountain massif, a subrange of craggy peaks rising to the west above the Cle Elum River. Davis Peak is the site of a former fire lookout and like all lookout sites provides panoramic views of the surrounding wilderness landscape. If you come on a clear day, bring lots of film. There are high views of neighboring peaks, lakes, and valleys, and of wildflowers growing everywhere in early summer. The trail pulls no punches; it climbs relentlessly from the river bottom to the summit, gaining almost 4,000 feet in 2 linear miles, with 4 miles of nearly unrelenting switchbacks. If you hike this trail on a summer day, come early before the heat becomes unbearable. Bring plenty of water; by late summer the trail is dry.

From the trailhead, Davis Peak Trail descends some 300 feet in 0.4 mile to the Cle Elum River, crosses a footbridge, then contours upstream along the opposite slope another 0.5 mile through fir and hemlock forest. The trail switches back once, then again, and again, and pretty soon you're hiking up a trail that on the topo map looks like a seismograph printout after a long, low-magnitude earthquake. The trail zigzags directly up the ridge for more than 2 miles, switching back seemingly forever up the forested ridge. As you climb higher, the trees thin out, and you pass through steep, grassy meadows. There are wildflowers galore here in early summer: lupine, Indian paintbrush, aster, penstemon, to name only a few. The trail stops switching back briefly as it angles leftward, away from the ridge, but is soon at it again, climbing a short series of tight switchbacks that lead to the ridge crest, elevation 5,700 feet. Here the trail levels out and contours a high basin and crosses a streambed (there is water here until late August most years), then starts climbing switchbacks again up the final open ridge slope to trail's end at the lookout site. There are great views, north to Mount Daniel, west to Chimney Rock and other crest peaks, east to Mount Stuart, south to Mount Rainier, a panorama of high peaks, too many to name here. More flowers, too, clinging to the thin, rocky soil.

**Options:** The official trail ends at a false summit of Davis Peak, which is far enough for most hikers. The actual summit is 0.5 mile to the west. If you feel the need—or desire—to climb to the very top of Davis Peak, you can either traverse

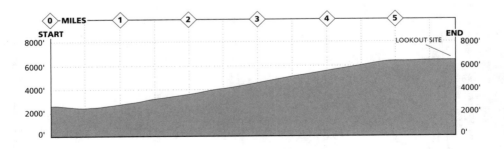

the ridge dividing the two peaks, a rocky but relatively easy scramble following a boot path, or leave the trail at the upper stream crossing and climb west to the saddle between the summit and the 5,900-foot point just south, then ascend the ridge northward to the top.

If you're looking for an overnight trip away from the crowds, here's one. A bivouac on top of Davis Peak on a starry night would be sublime. Hiking up Davis Peak with a pack full of gear and extra water would not be much fun, though, which may explain why very few people camp here. So much the better for those who do.

# 25 Cathedral Pass

**Overview:** *A scenic hike to Cathedral Pass.*

**Distance:** 8.0 miles round-trip.
**Difficulty:** Moderate.
**Best season:** Summer through fall.
**Traffic:** Foot and stock use; moderate to heavy traffic.

**High point:** About 5,600 feet.
**Maps:** USGS Mount Daniel, The Cradle; Green Trails No. 176 (Stevens Pass).
**For more information:** USDA Forest Service, Cle Elum Ranger District Office.

**Finding the trailhead:** Cathedral Pass Trail 1345 begins from Cathedral Pass trailhead near the end of Cle Elum River Road. To get there, drive I–90 to exit 80, marked Roslyn/Salmon la Sac. From the exit, drive north 2.8 miles to the State Route 903 junction. Turn left and follow SR 903 through Roslyn and Ronald and along Cle Elum Lake, 16.5 miles to pavement's end. The road forks here; take the right fork and continue another 12.3 miles on Forest Service Road 4330 to the Cathedral Pass trailhead, on the left, just 0.1 mile from road's end. This road has two stream crossings that can be difficult when water is running high. Those with low-clearance vehicles sometimes park at the stream crossings and hike or bike up to the trailhead. A Northwest Forest Pass is required.

## Key points:
   **0.1**  Bridge crossing Cle Elum River.
   **1.8**  Trail Creek Trail junction.
   **2.3**  Squaw Lake.
   **3.8**  Pacific Crest Trail junction.
   **4.0**  Cathedral Pass.

# Cathedral Pass

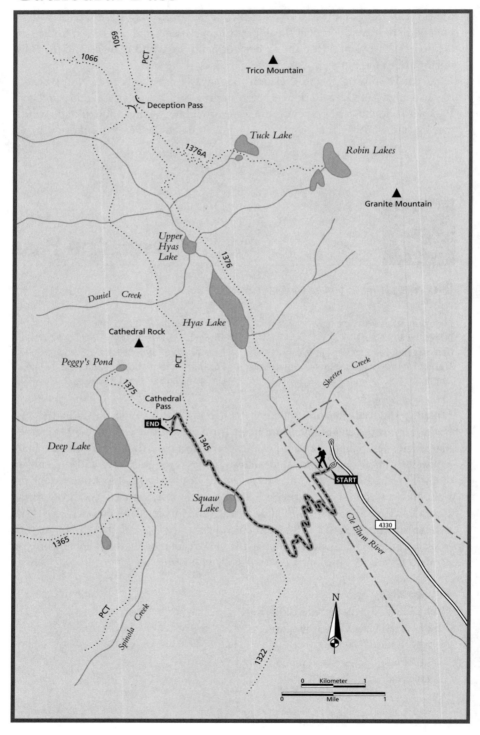

1059

1066

PCT

Trico Mountain

Deception Pass

1376A

Tuck Lake

Robin Lakes

Granite Mountain

Upper Hyas Lake

1376

Daniel Creek

Cathedral Rock

Hyas Lake

Peggy's Pond

PCT

Skeeter Creek

1375

Cathedral Pass

END

1345

Deep Lake

Squaw Lake

START

Cle Elum River

4330

1365

PCT

Spinola Creek

1322

N

| 0 | Kilometer | 1 |

| 0 | Mile | 1 |

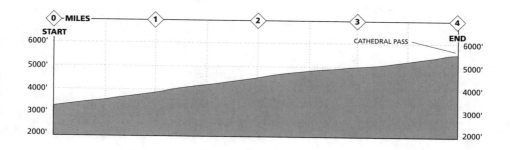

**The hike:** Cathedral Pass is a scenic high pass above the Cle Elum River valley, with views of the Wenatchee Mountains, Mount Daniel, and the lush meadows surrounding Deep Lake. The hike to Cathedral Pass is a good day hike, with lakes, meadows, craggy peaks, and views, and several options.

Get your permit and start hiking down the trail, which begins from the Cle Elum River valley bottom, crosses the river via a footbridge, then climbs, switching back several times through silver fir and hemlock forest, vanilla leaf, twinflower, and bunchberry lining the trail, devil's club and ferns in streambeds. This portion of the trail is cool in the morning and late afternoon but can be hot by midday. The slope tapers off noticeably as you near the ridge crest, and at 1.8 miles, just across a rocky divide, is the junction with Trail Creek Trail 1322, the turnoff for Lake Michael Trail, a popular horse packing trip.

Continuing from the junction, the trail leads northward, level at first but soon climbing through subalpine forest, with rhododendron, huckleberry, and mountain-ash lining the trail. The trail levels off again and just 0.5 mile from the junction reaches Squaw Lake, elevation 4,841 feet, a nice lake set on a talus- and cliff-rimmed shelf. There are several campsites here, none very private. Squaw Lake makes a convenient turnaround point for casual day hikers, a 4.6 mile round-trip.

From the lake, the trail climbs a bit, then crosses a divide and levels off, traversing a grassy meadow, then a subalpine bench dotted with tarns, with views across the valley to the Wenatchee Mountains and ahead to Cathedral Rock. There are campsites hidden among the trees here on the edge of the meadows; don't camp on the meadows, please. Look for lupine, lousewort, and shooting star among the many wildflowers growing here.

Once past the biggest tarn, the trail climbs briefly to the Pacific Crest Trail (PCT) junction. Go left from the junction, climbing a couple of switchbacks to Cathedral Pass, a rocky divide just below Cathedral Rock, elevation 5,600 feet. There are several places to sit and enjoy the views east to the Wenatchee Mountains and Stuart Range and west to Deep Lake, Mount Daniel, and the Snoqualmie Crest peaks.

**Options:** Ambitious day hikers can continue another 2 miles or so down to Deep Lake. It's a 13-mile round-trip, strenuous both ways, and more popular as an

*Peggy's Pond and Cathedral Rock*

overnight or weekend backpack. A more feasible day trip is to hike the 0.5 mile spur trail to Peggy's Pond, a small lake set in a cirque below the imposing cliffs of Cathedral Rock. This trail leads off from the second switchback below Cathedral Pass. The trail is unmarked except for a sign that says the trail is not suitable for stock travel, and it isn't. The trail contours below the cliffs of Cathedral Rock, crossing steep talus and exposed ledges, and is pretty rough as hiking trails go. Peggy's Pond is pretty and secluded, but there's little solitude as this is a popular and heavily abused campsite.

Another option is to hike the "Rainier Vista" trail, an old trail that doesn't show up on current topo maps. The route basically follows an abandoned trail along the flat divide southward from Cathedral Pass before dropping down to an unnamed lake above Squaw Lake, then descending to Trail Creek and looping back to Cathedral Pass Trail. The route is easy to follow to the 5,670-foot ridge point about 1.5 miles south of Cathedral Pass, and another 0.2 mile down to the lake. It can be done the other way, uphill from Trail Creek Trail. Find the trail about 0.5 mile from the Cathedral Pass–Trail Creek Trail junction. A blazed tree marks the junction. This route has some challenging route-finding and may be a bit much for casual hikers, although horses have been known to manage it just fine.

# 26

# Deception Pass

**Overview:** *A hike to Deception Pass, with several options.*

**Distance:** 8.8 miles round-trip.
**Difficulty:** Moderate.
**Best season:** Summer through fall.
**Traffic:** Foot and stock traffic; moderate to heavy use.

**High point:** 4,470 feet.
**Maps:** USGS Mount Daniel; Green Trails No. 176 (Stevens Pass).
**For more information:** USDA Forest Service, Cle Elum Ranger District Office.

**Finding the trailhead:** Deception Pass Trail 1376 begins at the end of Cle Elum River Road (Forest Service Road 4330). To get there, drive I–90 to Roslyn/Salmon La Sac, exit 80. From the exit, drive north 2.8 miles to the State Route 903 junction. Turn left and follow SR 903 through Roslyn and Ronald and along Cle Elum Lake, 16.5 miles to pavement's end. The road forks here; take the right fork and continue another 12.4 miles on FS 4330 to the Deception Pass trailhead at road's end. The road crosses two streams, which run high in early season. If you don't have a high-clearance vehicle, consider parking and fording the creeks on your walk or bike ride up the road to the trailhead. A Northwest Forest Pass is required.

# Deception Pass

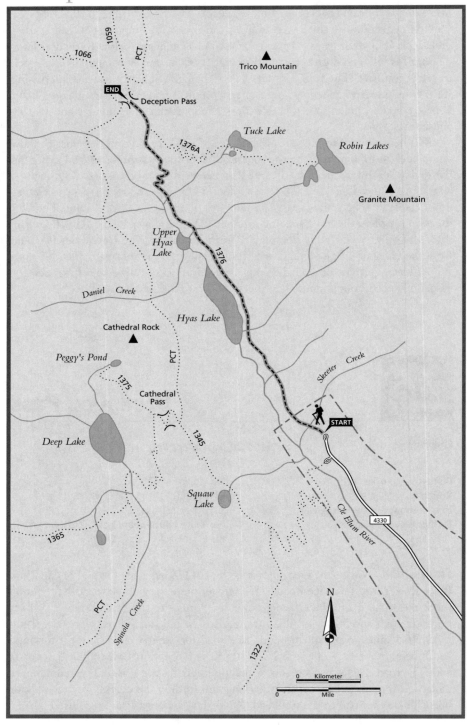

## Key points:
**0.2** Alpine Lakes Wilderness boundary.
**2.0** Hyas Lake.
**3.2** Side trail to upper Hyas Lake.
**4.2** Tuck Lake Trail junction.
**4.4** Deception Pass.

**The hike:** Deception Pass, a 4,470-foot-elevation pass located about midway between Stevens Pass and Snoqualmie Pass, is one of the major divides of the Alpine Lakes Wilderness. It is reached and crossed by several hiking trails, including the Pacific Crest Trail (PCT). The most popular route is a 4.4-mile hike up Cle Elum River. It is best done as a backpacking trip with stops at Deception or Marmot Lakes, or as a loop including a segment of the PCT.

The hike begins from the Deception Pass trailhead at the end of Cle Elum River Road. Register at the trailhead, then start hiking northward along the Cle Elum River bottom. The trail is fairly flat and wide, leading at first through lush meadows, then through silver fir and cedar forest. In 0.2 mile, the trail crosses the Alpine Lakes Wilderness boundary at Skeeter Creek. In early summer, there's no mystery how the creek got its name. Splash on the bug juice liberally or suffer the consequences! Continue up the trail, which climbs and drops a little, but fails to gain even 100 feet elevation in the first mile, then actually loses a few feet of elevation in the second mile, where it reaches Hyas Lake, a mile-long lake near the headwaters of Cle Elum River. The hike this far is a pleasant one-hour walk through shady forest and grassy meadows. There are several campsites along the lakeshore, none very private.

Keep hiking up the lakeshore to the north end of Hyas Lake. In another 0.2 mile is Upper Hyas Lake, a tiny marsh by comparison, invisible from the trail. An unmarked side trail (or two) leads to the lakeshore and a few more campsites. About 0.5 mile past Upper Hyas Lake, the trail crosses a creek and then crosses Cle Elum River, a mere stream here, just before leaving the river basin and climbing steep forest slopes to Deception Pass. The trail climbs steadily and steeply for 0.5 mile, switching back most of the way, then crosses a creek and curves into a brushy basin, where the angle abates. A trail (1376A) to Tuck and Robin Lakes departs here.

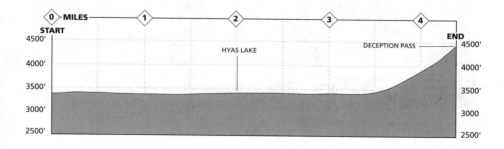

*Hyas Lake from Tuck Lake Trail*

Continue gradually upward through brushy open forest and increasingly subalpine meadows to Deception Pass, elevation 4,470 feet. The pass is a low, broad wooded bench, with trails leading off in all directions.

**Options:** From the pass, there are several options, most of which are not suitable as day hikes except for the hardiest of hikers. You can continue 3.5 miles northward along the PCT to Deception Lakes and Surprise Mountain or 3.4 miles to Marmot Lake. A popular variation of this hike is to do a loop via the PCT southward from the pass to join Cathedral Pass Trail 1345 (Hike 25) for a 14-mile loop.

# 27

# Paddy-Go-Easy Pass

**Overview:** *A steep hike to a high pass in the Wenatchee Mountains.*

**Distance:** 6.0 miles round-trip.
**Difficulty:** Strenuous.
**Best season:** Summer through fall.
**Traffic:** Foot and stock traffic; heavy use.
**High point:** About 6,100 feet.

**Maps:** USGS The Cradle; Green Trails No. 176 (Stevens Pass).
**For more information:** USDA Forest Service, Cle Elum Ranger District Office.

**Finding the trailhead:** Paddy-Go-Easy Pass Trail 1595 begins from Cle Elum River Road (Forest Service Road 4330). To get there, drive I–90 to Roslyn/Salmon La Sac, exit 80. From the exit, drive north 2.8 miles to the State Route 903 junction. Turn left and follow SR 903 through Roslyn and Ronald and along Cle Elum Lake, 16.5 miles to pavement's end. The road forks here; take the right fork and continue another 10.4 miles on FS 4330 to the Fish Lake guard station. The Paddy-Go-Easy Pass trailhead is 0.9 mile past the guard station, on the right. The road crosses two streams, which run high in early season. If you don't have a high-clearance vehicle, consider parking and fording the creeks on your walk or bike ride up the road to the trailhead. A Northwest Forest Pass is required.

## Key points:
**0.6** Stream crossing.
**1.5** Stream gully.
**3.0** Paddy-Go-Easy Pass.

# Paddy-Go-Easy Pass

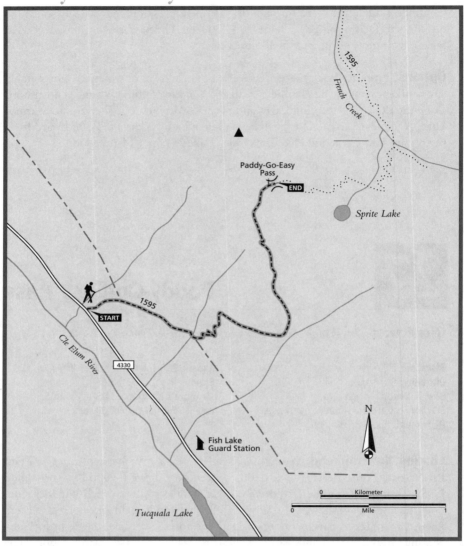

**The hike:** Paddy-Go-Easy Pass Trail is one of the shortest view hikes in the Cle Elum River valley, making it very popular. It's a steep trail, though, leading 3 miles up through dusty pine and fir forest to the 6,100-foot pass, gaining 900 feet per mile on average. It is worth the effort; the views are excellent.

From the trailhead, the trail crosses a stream and leads east, angling up moderately steep forested slopes. At 0.6 mile, the trail crosses a small stream, then turns up slope and gains a quick 500 feet in 0.4 mile to a switchback. From the switch-

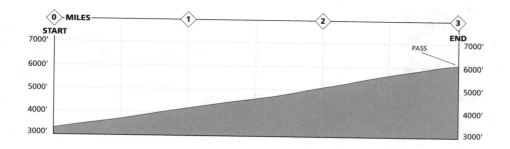

back, the trail traverses for another 0.5 mile, still in forest, climbing a steeper slope to a steep stream gully. From the stream gully, the trail angles northward, traversing an even steeper slope for another mile, contouring occasionally but usually climbing through increasingly subalpine forest with views down to Tucquala Lake and across the valley to Cathedral Rock and Mount Daniel and other peaks. At 2.5 miles, the trail levels out some, contouring meadows into the basin below the pass. There is a path leading off to a mining claim; stay left at the trail fork and proceed a final 0.5 mile to Paddy-Go-Easy Pass, elevation 6,100 feet, and grand views to the east and west.

**Options:** For better views, follow a path up the 6,573-foot peak just 0.5 mile north of the pass or the 6,395-foot high point 0.3 mile south of the pass. As always, exercise caution when you hike off-trail.

An obligatory side trip is to descend 0.3 mile from the pass and take a short path to Sprite Lake. If you're doing this as an overnight hike, Sprite Lake is the popular campsite, which means it gets crowded, especially on summer weekends. The trail descends steeply from the pass 2 miles to French Creek. From here, several options are possible.

# 28

# Jolly Mountain

**Overview:** *A hike to the summit of 6,443-foot Jolly Mountain.*

**Distance:** 11.2 miles round-trip.
**Difficulty:** Moderate.
**Best season:** Midsummer through fall.
**Traffic:** Multiple-use trail; moderate use.
**High point:** 6,443 feet.

**Maps:** USGS Davis Peak; Green Trails No. 208 (Kachess Lake).
**For more information:** USDA Forest Service, Cle Elum Ranger District Office.

**Finding the trailhead:** Jolly Mountain Trail 1307 is approached via Cle Elum River Road from Roslyn. To get there, drive I–90 to Roslyn-Salmon la Sac, exit 80. From the exit, drive north 2.8 miles to the State Route 903 junction. Turn left and follow SR 903 through Roslyn and Ronald and along Cle Elum Lake, 16.3 miles to Salmon La Sac Creek. Turn right into Cayuse Horse Camp and follow the loop through the campground to the corrals near the back. The trailhead is just left of the horse stables and corrals. A Northwest Forest Pass is required.

## Key points:

**0.3** Service road.
**0.8** Logging road and clearcut.
**1.2** Another logging road.
**2.5** Salmon la Sac Creek crossing.
**3.1** South Fork Paris Creek Trail junction.
**4.0** Sasse Ridge Trail junction.
**4.4** West Fork Teanaway River Trail junction.
**5.0** Jolly Creek Trail junction.
**5.6** Jolly Mountain.

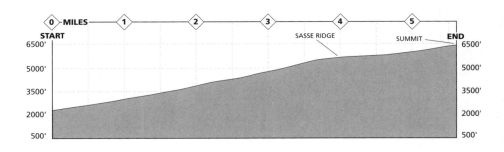

# Jolly Mountain

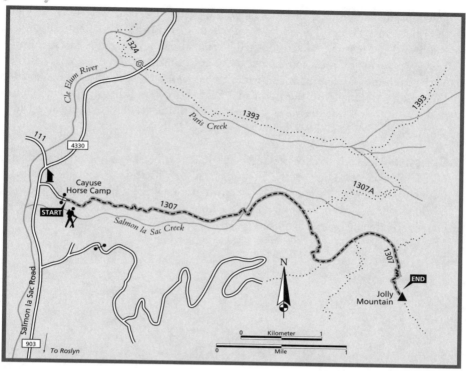

**The hike:** Jolly Mountain lies outside the Alpine Lakes Wilderness but is a some-what popular hike to a 6,443-foot summit that offers incredible views of the Stuart Range and Snoqualmie Crest peaks. The trail suffers from logging activity and passes through clearcut areas. The trail is open to all use, including trail bikes, and is heavily abused. Because of the multiuse status, this hike is best done on a week-day. Pick a sunny day so you don't miss out on the views, but start early so you don't bake in the sun.

The trail begins from beside the Cayuse Horse Camp corral and climbs gradu-ally up moderately steep, grassy pine and fir forest slopes, crossing service roads and logging spurs and clearcuts new and old, where the trail is gravelly and steep and generally not pleasant to hike on. The trail continues up through logged-over forest, then contours toward Salmon la Sac Creek, which is soon crossed. After a switchback, the trail climbs the opposite bank, then contours along the creek another 0.6 mile to the South Fork Paris Creek Trail (1307A) junction, the first of several trail junctions. Take the right fork and continue almost a mile up the steep subalpine forest slope to the head of Salmon la Sac Creek basin and the crest of Sasse Ridge, elevation 5,600 feet, and the best views so far. The Sasse Ridge Trail junction is here; stay on the ridge, traversing. In another 0.4 mile is yet another trail junction, this one leading 11 miles down the West Fork Teanaway River. Stay on the ridge crest, rising in a southward arc with increasing views. The trail curves southward and reaches a 5,980-foot saddle and a final trail junction, this one leading down to Jolly Creek and 12 miles out to the Middle Fork Teanaway River. Views from the saddle are far and wide, including a look at the Stuart Range and Wenatchee Mountains to the east and Mount Daniel and the Snoqualmie Crest peaks to the west, but the views get better. From the saddle, continue along the ridge and climb a final 0.6 mile to the summit of Jolly Mountain.

**Options:** There is a shorter version of this hike that begins up a logging road just off of the main road south of the Salmon la Sac guard station. Although shorter, it leads through more clearcuts and is not any better than the trail. This hike also can be done starting from Paris Creek; it's a little longer and has a clearcut, but is equally worthwhile, perhaps more so.

# Teanaway
# RIVER AREA

# 29 Esmerelda Basin–Lake Ann

**Overview:** *A hike through a flowery basin to Lake Ann, with views of Ingalls Peak.*

**Distance:** 9.2 miles round-trip.
**Difficulty:** Moderate.
**Best season:** Summer through fall.
**Traffic:** Foot and stock traffic; moderate to heavy use.

**High point:** About 6,470 feet.
**Maps:** USGS Mount Stuart; Green Trails No. 209 (Mount Stuart).
**For more information:** USDA Forest Service, Cle Elum Ranger District Office.

**Finding the trailhead:** The hike to Lake Ann begins from the Esmerelda trailhead, which is approached from near Cle Elum via Teanaway River Road, about 6.8 miles east of Cle Elum, exit 85 on State Route 970. Turn up Teanaway River Road and follow 13 miles to pavement's end, where the road forks. Take the right fork and follow Forest Service Road 9737 about 9.5 miles to the Esmerelda trailhead at road's end. A Northwest Forest Pass is required.

## Key points:
- **0.3** Ingalls Way Trail junction.
- **2.0** Esmerelda Basin.
- **3.0** County Line Trail junction.
- **4.3** High pass above Lake Ann.
- **4.6** Lake Ann.

**The hike:** Lake Ann is a small lake set in a quiet basin on the western flank of Ingalls Peak, just outside the Alpine Lakes Wilderness. A 4.6-mile trail leads to the lake. Most hikers don't visit Lake Ann but stop short in Esmerelda Basin, one of the most popular wildflower hikes in the Teanaway region.

Get your permit and start hiking up the Esmerelda Basin Trail 1394, a rocky old roadbed beside the upper North Fork Teanaway River. In 0.3 mile is the Ingalls Way Trail (1390) junction. Continue up the river, following the old road through

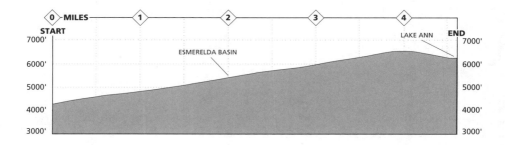

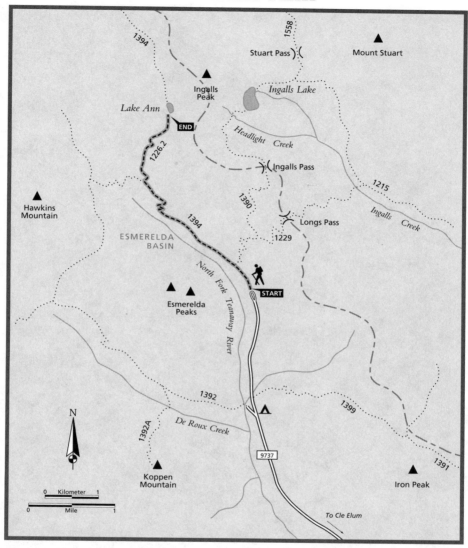

grassy meadows and pine and fir groves into Esmerelda Basin, a flowery meadow basin. The road soon leads up the north slope of the basin, away from the creek, switching back a few times as it climbs through rocky meadows to a junction with the old County Line Trail (Forest Service Trail 1226.2). This is an abandoned trail, not maintained but not too difficult to follow for experienced hikers.

Follow the old trail through more meadows that are thick with wildflowers in season, then up switchbacks to a 6,470-foot pass overlooking Lake Ann, with good

125

*Ingalls Way Trail*

views down Fortune Creek basin and up to Ingalls Peak. There is a fine campsite on the ridge, although it is dry. The nearest water is at the lake, just below.

From the pass, descend a quick 0.3 mile to diminutive Lake Ann, elevation 6,140 feet. The lake is set in a broad, rocky meadow basin beneath Ingalls Peak, with spectacular mountain views. You can find a suitable campsite near the outlet or on snow closer to the lake in early season, although camping at the lake is not encouraged. If you're backpacking, use the campsite back at the pass or find a spot farther along the trail.

**Options:** A day hike to Lake Ann is a reasonable 9.2-mile round-trip, which is far enough for most hikers. There are several multiday loop options via Esmerelda Basin and Lake Ann.

# Ingalls Lake

**Overview:** *A hike up Ingalls Way Trail to lovely Ingalls Lake.*

**Distance:** 8.0 miles round-trip.
**Difficulty:** Strenuous.
**Best season:** Summer through fall.
**Traffic:** Foot traffic only; heavy use. No dogs.
**High point:** About 6,500 feet.

**Maps:** USGS Mount Stuart; Green Trails No. 209 (Mount Stuart).
**For more information:** USDA Forest Service, Cle Elum Ranger District Office.

**Finding the trailhead:** Ingalls Way Trail 1390 is approached via Teanaway River Road from Cle Elum. Take Teanaway River Road, about 6.8 miles east of Cle Elum, exit 85 on State Route 970. Turn up Teanaway River Road and follow 13 miles to pavement's end, where the road forks. Take the right fork and follow Forest Service Road 9737 about 9.5 miles to the Esmerelda trailhead at road's end. A Northwest Forest Pass is required.

## Key points:
**0.3** Ingalls Way Trail junction.
**1.3** Longs Pass Trail junction.
**2.8** Ingalls Pass.
**3.8** Headlight Creek crossing.
**4.0** Ingalls Lake.

# Ingalls Lake

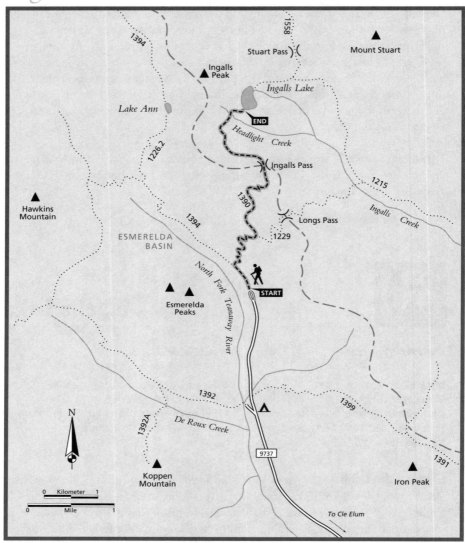

**The hike:** Ingalls Lake is one of the loveliest lakes in the Alpine Lakes Wilderness. A strenuous 4-mile trail leads to the lake through some of the most sublime parkland in the wilderness. All of the superlatives that could be heaped upon this hike would be understatements. It is a short hike, but packs a lot of scenery in only 4 miles, and is exceedingly popular. You won't find much solitude here, but you probably won't complain.

Get your permit at the trailhead register, then start hiking up Esmerelda Basin Trail 1394, a rocky old road grade that climbs steadily from the start through dusty

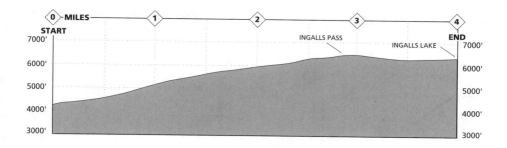

0 MILES 1 2 3 4
START
7000'
INGALLS PASS
INGALLS LAKE
END
7000'

6000'
6000'

5000'
5000'

4000'
4000'

3000'
3000'

pine forest alongside the North Fork Teanaway River. At 0.3 mile is the Ingalls Way Trail junction. Take the right fork and hike up Ingalls Way Trail 1390, which climbs abruptly out of the river basin via a series of switchbacks through fairly open silver fir and western white pine forest, gaining 900 feet elevation in a long mile to the Longs Pass Trail (1229) junction in a rocky basin.

Continuing from the Longs Pass junction to Ingalls Lake, contour northward across ridges and basins toward Ingalls Pass. This section of the trail is rocky and dusty going much of the way, with views down to Esmerelda Basin and across to the Esmerelda Peaks and beyond. There are some wildflowers, including lupine, Indian paintbrush, aster, skyrocket, phlox, and countless others. About a mile along this traverse, the trail switches back near a small stream and climbs through a grove of subalpine firs and pines set amid orange rock ridges and domes. A few more switchbacks lead to the Alpine Lakes Wilderness boundary at Ingalls Pass, elevation 6,500 feet. There are several campsites near the pass.

As you cross the pass, you enter a different world. Golden granite domes, slabs, and talus frame heather meadows and larch groves in the broad subalpine basin below. Mount Stuart and Ingalls Peak rise up beyond in splendid majesty. Descend through talus, contouring into the basin, then traverse some of the loveliest terrain imaginable. Here is a grove of larches set on a dome-top rock garden; there is a stream meandering through a heather park and cascading down granite slabs. Succulent purple flowers spring out of every rock crevice; bright red shooting star explodes in the meadows; marmots scurry amid the talus. The beauty of this basin can scarcely be described in the space given here. It is like a little slice of the Enchantment Lakes only 3 miles from the road. In autumn, when the larches turn from green to gold, hikers and photographers swarm in.

The trail descends briefly through a talus field that conceals Headlight Creek, where it is easy to lose the trail. Cairns mark the true path, although those who lose the trail will have little trouble picking it up again, if they are watchful. After traversing briefly across more talus and gullies awash in heather and other wildflowers, the trail climbs a rocky slope to Ingalls Lake, elevation 6,463 feet. You have to be careful here to take a sharp left turn up a gully; if you stray too far rightward you may find yourself rock climbing. Ingalls Lake is a turquoise jewel set amid golden granite domes and slabs. Because of its rare beauty and easy accessibility, the lakeshore has been abused, and camping is no longer permitted. There aren't many

*Ingalls Peak above Headlight Basin*

places you could camp at the lake anyway, so camp at the pass, in Headlight basin, or beyond the lake. Please camp on snow or rock or at existing campsites and stay off the meadows to help preserve this area for those who follow.

**Options:** Longs Pass Trail 1229 climbs 800 feet in 0.9 mile of dry, open switchbacks to Longs Pass, elevation 6,220 feet, for spectacular views of Mount Stuart, providing an interesting albeit rugged loop option. From Ingalls Pass, a quick scramble up the unnamed 6,878-foot peak 0.4 mile to the east provides excellent views. It's a rocky scramble but not too difficult for experienced hikers. Adventuresome hikers can scramble about on the granite slabs above the lake or climb snow fields and talus to the 7,300-foot saddle between the south and middle summits of Ingalls Peak. That's far enough for mere hikers; the cliffs above the gap are strictly for experienced alpine scramblers and rock climbers.

From Ingalls Lake, the trail continues 0.6 mile to 6,400-foot Stuart Pass, the divide between Ingalls and Jack Creeks. A loop hike via Longs Pass is possible; hike down Ingalls Creek Trail about 2 miles to the junction, then climb 1,200 feet in under 2 miles to Longs Pass and down the other side to rejoin Ingalls Way Trail. Given the prospect of losing and regaining an extra 1,200 feet of elevation, most hikers are content to return the way they came.

# Iron Peak

**Overview:** *A strenuous but flowery hike to a saddle below Iron Peak.*

**Distance:** 5.6 miles round-trip.
**Difficulty:** Strenuous.
**Best season:** Summer through fall.
**Traffic:** Foot and stock traffic only; light use.
**High point:** About 6,120 feet.

**Maps:** USGS Mount Stuart; Green Trails No. 209 (Mount Stuart).
**For more information:** USDA Forest Service, Cle Elum Ranger District Office.

**Finding the trailhead:** Iron Peak Trail 1399 is approached via North Fork Teanaway River Road (Forest Service Road 9737) north of Cle Elum. Take Teanaway River Road, about 6.8 miles east of Cle Elum, exit 85 on State Route 970. Turn up Teanaway River Road and follow 13 miles to pavement's end, where the road forks. Take the right fork and follow FS 9737 for 8.4 miles to the Iron Creek trailhead, on the right, just past the De Roux Campground turnoff. A Northwest Forest Pass is required.

# Iron Peak

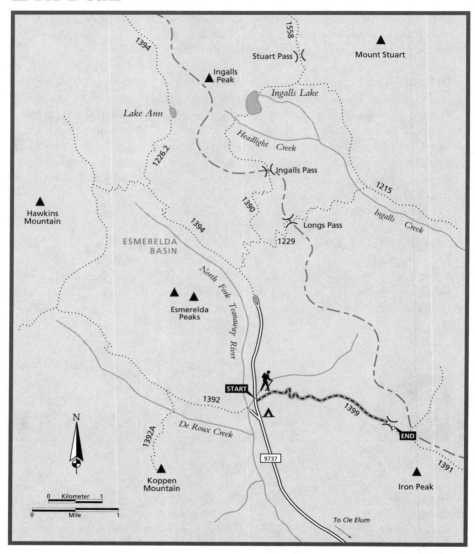

- 1394
- 1558
- Stuart Pass
- Mount Stuart
- Ingalls Peak
- Ingalls Lake
- Lake Ann
- *Headlight Creek*
- 1226.2
- Ingalls Pass
- 1215
- *Ingalls Creek*
- Hawkins Mountain
- 1390
- Longs Pass
- 1394
- 1229
- ESMERELDA BASIN
- *North Fork Teanaway River*
- Esmerelda Peaks
- START
- 1399
- N
- 1392
- *De Roux Creek*
- 1392A
- END
- 9737
- 1391
- Koppen Mountain
- Iron Peak
- 0 Kilometer 1
- 0 Mile 1
- To Cle Elum

## Key points:
**1.8** Eldorado Creek basin.
**2.8** Iron Peak saddle.

**The hike:** Iron Peak is a craggy 6,507-foot summit rising from the North Fork Teanaway River. A hiking trail leads 2.8 miles up from the road to a saddle overlooking Beverly Creek basin. It is not a popular hike, relatively speaking, probably

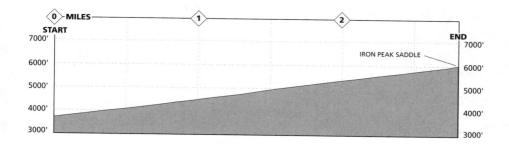

because of the fact that other nearby trails lead through wildflower meadows to more scenic viewpoints without as much elevation gain. The western slopes of Iron Peak are imposing, rising up in a series of craggy cliffs, but the trail isn't nearly as steep as one might guess, gaining only 2,200 feet elevation in just over 3 miles. However, Iron Peak Trail is regarded as one of the best short wildflower and view hikes in the Teanaway region.

The switchbacks begin right from the start and scarcely let up all the way to the pass. The trail climbs a sparsely wooded rib next to an intermittent stream, gaining elevation steadily, with increasing views across to the Teanaway peaks, including Koppen Mountain, the Esmerelda Peaks, and Mount Rainier in the distance, as well as down into the Teanaway River valley. In about 1.8 miles, the trail levels out some as it traverses Eldorado Creek basin, then starts climbing again a final mile to the pass, elevation 6,100 feet.

**Options:** You may scramble up 6,507-foot Iron Peak by traversing the ridge southward from the saddle, following a climbers' trail up the rocky ridge slope to the summit. There is just a little bit of scrambling. As always, alpine scrambling is not recommended for casual hikers, but seasoned hikers and scramblers should have no difficulty reaching this summit.

# 32

# Beverly-Turnpike

**Overview:** *A hike to Beverly Pass.*

**Distance:** 7.6 miles round-trip.
**Difficulty:** Moderate.
**Best season:** Summer through fall.
**Traffic:** Foot and stock traffic only; heavy use.
**High point:** About 5,800 feet.

**Maps:** USGS Mount Stuart; Green Trails No. 209 (Mount Stuart).
**For more information:** USDA Forest Service, Cle Elum Ranger District Office.

**Finding the trailhead:** Beverly-Turnpike Trail 1391 is approached via North Fork Teanaway River Road (Forest Service Road 9737) north of Cle Elum. If approaching via I–90, turn off at exit 85 and follow State Route 970 east 6.8 miles to Teanaway River Road. If approaching via U.S. Highway 97, follow to the 97–970 junction and drive west on SR 970 just 3.4 miles to the Teanaway River Road turnoff. Follow Teanaway River Road about 13 miles to pavement's end, where two dirt roads fork off. Take the right fork (FS 9737) and follow 3.6 miles to the Beverly Creek spur road (Forest Service Road 9737-112), then take the right fork and follow 1.1 miles to the Beverly Creek trailhead at road's end. A Northwest Forest Pass is required.

## Key points:

**0.2**  Bean Creek junction.
**2.7**  Fourth Creek Trail junction.
**3.3**  Iron Peak Trail junction.
**3.8**  Beverly Pass.

**The hike:** Beverly-Turnpike Trail is a popular hike since it provides one of the shortest routes to the foot of Mount Stuart. Although it is traveled heavily by mountain climbers, day hikers are rewarded by views of the Stuart Range and a

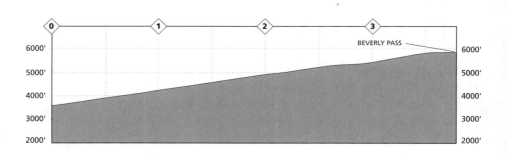

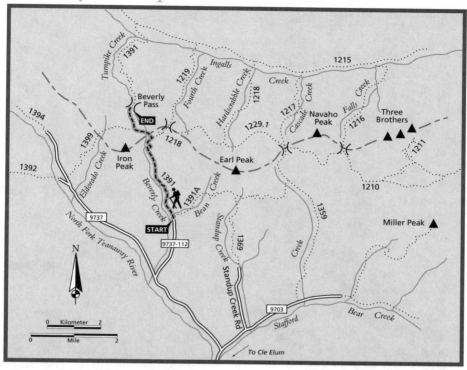

bounty of wildflowers, but they may suffer from a distinct lack of solitude on summer and fall weekends.

Get your permit and start up the trail, crossing a sturdy footbridge across Beverly Creek, then hiking up an old road grade until it narrows into a trail proper. Not far up the trail is a junction with Bean Creek Trail (Hike 33). Stay left, crossing Bean Creek and continuing up Beverly-Turnpike Trail. In early season, high water may make this creek crossing a bit difficult. Once across the creek, the trail climbs steadily through a stand of big pines flanked by grassy meadows, then traverses close above the creek through open fir, hemlock, and pine forest. After a mile or so, the trail breaks out in a rocky basin below a rust-tinted shoulder of Iron Peak. Wildflowers bloom in abundance here in early summer, adding color to the dirt and rocks. In late season, the creek becomes strangely silent and seems to have run dry. It's still there, just running underground for a few hundred yards. The trail climbs away from the creek, dusty and rocky going, then contours below a craggy ridge awhile before entering open forest once more. At 2.7 miles is a junction with Fourth Creek Trail 1219 and a campsite. The right fork leads 0.4 mile to the Fourth Creek divide and views. Stay left here, dropping briefly to cross Beverly Creek, then climbing rocky slopes to the Iron Peak Trail junction (Hike 31). Wildflowers here include the familiar lupine, aster, arnica, pearly everlasting, and occasional bright-red skyrocket. Take the right fork this time and contour across the

*Mount Stuart from near Beverly Pass*

head of Beverly Creek basin to the Alpine Lakes Wilderness boundary and the high point of the hike—literally and figuratively—at Beverly Pass, elevation 5,800 feet. Take a moment to catch your breath, not only from the hike up here but from the sudden appearance of Mount Stuart and the other peaks of the Stuart Range and Enchantments directly across the valley.

**Options:** Day hikers usually turn around at the divide, content with the views, but the trail continues another 2.5 miles down Turnpike Creek to Ingalls Creek Trail 1215. Another option is to hike up to Fourth Creek Pass, just 0.5 mile up a side trail from upper Beverly Creek basin.

# 33

# Bean Creek

**Overview:** *A hike up Bean Creek to a high ridge.*

**Distance:** 4.6 miles round-trip to meadows; 6.0 miles round-trip to Earl Peak saddle.
**Difficulty:** Moderate to strenuous.
**Best season:** Summer through fall.
**Traffic:** Foot and stock traffic only; heavy use.

**High point:** About 6,600 feet.
**Maps:** USGS Mount Stuart; Green Trails No. 209 (Mount Stuart).
**For more information:** USDA Forest Service, Cle Elum Ranger District Office.

**Finding the trailhead:** Bean Creek Trail 1391.1 is approached via North Fork Teanaway River Road (Forest Service Road 9737) north of Cle Elum. If approaching via I–90, turn off at exit 85 and follow State Route 970 east 6.8 miles to Teanaway River Road. If approaching via U.S. Highway 97, follow to the 97–970 junction and drive west on SR 970 just 3.4 miles to the Teanaway River Road turnoff. Follow Teanaway River Road about 13 miles to pavement's end, where two dirt roads fork off. Take the right fork (FS 9737) and follow 3.6 miles to the Beverly Creek spur road (Forest Service Road 9737-112), then take the right fork and follow 1.1 miles to the Beverly Creek trailhead at road's end. A Northwest Forest Pass is required.

## Key points:
**0.2** Bean Creek junction.
**1.8** Meadow trail junction.
**3.0** Earl Peak saddle.

# Bean Creek

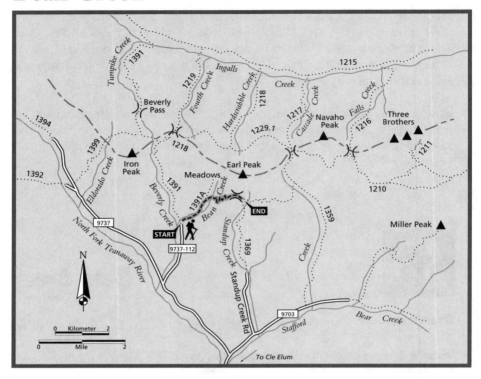

**The hike:** Bean Creek is a tributary of Beverly Creek, with a popular hiking trail forking off from Beverly-Turnpike Trail and leading up a dusty canyon to a high pass below 7,036-foot Earl Peak.

Get your permit and start up Beverly-Turnpike Trail (Hike 32), crossing a sturdy footbridge across Beverly Creek, then hiking up an old road grade until it narrows into a trail proper. About 0.2 mile up the trail is a junction with Bean Creek Trail 1391A (officially 1391.1 but the sign says 1391A). Beverly-Turnpike Trail veers leftward, crossing Bean Creek and continuing up the canyon. Stay right and climb gradually alongside Bean Creek. The trail crosses the creek a short distance above. This crossing may be difficult in early season, when the water runs high. By late summer of most years, it's an easy boulder hop across. Continue along the stream bank, climbing through dusty old-growth pine and fir forest, always within a stone's throw of the chattering creek. The trail eventually breaks out of the woods for views of the surrounding ridges, including Earl Peak to the east, then forks. One trail drops down to and crosses the creek, the other keeps climbing up the basin.

The majority of hikers follow the upstream trail, which is not a designated trail but still gets most of the traffic. It leads another 0.5 mile, gaining 400 feet, to the

138

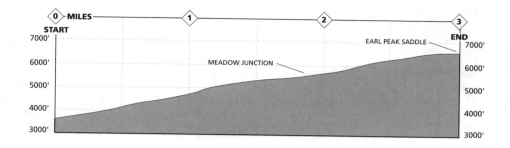

upper Bean Creek basin and fabulous meadows at an elevation of 6,200 feet. In early summer, these grassy meadows sprout wildflowers like weeds. At only 2.3 miles from the trailhead, Bean Creek's meadows are among the most accessible in the area and are usually much less crowded than nearby Esmerelda Basin.

The other fork is the official trail. It dips down and crosses Bean Creek, climbs briefly through rocky meadows thick with wildflowers in early summer, then starts climbing a wooded slope. The narrow, dusty trail switches back steeply upward, although it is pleasant enough early in the day, before the sun's rays hit the slope. Views increase as you climb higher. First you see the upper meadows and high ridges across the basin, then the tips of the Stuart Range peaks. After 1.2 miles and 1,000 feet of elevation gain from the fork, the trail tops out on a high ridge of Earl Peak. For easy views, follow this ridge southward a short distance to a viewpoint, but not too far, as it gets rocky and steep.

**Options:** A climbers' trail leads up from the ridgetop to the 7,036-foot summit of Earl Peak. Although the trail is rough and rocky and not recommended for hikers without alpine scrambling experience, a majority of hikers who reach the ridge continue up Earl Peak to spectacular views.

# 34

# Standup Creek

**Overview:** *A hike up lonesome Standup Creek.*

**Distance:** 8.8 miles-round trip to Earl Ridge.
**Difficulty:** Moderate.
**Best season:** Summer through fall.
**Traffic:** Foot and stock use; light traffic.
**High point:** About 6,200 feet.

**Maps:** USGS Enchantment Lakes; Green Trails No. 209 (Mount Stuart).
**For more information:** USDA Forest Service, Cle Elum Ranger District Office.

**Finding the trailhead:** Standup Creek Trail 1369 is approached via Teanaway River Road from Cle Elum. If approaching via I–90, turn off at exit 85 and follow State Route 970 east 6.8 miles to Teanaway River Road. If approaching via U.S. Highway 97, follow to the 97–970 junction and drive west on SR 970 just 3.4 miles to the Teanaway River Road turnoff. Follow Teanaway River Road about 13 miles to pavement's end, where two dirt roads fork off. Take the right fork (Forest Service Road 9737) and follow 1.2 miles to the Stafford Creek Road fork (Forest Service Road 9703). Turn right on FS 9703 and follow just 0.7 mile to Standup Creek Road (spur 112). Turn left up the spur and follow just over 1 mile to the Standup Creek trailhead. The spur road is rugged and not recommended for any but high-clearance vehicles. Many hikers park on Stafford Creek Road and walk the mile up to the trailhead. A Northwest Forest Pass is required.

## Key points:

**2.3** Avalanche swath.
**3.9** Bean Creek Trail junction.
**4.4** Earl Peak saddle.

**The hike:** Standup Creek Trail is an overlooked and lightly traveled trail in the Teanaway River region on the southeast boundary of the Alpine Lakes Wilderness.

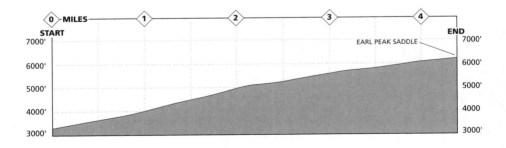

# Standup Creek

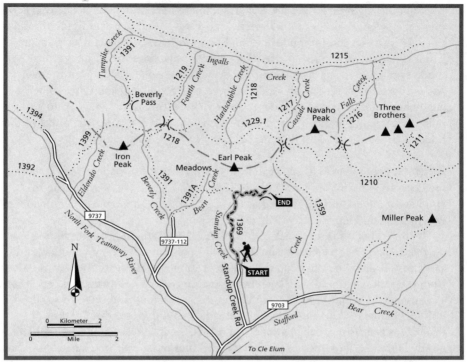

The trail climbs 4.4 miles to a 6,200-foot saddle on the Standup–Stafford Creek divide, the usual turnaround point for day hikers, and continues down into Stafford Creek basin. If you started from Stafford Creek Road, add a mile to your one-way distance.

Get your day-use permit at the trailhead register and start hiking. From the official trailhead, the trail follows an old road grade upstream. The going is always up but gradually, through open hemlock, fir, and pine forest. In the first 2 miles, the trail crosses Standup Creek several times, potential trouble in early season when water may be running high, but usually not a problem in late summer and fall. A few switchbacks lead up to a viewpoint about halfway up the trail, from where you can look down the canyon or up toward Earl Peak.

Just over 2 miles up the trail is the avalanche crossing. A big slide came ripping down the gully from Earl Peak a few years back and wiped out everything in its path in a narrow swath down the creek bed. Avalanche debris is scattered across the slope, but the woods weren't too thick so there isn't so much debris that the trail is impassable. Even so, cross with care and continue up the basin. Once past the avalanche swath, the trail climbs a bit more steeply through thinning forest, with increasing views up the basin, then traverses open meadows to the junction with Bean Creek Trail 1391A (or 1391.1, the official designation).

Continue right on Standup Creek Trail, to the Earl Peak saddle. The trail contours the steep, rocky meadows briefly and crosses Standup Creek for the final time. This stream runs faithfully even in late season, fed by a perennial spring, providing a narrow strip of lush greenery amid the otherwise dry meadows. Just past the stream, the trail starts switching back up a steep, wooded slope, but the switchbacks end soon at Earl Peak saddle. There is a good campsite here, sometimes windy but fairly sheltered by the trees. For views, step out of the woods to a rocky point overlooking Stafford Creek basin, from where you can see the peaks of the Stuart Range over Navaho Pass, and more.

**Options:** From the saddle, you can drop down 1.5 miles through lovely, lonesome meadows to join Stafford Creek Trail 1359 (Hike 35) and loop back to the road. If you have a mountain bike stashed at the trailhead, or can swap cars with another group, this semiloop is more easily done.

If you go left on Bean Creek Trail 1391A (1391.1), the trail climbs up to a saddle overlooking Bean Creek basin. This section of the trail is hard to follow and is easily lost. Follow the cairns up the meadows from a streambed just a few minutes from the trail junction; if you keep traversing on the obvious path, you end up on a dead-end ridge and have to scramble up steep meadows and scree to regain the trail. A climbers' trail leads up from the saddle to the summit of 7,036-foot Earl Peak. This is little more than a rocky ridge hike, steep and strenuous but not technically difficult. Not recommended for the inexperienced, of course, but that scarcely deters them from trying.

# 35

# Stafford Creek

**Overview:** *A hike or backpack up Stafford Creek to Navaho Pass.*

**Distance:** 11.2 miles round-trip.
**Difficulty:** Moderate.
**Best season:** Early summer through fall.
**Traffic:** Foot and stock traffic; moderate use.
**High point:** About 6,040 feet.

**Maps:** USGS Enchantment Lakes; Green Trails No. 209 (Mount Stuart).
**For more information:** USDA Forest Service, Cle Elum Ranger District Office.

**Finding the trailhead:** Stafford Creek Trail 1359 is approached via Teanaway River Road from Cle Elum. If approaching via I–90, turn off at exit 85 and follow State Route 970 east 6.8 miles to Teanaway River Road. If approaching via U.S. Highway 97, follow to the 97–970 junction and drive west on SR 970 just 3.4 miles

# Stafford Creek

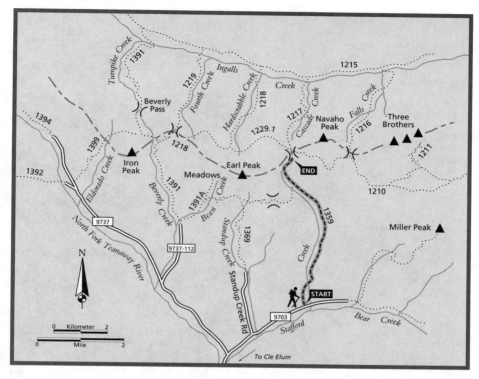

to the Teanaway River Road turnoff. Follow Teanaway River Road about 13 miles to pavement's end, where two dirt roads fork off. Take the right fork (Forest Service Road 9737) and follow about 1.2 miles to the Stafford Creek Road fork (Forest Road 9703). Turn right on FS 9703 and follow 2.5 miles to the Stafford Creek trailhead on the left; parking is on the right. A Northwest Forest Pass is required.

## Key points:
**4.0** Standup Creek Trail junction.
**5.0** Meadow.
**5.6** Navaho Pass.

**The hike:** Stafford Creek Trail is a popular hike in the Teanaway River region of Mount Baker–Snoqualmie National Forest. The trail climbs 5 miles up a chuckling creek to a lush meadow basin, then climbs a bit more to a high pass at the southeastern boundary of the Alpine Lakes Wilderness, with views of the Stuart Range and more.

Cross the road to the trailhead register, get your permit, then start hiking. Typical of trails in this area, the trail initially follows an old road grade up the canyon,

*Stafford Creek Trail*

climbing gradually through dusty, open pine, hemlock, and fir forest. The trail starts on the western side of Stafford Creek, but within the first mile crosses the creek and then contours the east bank, gaining only a little elevation. If you are on the trail early, the first 2 miles are in shady forest up the steep-walled canyon. At 1.2 miles, the trail crosses a bridge, then continues as before, closely above the streambank, a little steeper than before, gaining 500 feet elevation in the second mile, with increasing views up and down the valley. At 2.6 miles, the trail crosses another creek, then proceeds along Stafford Creek, more steeply now, with increasing views including Navaho Peak and, as you round the corner into the upper basin, Earl Peak. At 4 miles is the Standup Creek Trail junction.

The sign says Navaho Pass is 2 miles from the junction, but it is really only about 1.6 miles. The trail switches back a couple of times as it climbs a dusty forest slope just over 1 mile to a broad, grassy meadow with a couple of good campsites in the trees bordering the meadows. In early summer, the meadows are bursting with wildflowers, including shooting star and aster, with Indian paintbrush, lupine, and skyrocket on the fringes. Above the meadow, the trail continues climbing more gradually through subalpine meadows, then crosses a gravelly shelf before curving rightward and climbing a final slope to Navaho Pass, the 6,040-foot divide at the head of Stafford Creek. Navaho Pass is the usual turnaround point for day hikers. If the sky is clear, expect great views of the Enchantment and Stuart Range peaks, although Mount Stuart itself is hidden behind an intervening ridge.

**Options:** Better views, including stunning views of Mount Stuart, can be had from the pass just west of Navaho Pass, on the Stafford–Hardscrabble Creek divide. Take a left at the top of Navaho Pass and follow County Line Trail 1229.1 westward to the pass, or follow the faint trail leading west from the cairn just before the final turn up to Navaho Pass.

A recommended option is to follow the County Line Trail east beyond Navaho Peak to the trail junction at Falls Creek Pass, then up a way trail (1210) up the rocky ridge to the top of the Three Brothers, a 7,303-foot summit. Although this "trail" is actually a climbers' trail, it is really just steep, rocky, ridge hiking. For that matter, the summit of 7,223-foot Navaho Peak is a fairly easy and straightforward scramble via either of two ridges crossed by the County Line Trail as you hike east from Navaho Pass. These summits are not recommended for casual hikers, but experienced, conditioned hikers should have no trouble once the snow is gone.

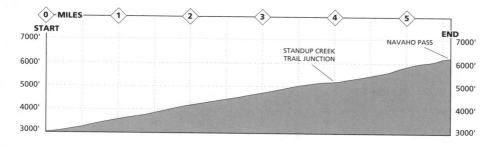

# 36     Swauk Discovery Trail

**Overview:** *An interpretive loop near Blewitt Pass.*

**Distance:** 3.0-mile loop.
**Difficulty:** Easy.
**Best season:** Summer through fall.
**Traffic:** Foot traffic only; moderate use.
**High point:** About 4,200 feet.

**Maps:** USGS Blewitt Pass; Green Trails No. 210 (Liberty).
**For more information:** USDA Forest Service, Cle Elum Ranger District Office.

**Finding the trailhead:** Swauk Discovery Trail 1334 begins just south of Blewitt Pass. Drive U.S. Highway 97 to Blewitt Pass. From the wide gravel parking area just east of the pass, turn up Forest Service Road 9716 and follow 0.5 mile to the Swauk Discovery trailhead. A Northwest Forest Pass is required.

## Key points:
**3.0**   End of loop at trailhead.

**The hike:** Swauk Discovery Trail is a short, interpretive, loop hike located just south of Blewitt Pass, about 0.5 mile off of US 97. This hike is not located within the Alpine Lakes Wilderness but is a fairly easy forest hike with views, suitable for hikers of all ages and ambitions. The loop is described in counterclockwise fashion beginning from the trailhead. The main loop is 3 miles around, but an eastern trail section can lengthen the hike by about 0.7 mile. The trail features a variety of trees and brush, including grand and Douglas fir, western larch, ponderosa, lodgepole, and western white pine, Engelmann spruce, and others, with interpretive signs all along the way. A self-guiding brochure may be available at the trailhead; it provides information about each feature of the trail. Once you've hiked the trail, return the brochure so others may use it. The trail has some views, including a faraway look at the Stuart Range peaks and Mounts Rainier and Adams.

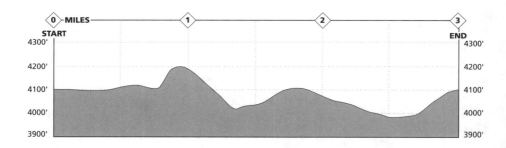

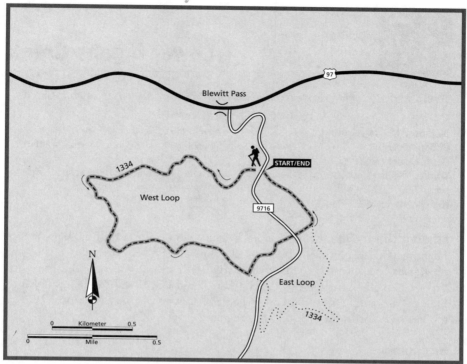

The loop begins from the trailhead and meanders westward for about a mile to a stand of ponderosa pine before curving southward briefly and then eastward for a mile to a cutoff trail junction. The short loop follows this trail across the road and up the other side back to the trailhead. If you stay right at this junction, you follow the road a short distance, then switchback up to a ridge and loop around to rejoin the short loop about 0.3 mile short of the trailhead. The eastern loop has the steepest hiking and few interpretive signs, but it also has the fewest other hikers in case you want to get away from the crowds for a few minutes.

**Options:** By hiking the east loop, you add 0.7 mile to the loop hike. It takes only about fifteen minutes more to do the entire loop, so why not?

# 37

# Lower Ingalls Creek

**Overview:** *A popular, early-season flower hike along Ingalls Creek to Falls Creek.*

**Distance:** 11.4 miles round-trip.
**Difficulty:** Easy.
**Best season:** Late spring to late fall.
**Traffic:** Foot and stock use; moderate use. No dogs.
**High point:** About 3,300 feet.

**Maps:** USGS Blewitt, Enchantment Lakes, Mount Stuart; Green Trails No. 210 (Liberty), 209 (Mount Stuart).
**For more information:** USDA Forest Service, Leavenworth Ranger District Office.

**Finding the trailhead:** Ingalls Creek Trail 1215 begins just off the Blewitt Pass Highway (U.S. Highway 97) between Cle Elum and Leavenworth. Drive US 97 to the Ingalls Creek Road (Forest Service Road 7310) turnoff, which is 7.1 miles south from the "Big Y" junction of U.S. Highway 2 and US 97 and 14.2 miles north of Blewitt Pass, at milepost 178. Follow FS 7310 about 1.2 miles to the Ingalls Creek trailhead. A Northwest Forest Pass is required.

## Key points:
**0.5** Alpine Lakes Wilderness boundary.
**5.7** Falls Creek Trail junction.

**The hike:** Ingalls Creek Trail is one of the longest and loneliest trails in the Alpine Lakes Wilderness. Few hikers complete the entire trail. Early-season hikers go 5 or 6 miles before they are turned back by snow. Late-season hikers usually bypass the first dozen miles of the trail, favoring a shortcut into the upper canyon via Beverly-Turnpike or Ingalls Way Trails, which allow quicker access to the "best" part of the hike. But the lower portion of the trail, though lacking in sublime views, has its own rewards. Wildflowers are everywhere along the trail in early season; fall colors are spectacular. Throw in a few waterfalls and some impressive mountain views, and you have a good, easy day hike that deserves your attention.

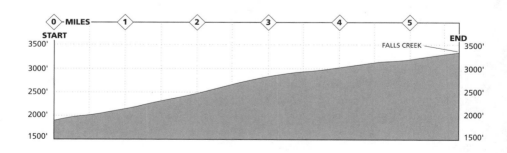

# Lower Ingalls Creek

START

END

7310

97

Peshastin

Creek

Creek

To Leavenworth

To Cle Elum

N

Kilometer    1
0

Mile
0

Stuart Pass

Ingalls Lake

Mount Stuart

Sherpa Peak

Argonaut Peak

Colchuck Peak

Dragontail Peak

Little Annapurna

McClellan Peak

Three Brothers

Navaho Peak

Earl Peak

Iron Peak

1215

1216

1211

1210

Falls Creek

Cascade Creek

1217

1218

Hardscrabble Creek

Ingalls Creek

Fourth Creek

1219

Turnpike Creek

1391

1391

1359

1369

1391A

1399

Get your permit at the trailhead register and start hiking. The trail begins along Ingalls Creek's north bank and stays there, always close above the creek, leading gradually upward through deep fir, hemlock, and cedar forest for the first 3 miles or so, with only occasional window views of the canyon slopes and ridge points. At 3.6 miles, the trail crosses a stream, then meanders through a basin, crossing open slopes below talus slides that offer glimpses of McClellan Peak and the Three Brothers. After a short climb out of the basin, including a rare switchback, the trail levels out again and contours along the creek as before, in and out of woods.

At 5.7 miles is the Falls Creek Trail (1216) junction, the usual turnaround point for day hikers, especially early-season hikers who can expect to be slowed down looking at the abundant wildflowers, including the to-be-expected lupine, penstemon, bead lily, and trillium, as well as varieties of orchids and other flowers. In early season, avalanche-piled snow may linger in the gully crossings in the last couple of miles to the Falls Creek junction. Those not prepared for snow crossings should turn back. In 5.7 miles the trail has gained only about 1,300 feet, making for a reasonably easy 11.4-mile round-trip.

**Options:** You can continue on to Stuart Pass, 31 miles round-trip. Several side trails offer interesting loop options. Many of these trails are infrequently, if ever, maintained, and are best left to those experienced in and willing to endure miles of poor trail in the pursuit of solitude.

# Leavenworth
## AREA

# 38

# Snow Creek–Nada and Snow Lakes

**Overview:** *A hike up Snow Creek canyon to Nada Lake and the popular Snow Lakes.*

**Distance:** 13.4 miles round-trip to Snow Lakes.
**Difficulty:** Moderately strenuous.
**Best season:** Summer through fall.
**Traffic:** Foot traffic only; heavy use. No dogs.
**High point:** About 5,450 feet.

**Maps:** USGS Leavenworth, Blewett, Enchantment Lakes; Green Trails No. 209S (The Enchantments).
**For more information:** USDA Forest Service, Leavenworth Ranger District Office.

**Finding the trailhead:** Snow Creek Trail 1553 is approached from Leavenworth via Icicle Creek Road (Forest Service Road 76). Drive U.S. Highway 2 to Icicle Junction at the west end of Leavenworth. Follow Icicle Creek Road 4.1 miles to the Snow Creek Trail parking lot. The parking lot is big but gets crowded on summer and fall weekends, when everybody seems to be hiking Snow Creek Trail to the Enchantments. Theft is common at this trailhead, so park and lock your car, leaving no valuables behind. A Northwest Forest Pass is required. This is one trailhead where you can count on getting ticketed if you don't display a pass.

## Key points:

**0.1**  Footbridge across Icicle Creek.
**0.3**  Aqueduct crossing.
**1.3**  Alpine Lakes Wilderness boundary.
**2.0**  Snow Creek Wall.
**5.1**  Nada Lake.
**6.7**  Snow Lakes.

**The hike:** Snow Creek Trail is one of the most popular hikes in the Leavenworth area—and for good reason. Tourists and trail runners hike the first mile or two for views or a workout. Rock climbers hike the trail to access several crags, including Snow Creek Wall, a 900-foot-high granite cliff. Day hikers swarm to Nada Lake

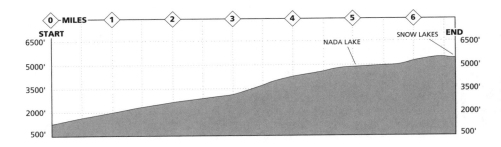

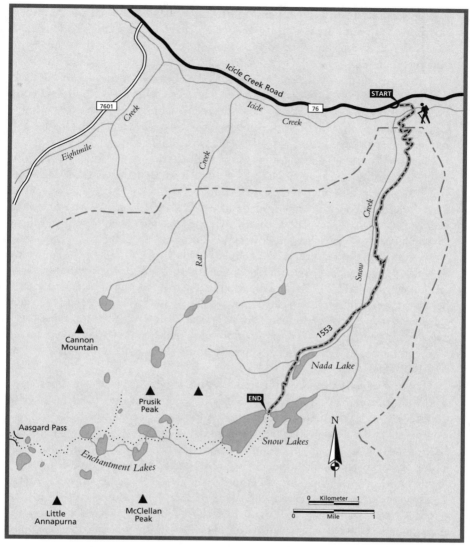

and Snow Lakes on late summer and autumn weekends. And determined backpackers and wilderness adventurers trek in droves to the Enchantment Lakes, the
quintessential Alpine Lakes Wilderness destination. The downside is that Snow
Creek Trail is often crowded, but it's a price that many are willing to pay.

The trail begins from the kiosk at the south end of the parking lot and descends
briefly to cross Icicle Creek via an oversized footbridge, then meanders up a dusty
road grade to an aqueduct channel, crosses the aqueduct channel, then starts climb-

ing a series of hot, dusty switchbacks. The firestorm of 1994 burned the old bridge, closing the trail until the new bridge was completed two years later. The fires also left these initial slopes exposed to the sun, so begin your hike early in the day to beat the heat, and bring plenty of water. The fire left behind charred trees and other hazards, so stay on the trail in this area. The brush has started growing back, as have the wildflowers. Eventually the switchbacks abate and the trail levels out, contouring rocky, occasionally brushy, slopes just across the canyon from Snow Creek Wall. Scan the cliff for rock climbers; on a sunny day you'll probably see several rope teams in action.

The trail continues up the canyon, leaving the burn area and entering shady fir and pine forest, soon passing a side trail leading down to a shady spot beside Snow Creek at a campsite sometimes used by climbers. Ascend gradually up the canyon for a distance, then start climbing again up a few switchbacks. The path levels out in a brushy basin, briefly, then begins switching back once more, up the dusty canyon slope through open pine forest, then contours the slope and soon crosses Snow Creek via a good bridge and parallels Nada Creek for a short mile, with a final few switchbacks to overcome before easing through grassy marshes to Nada Lake, elevation 4,800 feet. Nada Lake is a long, narrow lake lined by talus and timber, set in a narrow, granite-walled canyon. There are several campsites at Nada Lake near the outlet stream and halfway up the lakeshore. Although most backpackers are in a hurry and continue on to Snow Lakes to get a head start to the Enchantment Lakes, Nada Lake is usually a quiet lake worthy of a day visit or overnight stay.

Those who continue follow the trail from the outlet stream around the western lakeshore, through subalpine and Douglas fir and Engelmann spruce, past giant granite boulders, then across Nada Creek on footlogs. Beyond, the trail climbs an exposed talus slope, strenuous but not unpleasant early or late in the day; in the heat of the day, suffer upward. After several rocky switchbacks, the trail levels off and traverses subalpine forest over a rise and down to Snow Lakes, elevation 5,417 feet. The lakes are separated by a masonry dam, which keeps the upper lake from flooding the lower lake. The upper lake is drawn down during the summer to ensure a steady water supply for the fish hatchery miles downstream. By late summer, the upper lake may be several dozen feet low; in drought years, it is a blight on the otherwise pristine wilderness landscape.

Although 6.7 miles from the car, many hikers make a round-trip in a day. For those who suffered under the weight of a full pack, there are numerous campsites at Snow Lakes, the traditional basecamp for exploration of the Enchantment Lakes, which are worthy of their own volume. If you camp here, please try to avoid adverse impacts by using the low-impact techniques discussed in the Introduction.

A permit is required for overnight camping at Nada Lake, Snow Lakes, and everywhere else in the vicinity. Permits are available by mail while supplies last, and a few are given out each morning at the Leavenworth Ranger Station; they go fast, so get yours early or try your luck in the daily lottery. Refer to the Enchantment

Lakes Wilderness Permit section in Appendix A, or call the Leavenworth Ranger Station for permit information.

**Options:** From Snow Lakes, the fabled Enchantment Lakes are a virtual hop and a step away. A well-established high route leads up between the Snow Lakes to the Enchantment basin, a virtual wonderland of little alpine lakes, tarns, and ponds surrounded by white granite peaks, walls, domes, and spires. Hikers camped at Snow Lakes can and usually do make a day jaunt up into the Enchantments.

# 39   Colchuck and Stuart Lakes

**Overview:** *A hike to two alpine lakes nestled beneath the rugged peaks of the Stuart Range.*

**Distance:** 13.4 miles round-trip to both lakes.
**Difficulty:** Moderate.
**Best season:** Summer through fall.
**Traffic:** Foot traffic only; moderate to heavy use. No dogs.
**High point:** 5,600 feet.

**Maps:** USGS Enchantment Lakes; Green Trails No. 177 (Chiwaukum Mountains) or 209S (The Enchantments).
**For more information:** USDA Forest Service, Leavenworth Ranger District Office.

**Finding the trailhead:** Stuart Lake Trail 1599 and Colchuck Lake Trail 1599A are approached from Leavenworth via Icicle Creek Road (Forest Service Road 76). Drive U.S. Highway 2 to Icicle Creek Road at the western end of Leavenworth. Follow Icicle Creek Road 8.3 miles to Bridge Creek Campground. Turn left and follow Eightmile Creek Road (Forest Service Road 7601) 3.9 miles to the Mountaineer trailhead at road's end. A Northwest Forest Pass is required.

## Key points:

**0.7**   Alpine Lakes Wilderness boundary.
**1.5**   Mountaineer Creek crossing.
**2.4**   Trail forks; bear left to Colchuck Lake.
**3.7**   Colchuck Lake.
**5.0**   Trail junction; bear left to Lake Stuart.
**8.0**   Lake Stuart.

**The hike:** Colchuck and Stuart Lakes are two of the most popular destinations in the Alpine Lakes Wilderness. These lovely lakes lie nestled in high granite basins

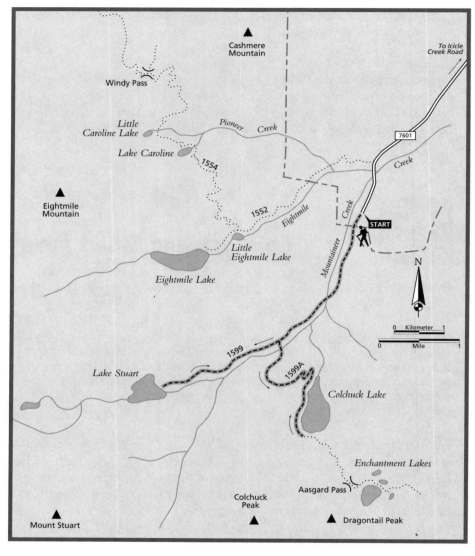

beneath the rugged north walls of the Stuart Range peaks, yet are reached via relatively short trails that begin only a few minutes' drive from Leavenworth. You won't find solitude here except on rare weekdays, but you, like most other hikers who visit, probably won't mind. The hike to Colchuck Lake is rocky and steep; Lake Stuart is a gentle meander through boulders and meadows. Choose one or the other or both.

This hike is described as a day hike including a trip to each lake. You may hike to either lake, or both, as a day hike or backpack. Whatever you decide, register at

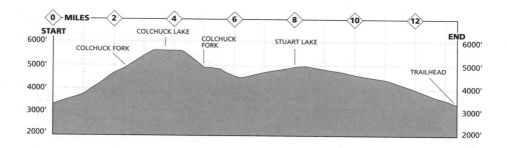

the trailhead and start hiking up Trail 1599, which contours above Mountaineer Creek through fir and pine forest, soon crossing a side stream and at 0.7 mile passing the wilderness boundary marker. The trail is fairly gentle at first, climbing gradually, winding through firs, pines, and cedars, staying close to the creek, then wandering away. Bead lily and twinflower line the trail. At 1.5 miles the trail crosses Mountaineer Creek via a sturdy bridge spanning a pool just below a cascade, then climbs the opposite slope, passing many large granite boulders before leveling off at the edge of a burn area and reaching a trail junction.

To reach Colchuck Lake, the more popular of the two lakes, take the left fork onto Trail 1599A, which drops down and crosses another well-built footbridge anchored by big boulders, then leads along the toe of a talus field along marshy meadows before it starts climbing a timbered slope. The trail crosses a cascading creek, then switches back and crosses it again higher up, then climbs steeply up rocky steps and benches. There is a granite dome beside the trail that is a good rest stop with a great view of the canyon and the peaks above Lake Stuart. Higher up, the trail switches back just below a waterfall; a side trail leads closer. At one point the trail gains 600 feet of elevation in just over 0.5 mile, then crosses over a rocky ridge and contours along above the northern end of Colchuck Lake, elevation 5,570 feet. Colchuck Lake is a deep cirque lake bordered by subalpine fir and mountain-hemlock ridges, immense granite cliffs, and huge granite boulders. The glacier-draped north faces of Dragontail and Colchuck Peaks loom over the lake, providing a stunning backdrop to the cloudy turquoise lake waters. Colchuck Lake is fed by a small active glacier, which accounts for the lake's distinctive coloration. There is a spot where the trail crosses an open rocky shelf where everybody stops for a rest and to reload the camera after shooting pictures of the lake and Dragontail Peak. The trail continues along above the lake's rocky western shore to the southern shoreline, where it ends abruptly amid huge boulders. There are a few campsites above the lakeshore; hopefully you remembered to get a permit. If not, camp at the risk of a stiff fine.

To reach Lake Stuart, backtrack to the fork at Mountaineer Creek junction and head west up the basin for over a mile of fairly level hiking through meadows and alongside marshy meadows and granite boulders, with views of Colchuck and Argonaut Peaks, and the impressive north face of 9,415-foot Mount Stuart that shines

*Colchuck Lake*

stark white in the morning sun. The trail climbs briefly, drops some, and meanders through open, boulder-strewn subalpine fir and mountain-hemlock meadows, past marshes and through brush and grass meadows, before descending a bit to Lake Stuart, elevation 5,064 feet. The best views of Mount Stuart are not from Lake Stuart; wander up the slopes north of the lake or up the angler's trail toward Horseshoe Lake for better views. There are several campsites near the lake.

Horses are allowed on Stuart Lake Trail after Labor Day but not on Colchuck Lake Trail. They are infrequent trail users, judging by a lack of the usual evidence of horse traffic. Dogs are not allowed at either lake. Because of the popularity of these lakes, a permit is required for overnight camping. Get your permit at the Leavenworth Ranger Station. See the Enchantment Lakes Wilderness Permit section in Appendix A for details.

**Options:** Colchuck Lake is the starting point of the customary shortcut into the Enchantment Lakes, via Aasgard Pass, the wide saddle above the southeast corner of the lake, just left of Dragontail Peak. Skirt around the lake's southern shore, crossing the boulder field, and ascend a rocky trail up the broad gully to Aasgard Pass, staying left to pass the cliffs near the top. A trail of sorts can be followed to the pass, although the route is over sandy rock, talus, and snow, and although not technically difficult, it can be very dangerous, especially for those lacking alpine scrambling experience. An ice ax is a must if there is snow, and remember that most accidents happen on the way down. Crampons may be useful, especially early on fall mornings when snow is icy. At least one fatality has been reported here, so be very careful. A 19-mile day hike through the Enchantments, affectionately referred to as "the death march," is somewhat popular among hardcore hikers, especially since overnight permits are hard to get, although the Enchantments are best done as a multiday trip.

# Eightmile and Caroline Lakes

**Overview:** *A short hike to Eightmile Lakes or a longer hike to Lake Caroline.*

**Distance:** 6.2 miles round-trip to Eightmile Lake; 9.6 miles round-trip to Lake Caroline; 10.6 miles round-trip to both lakes.
**Difficulty:** Easy to Eightmile Lake; strenuous to Lake Caroline.
**Best season:** Summer through fall.
**Traffic:** Foot and stock traffic; moderate to heavy use. No dogs.
**High point:** About 6,400 feet.
**Maps:** USGS Cashmere Mountain; Green Trails No. 209S (The Enchantments).
**For more information:** USDA Forest Service, Leavenworth Ranger District Office.

**Finding the trailhead:** Eightmile Creek Trail 1552 and Lake Caroline Trail 1554 are accessed from the Eightmile Creek trailhead in Icicle Creek Canyon. Drive U.S. Highway 2 to Icicle Junction at the west end of Leavenworth. Turn onto Icicle Creek Road and follow 8.3 miles to Bridge Creek Campground. Turn left on Forest Service Road 7601 and follow 3 miles to the Eightmile Creek trailhead. A Northwest Forest Pass is required.

## Key points to Eightmile Lakes:
- **2.6** Little Eightmile Lake.
- **3.1** Eightmile Lake.

## Key points to Lake Caroline:
- **2.6** Little Eightmile Lake
- **4.0** Meadow camp.
- **4.8** Lake Caroline.

**The hike:** The hike to Lake Caroline is an Alpine Lakes Wilderness favorite, especially among those who enjoy hiking through high subalpine meadows and don't mind sweating a little to get there. This hike packs a lot into 4.8 miles, reaching two lakes in the first 3.1 miles, climbing through fire-scarred forest slopes and

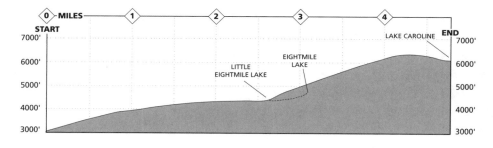

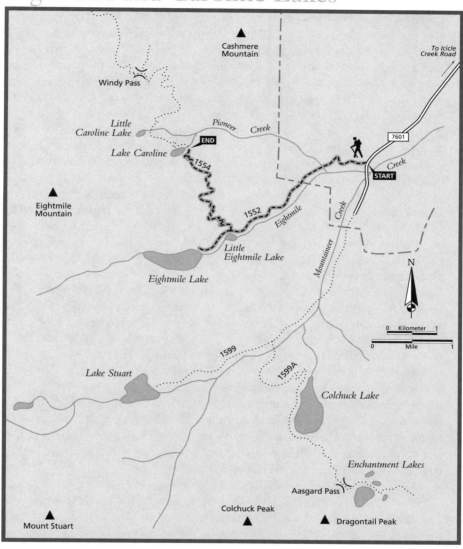

flower-strewn meadows, meandering through high lakes, and climbing wide-open meadows and basins.

Get your permit and begin hiking up the trail, which climbs up a grassy ridge above Eightmile Creek about 0.5 mile to a junction with an old logging road, follows the logging road briefly to a stream crossing, then departs the road and soon crosses the Alpine Lakes Wilderness boundary. The trail winds up the valley amid fire-ravaged snags and dense underbrush, coming near the creek here, climbing away there, until finally leveling out and descending slightly to Little Eightmile

Lake, 2.6 miles, elevation 4,404 feet. There are campsites here, but most hikers continue on to Eightmile Lake or Lake Caroline. The trail junction is just ahead. Continue on up the canyon another 0.5 mile to Eightmile Lake, elevation 4,641 feet, a big lake tucked into a craggy basin. A majority of hikers on this trail are bound for Eightmile Lake, which makes a nice 6.2-mile round-trip hike for families or day hikers who want to beat the traffic back across the mountains. However, enough overnight hikers visit to fill up the available campsites on summer weekends, so come early or on a weekday if you are planning to camp at Eightmile Lake.

Lake Caroline Trail 1554 climbs from the junction at Little Eightmile Lake in a series of switchbacks leading up the fire-razed slopes, then contours up canyon into a basin, then switches back again up the ridge and climbs even more steeply. If you get a late start, you'll be suffering on this part of the trail; with all the trees burned, there is no shade. Just over a mile from the lake, the trail reaches a rocky viewpoint, from where you get a good view of Eightmile Lake and, just now peeking over the intervening ridge, the peaks of the Stuart Range. Continue up amid rust-colored talus, then across a flat, boggy basin, from where the trail leaves the ghost forest behind and enters meadows, steep at first but soon tapering back. Wildflowers are here and everywhere in season, all the way to the divide above Lake Caroline—aster, lupine, paintbrush, skyrocket—framed by subalpine firs and sienna cliffs. You stand a good chance of seeing deer here, maybe a bear, or a redtail hawk swooping overhead scouting the meadows for chipmunks, ground squirrels, and deer mice. The trail passes a campsite (and a horse camp) midway up the meadows, then switches back twice to reach the divide. Pause for effect, taking in the views of the Stuart Range and Enchantment peaks, steep rock walls, craggy ridge lines, glaciers, and all—then drop over the divide and switchback abruptly down to Lake Caroline, 4.8 miles, elevation 6,190 feet, a lovely, quiet lake ringed by subalpine firs and silver snags. For those making an overnight trip, there are several good campsites near the outlet stream and beyond and a pit toilet nearby. (Day-use area only for stock; tie line just before outlet stream.)

Dogs are not allowed on this hike. Because of the popularity of this area, a permit is required for overnight camping at the lakes and elsewhere along this trail. Get your permit from the Leavenworth Ranger Station. A self-issued permit from the trailhead register is all that is required for day hiking here and elsewhere in the Alpine Lakes Wilderness.

**Options:** From Lake Caroline, the trail continues another 0.5 mile to Little Caroline Lake and then up through subalpine parkland for another 6.5 miles to 7,220-foot Windy Pass, a most scenic spot. Motivated hikers make the 14-mile round-trip in a day. The rest of us will find campsites near the lakes.

Experienced scramblers and climbers can make the ascent of 8,501-foot Cashmere Mountain. There is a reasonable route up the west ridge, although it is quite exposed and not at all recommended for hikers lacking mountaineering experience. Refer to *Climbing Washington's Mountains* (see Appendix E) for details.

# 41 Icicle Gorge Scenic Loop

**Overview:** *A scenic loop hike along an interpretive trail in the heart of Icicle Creek Canyon.*

**Distance:** 4.5-mile loop.
**Difficulty:** Easy.
**Best season:** Summer through fall.
**Traffic:** Foot traffic only; heavy use.
**High point:** About 3,000 feet.

**Maps:** USGS Jack Ridge; Green Trails No. 177 (Chiwaukum Mountains).
**For more information:** USDA Forest Service, Leavenworth Ranger District Office.

**Finding the trailhead:** Icicle Gorge Scenic Interpretive Trail 1596 begins far up Icicle Creek Road (Forest Service Road 76) from Leavenworth. From U.S. Highway 2 at Icicle Junction at the west end of Leavenworth, turn south and follow Icicle Creek Road 16.5 miles to Chatter Creek Guard Station. To reach the River Trail trailhead, continue 0.4 mile past the guard station; the trailhead is on your left A Northwest Forest Pass is required unless you are camped at Chatter Creek or Rock Island Campgrounds.

## Key points:
**0.4** River Trail trailhead.
**0.5** Chatter Creek bridge.
**1.2** Trout Creek.
**1.8** Rock Island.
**2.8** Rock Island bridge.
**3.5** Boggy Creek and View Trail junction.
**4.0** Upper View Trail fork.
**4.5** River Trail trailhead.

**The hike:** Icicle Gorge Scenic Interpretive Trail is an easy loop trail leading through the heart of Icicle Creek Canyon. The trail leads along the creek's edge

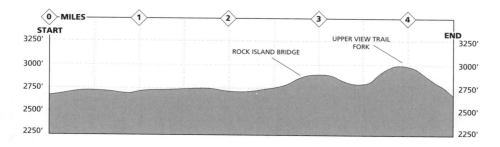

# Icicle Gorge Scenic Loop

*Icicle Creek Gorge*

and up away from the creek, offering both a close-up and faraway look at the diversity of plant and animal life and geology of the Icicle Gorge. Being an interpretive trail with a relatively gentle grade and exhibits explaining the varied plant and animal life and geologic features found along the trail, Icicle Gorge Trail is popular with adventuresome tourists and families. The hike described here is a loop beginning from and ending at the River Trail trailhead and includes a section of the View Trail 1596.1. Many full and semiloop options exist, making this hike as short or as long as you like.

From the River Trail trailhead, follow the trail down toward Icicle Creek to its junction with the loop trail, then turn left and contour above the creek, soon crossing Chatter Creek and proceeding between Icicle Creek and the road to Chatter Creek bridge. Cross the bridge and start up the south side of Icicle Creek, climbing briefly to an overlook. Continue upstream, contouring through shady pine and fir forest, crossing Trout Creek and dropping closer to the creek. Once across the east channel of Jack Creek, you're on Rock Island, hiking through granite boulders. The trail meanders to the creek's edge, then parallels the creek for some distance, crossing the west channel of Jack Creek and soon reaching Icicle Road. Hike beside the road, crossing Rock Island bridge, then pick up the trail on the other side. Continue downstream now, through dusty pine forest along the edge of Icicle Creek, across Boggy Creek, to a junction with the View Trail. From here, you can continue 0.5 mile down the River Trail to the trailhead for a shorter, 3.9-mile loop.

To complete the 4.5-mile loop, cross Icicle Creek Road and climb a series of switchbacks for 0.2 mile, then contour open slopes, which provide views down into Icicle Gorge. A fork is soon reached; the right fork arcs down to the River trailhead to complete the loop; the left fork continues up high for another 0.5 mile before descending to the Chatter Creek trailhead and rejoining the River Trail about 0.4 mile below the trailhead.

**Options:** A shorter loop may be done by hiking the View Trail only, then looping back along the River Trail to the trailhead. This loop is 1.2 miles; it has some elevation gain and loss, but should take only a half-hour or less for most hikers.

# Lower Icicle Creek

**Overview:** *A good early-season hike up the first few miles of Icicle Creek Trail.*

**Distance:** 9.8 miles round-trip to Icicle–Frosty junction.
**Difficulty:** Easy.
**Best season:** Early summer through fall.
**Traffic:** Foot and stock traffic; moderate use.
**High point:** About 3,400 feet.

**Maps:** USGS Chiwaukum Mountains, Stevens Pass; Green Trails No. 177 (Chiwaukum Mountains), 176 (Stevens Pass).
**For more information:** USDA Forest Service, Leavenworth Ranger District Office.

**Finding the trailhead:** Icicle Creek Trail 1551 begins from the end of Icicle Creek Road (Forest Service Road 76) just beyond Blackpine Campground. From Leavenworth, follow Icicle Creek Road just over 19 miles to road's end and the Icicle Creek trailhead. A Northwest Forest Pass is required.

## Key points:
- **0.3** Alpine Lakes Wilderness boundary.
- **1.5** French Creek Trail junction.
- **2.8** Old Frosty Pass Trail junction.
- **4.3** Doughgod Creek Trail.
- **4.9** Icicle Creek crossing and Frosty Pass Trail junction.

**The hike:** Icicle Creek is the major drainage of the northeastern portion of the Alpine Lakes Wilderness. The creek flows through one of the deepest canyons in the Cascade Range, more than 5,000 feet as measured from the top of Icicle Ridge to the depths of Icicle Creek. A popular hiking trail follows the creek some 11 miles

# Lower Icicle Creek

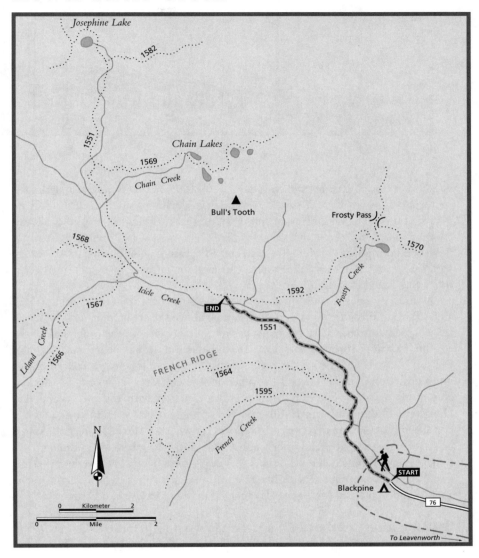

to its source at Josephine Lake. The hike is not popular in its own right so much as it is heavily used to access the many trails leading to sparkling lakes and scenic ridges in this corner of the wilderness. Hikers, horseback riders, and anglers swarm up the trail all summer. While most of the Icicle Creek trails are multiday backpacks, day hikers venture as far up the trail as they like, especially in early season before the higher trails melt out.

From the trailhead, cross Blackpine Creek and continue along the trail through dusty, open pine forest. In 0.3 mile is the wilderness boundary; the trail continues

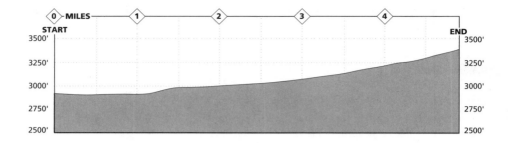

as before, crossing streams and traversing dusty forest. In 1.5 miles, just across the footbridge crossing French Creek, is the junction with French Creek Trail 1595. The trail this far is a popular late spring hike, at least among those who can't wait another month for the snow to melt out. Bright yellow and orange balsamroot flowers bloom profusely along the trail in early season, adding color to the otherwise drab forest. There is a campsite at this junction and one or two more at every other trail junction along the way.

A short distance farther up the trail is the junction with French Ridge Trail 1564. Beyond this junction, the trail climbs up above the creek, then descends back to the creek bottom, where the creek has meandered away to the other side of the canyon. Continue through quiet forest to the junction with an abandoned segment of Frosty Pass Trail. The bridge washed out, and the trail was relocated a couple of miles upstream. Not far beyond the junction, the creek reappears and is followed closely for another mile. The trail passes a junction with the old, abandoned Doughgod Creek Trail, which still shows up on some maps as leading up to Doelle and Chain Lakes. One hiker tried to follow it down from the lakes once; he told a tale of wading through miles of brush. Enough said. Pass it by and continue up the trail another 0.6 mile to a footbridge over Icicle Creek. There are several campsites near the crossing, popular with hikers and horseback riders. The trail this far is about 5 miles, making for a good day hike of about 10 miles round-trip.

**Options:** Icicle Creek Trail gives access to several long, lonely hikes, including French Creek, French Ridge, Frosty Pass, Leland Creek, Square Lakes, Lake Lorraine, and Chain Lakes. A round-trip to trail's end at Josephine Lake is 22 miles. The trail may also be hiked as a one-way hike of about 17 miles to or from Stevens Pass, a bit long for a day hike, but a good two- or three-day backpack.

**Overview:** *A steep hike up Chatter Creek basin to the crest of Icicle Ridge.*

**Distance:** 11.4 miles round-trip to Lake Edna.
**Difficulty:** Strenuous.
**Best season:** Summer through fall.
**Traffic:** Foot and stock traffic only; light to moderate use.

**High point:** About 6,800 feet.
**Maps:** USGS Chiwaukum Mountains; Green Trails No. 177 (Chiwaukum Mountains).
**For more information:** USDA Forest Service, Leavenworth Ranger District Office.

**Finding the trailhead:** Chatter Creek Trail 1580 begins from Icicle Creek Road. Drive U.S. Highway 2 to Icicle Junction at the west edge of Leavenworth. Follow Creek Road about 15.5 miles to Chatter Creek Campground. Continue 0.2 mile beyond the campground entrance and take the first right up Spur Road 515, just across Chatter Creek bridge, and follow 0.3 mile to Chatter Creek trailhead. A Northwest Forest Pass is required.

## Key points:

**1.5** Chatter Creek crossing.
**2.5** Chatter Creek basin.
**4.0** Icicle Ridge.
**4.3** Index Creek basin.
**5.0** Lower bypass trail junction.
**5.3** Icicle Ridge Trail junction.
**5.7** Lake Edna.

**The hike:** Chatter Creek Trail is one of the steeper creek hikes in the Alpine Lakes Wilderness. In its first 4 miles, the trail gains nearly 4,000 feet elevation, mostly in spurts, including a 1,250-foot gain in the final 0.8 mile from Chatter Creek basin to Icicle Ridge. But it is worth the strain and sweat. The trail climbs to the crest of

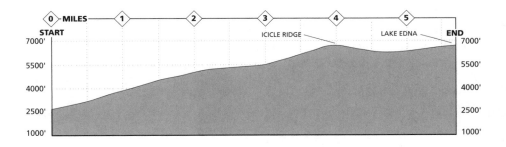

# Chatter Creek

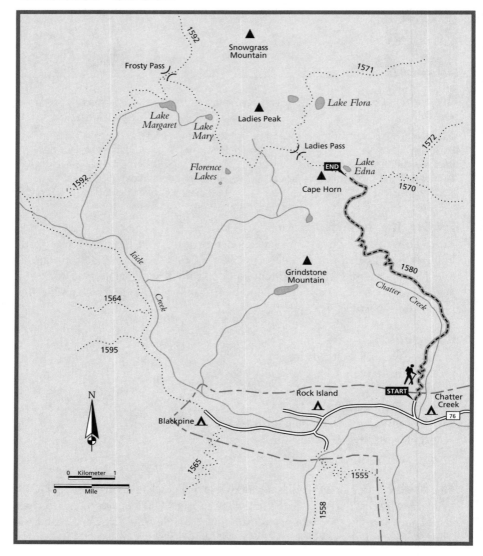

Icicle Ridge and over, traversing alpine meadows beneath granite peaks and ridges to a high pass and a klatch of pretty lakes.

From the trailhead, elevation 2,700 feet, the trail leads gradually uphill through ponderosa pine and Douglas fir forest, soon crossing the wilderness boundary. From there, the trail swings sharply eastward toward Chatter Creek, then switches back and climbs, sometimes via switchbacks and sometimes not, up the steep canyon slopes beside the creek. At 1.5 miles the trail crosses Chatter Creek and continues climbing on the opposite slope. In another 0.5 mile, the trail eases off and enters a broad meadow basin below Grindstone Mountain. A round-trip day hike to Chatter Creek basin and back is about 5 miles, farther if you explore or hike up to the Icicle Ridge divide.

From the upper end of the basin, the trail climbs steeper than ever, gaining 1,250 feet during 0.8 mile of rocky hiking from the basin to the crest of Icicle Ridge, elevation 6,650 feet. If you've come for views, stop here or wander eastward along the ridge crest. If you're aiming for Lake Edna, continue from the divide and descend briefly to upper Index Creek basin, a broad meadow shelf dotted with tarns. Cross the upper meadows of a high basin to a fork. Hikers can take the left fork, which leads 0.3 mile to Icicle Ridge Trail 1570, just 0.3 mile above Lake Edna. This is a hiker-only trail, not suitable for stock. Parties with horses should take the right fork, which leads 0.3 mile to Icicle Ridge Trail, then another 0.3 mile to reach the upper hiker trail junction. The shortcut trail is marked with cairns, where it disappears in the rocky meadows. The other trail is faint in places. It's not too difficult to stay on course here during good weather; if the weather turns, or in darkness, pay close attention.

Whichever option you choose, follow Icicle Ridge Trail 1570 westward another 0.3 mile from the upper bypass trail junction, gaining just over 300 feet of elevation, to Lake Edna, elevation 6,740 feet. Lake Edna is a tiny lake set in a rocky meadow basin amid subalpine firs, pines, and larches. If you're doing this as an overnight hike, no camping is allowed within 200 feet of the lake; camp back at Index Creek basin or farther along the trail.

As with other hikes leading to ridgetops in the eastern half of the Alpine Lakes Wilderness, beware of afternoon thunderstorms. Lightning strikes are frequent on Icicle Ridge and surrounding peaks and ridges. If a storm is moving in, get to a safe place quickly.

**Options:** While Chatter Creek is a good day hike, backpackers can spend several days exploring upper Icicle Ridge. You may continue to Ladies Pass, Lake Flora, Lake Mary, and Frosty Pass. There are several loop and long one-way options here for those who can arrange transportation.

# 44

# Fourth of July Creek

**Overview:** *A steep hike up a fire-scorched trail to the crest of Icicle Ridge.*

**Distance:** 10.4 miles round-trip.
**Difficulty:** Very strenuous.
**Best season:** Summer through fall.
**Traffic:** Foot and stock traffic only; light use.
**High point:** 6,780 feet.

**Maps:** USGS Big Jim Mountain, Cashmere Mountain; Green Trails No. 177 (Chiwaukum Mountains).
**For more information:** USDA Forest Service, Leavenworth Ranger District Office.

**Finding the trailhead:** Fourth of July Creek Trail 1579 is approached via Icicle Creek Road from Leavenworth. Drive U.S. Highway 2 to Leavenworth. Take Icicle Creek Road from the western end of town and follow 9.1 miles to the Fourth of July trailhead, on the right. This is a high car-prowl area, so leave nothing of value in your car. A Northwest Forest Pass is required.

## Key points:
**0.3** First creek crossing.
**0.6** Second creek crossing.
**3.8** Top of first switchbacks.
**4.2** More switchbacks.
**4.6** Upper meadows.
**5.2** Icicle Ridge Trail junction.

**The hike:** Fourth of July Creek Trail has a reputation for being a hot, dry, dusty, steep, and strenuous hike to a relatively unspectacular section of the Icicle Ridge crest. This reputation wasn't helped by recent forest fires, which burned much of Icicle Ridge, including the entire length of this trail. The hike wasn't especially popular before the fire; it did, though, have a following among hikers willing to suffer long, hot, uphill battles for views and solitude. It is sure to be less popular now. Be assured that it is still steep, hot, dry, and dusty, but also that the views remain

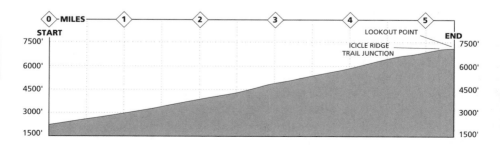

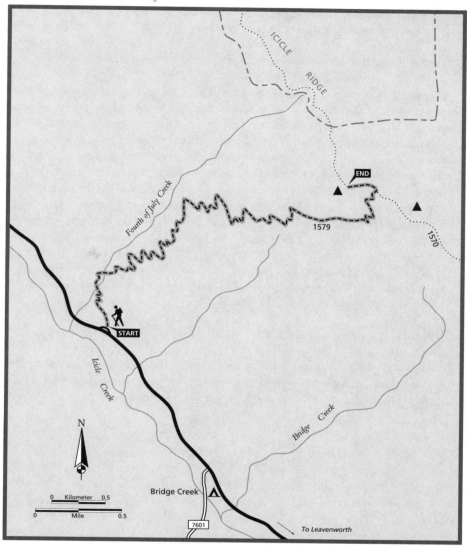

spectacular. Hike the trail when it is reopened in 2003, then in a few years, and so on, to watch the fire-scorched slopes come back to life. Be sure to check with the Forest Service prior to hiking this trail; until restored, the trail is too hazardous to recommend.

The trail begins in rocky, fire-scorched pine and fir forest, contouring along the base of the canyon wall to Fourth of July Creek, crossing, then circling back and crossing the creek again shortly above. Above the creek, the trail leads up through meadows—once and hopefully soon again bursting with lupine—and then starts up the switchbacks. Once the switchbacks start, they scarcely let up in the next 3 miles. The first mile above the creek is brutal, gaining 1,200 feet; it used to be in forest and somewhat shaded but now is more open and hot going. Higher up, the trail climbs through a brushy avalanche gully, pure torture on a hot summer day. Although the brush was razed by the fire, be sure it will grow back with a vengeance. After a mile of suffering, the trail goes back into what used to be woods and stays there as it climbs another several hundred feet to where the switchbacks end abruptly at 5,300 feet elevation and the trail contours eastward toward the ridge, still climbing. Once across the ridge, the trail switches back some more, gaining a quick 400 feet before contouring once more through fir and pine snags and open meadows just below the ridge crest. Aside from the uphill grind, the final mile is more enjoyable. The trail contours into a high meadow basin, with increasing views down to Icicle Creek and across to Cashmere and Cannon Mountains, the rock spires of the Lost World Plateau, and the high peaks of the Stuart Range. At the crest is the Icicle Ridge Trail (1570) junction at a saddle just a few feet shy of 6,800 feet elevation.

For the best views, hike 0.2 mile west and scramble up a 7,029-foot ridge point just off the trail. It's an easy scramble up boulders to this former lookout site. No question why they chose to build a lookout here. Enjoy the view!

**Options:** This is one of those trails with little else to do but hike up and back down, unless you are using the Fourth of July Trail as a shortcut to bypass the first 9 miles of Icicle Ridge Trail 1570. If so, continue up the ridge trail as far as you like. If you arrange transportation, you can loop out via Chatter Creek or Frosty Pass, or down Icicle Ridge to Leavenworth. There are several options.

# 45

# Lower Icicle Ridge

**Overview:** *A strenuous hike to the crest of Icicle Ridge.*

**Distance:** 9.6 miles round-trip.
**Difficulty:** Strenuous.
**Best season:** Late spring for first few miles; summer through fall for upper ridge.
**Traffic:** Foot and stock traffic; light use. Mountain bikes allowed on first 9 miles of trail.

**High point:** About 5,600 feet.
**Maps:** USGS Leavenworth, Cashmere Mountain, Big Jim Mountain; Green Trails No. 178 (Leavenworth), 177 (Chiwaukum Mountains).
**For more information:** USDA Forest Service, Leavenworth Ranger District Office.

**Finding the trailhead:** Icicle Ridge Trail 1570 begins from Icicle Creek Road (Forest Service Road 76) just south of Leavenworth. Drive U.S. Highway 2 to Leavenworth. Take Icicle Creek Road from the west end of town and follow 1.4 miles to what looks like a private road leading up to several houses. A small brown sign points to Icicle Ridge trailhead. Turn right, then left, and drive about 50 yards or so to the trailhead. A Northwest Forest Pass is required.

## Key points:
**2.0**  A saddle below Leavenworth viewpoint.
**4.8**  Ridge crest.

**The hike:** Icicle Ridge is one of the longest, highest hikes in the Alpine Lakes Wilderness. The ridge forms the divide between Tumwater and Icicle Creek Canyons, two of the deepest gorges in the Cascade Range. The relief is incredible; the trail begins from only about 1,600 feet elevation on the outskirts of the town of Leavenworth, then climbs up to and traverses along and beside a 7,000-foot-high ridge for over 20 miles. It goes without saying that the views from the ridge are far and wide. Although steep in places, especially in the first several miles, the majority of the trail is relatively gentle ridge hiking, with the usual ups and downs you might expect, sometimes steep. Wildflowers bloom in abundance in the spring and

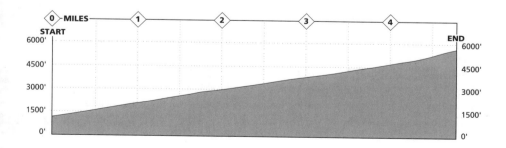

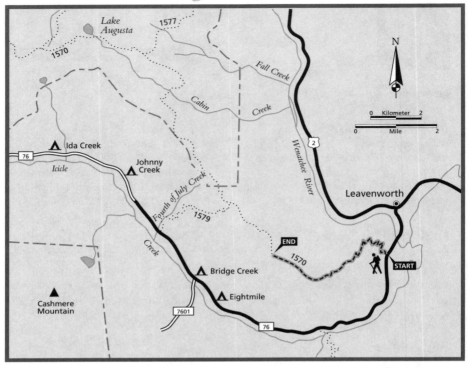

early summer on the lower ridge and stay late higher up. Because of its length, this hike is more popular with horse packers than backpackers. Few hike the entire trail in one push; most hike segments of the trail as part of other hikes. The first several miles of the trail are popular as a day hike, especially in early season before the high country melts out.

Get your permit at the trailhead register and start hiking. From the trailhead, the trail climbs through open pine forest that was burned over a decade ago, leaving grassy meadows in the place of brush. Pine needles litter the trail; in early season, yellow balsamroot flowers brighten the path. In 2 miles, after a healthy 1,600-foot gain, the trail reaches a saddle on the ridge, from where a quick trip along the ridge leads to a rocky viewpoint overlooking the town of Leavenworth and the highway snaking up Tumwater Canyon. There's a campsite here, offering a unique perspective of the sights and sounds of Leavenworth at night, but no water.

Continuing upward, the trail contours along the eastern side of the crest, switching back occasionally as it climbs through open pine and fir forest. In another 1.5 miles, sometimes on the ridge crest with views down into Tumwater Canyon, is the steepest part of the trail, climbing a series of tight switchbacks and gaining a quick 600 feet. The trail levels out just as suddenly, meandering through open forest and meadows along the gentle ridge crest to a 5,580-foot high point at 4.8 miles, a good place for a rest stop, with views down into Icicle Creek Canyon and beyond to the Stuart Range. This is a good place to turn back, for a 9.6-mile round-trip.

**Options:** Those with extra time or energy may continue along the ridge trail another 4 miles or so to the Fourth of July Creek Trail (1579) junction (Hike 44). This section of trail was burned over by a recent forest fire but should be open. A short distance beyond is the old lookout site, a supreme viewpoint at 7,029 feet elevation. At 18 miles, it's a bit far for a day hike, but with arranged transportation you can hike out via Fourth of July Creek Trail for a 14-mile, one-way trip, much more reasonable. Check with the Forest Service on trail status; forest fires left the trail scorched in places, and the trail may be closed for restoration.

# Chiwaukum Mountains
## AND LAKE WENATCHEE AREA

# Lower Chiwaukum Creek

**Overview:** *A hike up the first few miles of Chiwaukum Creek Trail.*

**Distance:** 10.8 miles round-trip to Chiwaukum Fork.
**Difficulty:** Mostly easy.
**Best season:** Late spring for lower Chiwaukum Creek Trail; summer through fall beyond Chiwaukum Fork.
**Traffic:** Foot and stock traffic; moderate to heavy use.

**High point:** About 3,400 feet.
**Maps:** USGS Big Jim Mountain, Chiwaukum Mountains; Green Trails No. 177 (Chiwaukum Mountains).
**For more information:** USDA Forest Service, Leavenworth Ranger District Office.

**Finding the trailhead:** Chiwaukum Creek Trail 1571 begins just off U.S. Highway 2 between Coles Corner and Leavenworth. Drive US 2 to Chiwaukum Creek Road (Forest Service Road 7908), 5 miles south of Coles Corner and 0.8 mile north of Tumwater Campground. Follow FS 7908 a short 0.3 mile to the Chiwaukum Creek trailhead loop. A Northwest Forest Pass is required.

## Key points:
**1.0** Trail forks off from access road.
**5.4** South Fork Trail junction.

**The hike:** Chiwaukum Creek, one of the major drainages of the Alpine Lakes Wilderness, has a reputation for being a long, lonely hike, and the reputation is partly right. The trail is over 13 miles long and leads to high meadows and lakes that are more readily reached via shorter trails coming up from Icicle Creek. Many hikers day hike the first 5 miles or so, especially in late spring and early summer, when the wildflowers are in bloom.

Chiwaukum Creek Trail begins at a gate blocking access to a private road that once upon a time could be driven about a mile farther up the canyon. Get your per-

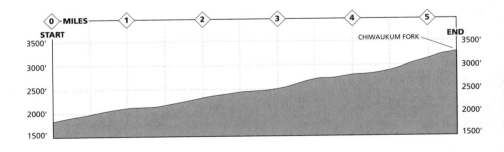

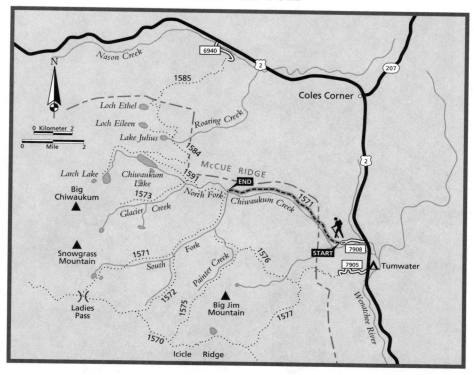

mit at the trailhead register, then hike up the road grade 1 mile to a gate, where signs point rightward to Chiwaukum Creek Trail. Continue up the canyon, staying on the north side of the creek another 4.4 up-and-down miles to a fork. The trail is relatively flat and easy going, gaining elevation gradually all the way but never too steeply. The trail ascends through fir and hemlock forest, passing frequent stands of mature pine. In early season, wildflowers bloom alongside the road and trail, including balsamroot, Tweedy's lewissia, and the usual lupine, paintbrush, bead lily, trillium, and bunchberry. The trail is well trodden by horse traffic, which is abundant. The loose, dusty soil can be irritating to walk on after awhile. For the most part, the trail stays well above the creek. The trail drops down to a campsite next to the creek in a couple of miles, then reaches the creek again at a bouldery spot a bit farther on. Just past the 5-mile mark, the trail forks. The horse ford is down to the left; the footlog crossing is off to the right. The footlog crossing is recommended for two-footed travelers. Once across the convenient cedar footlogs, the trail meanders to the junction of the South and North Fork Chiwaukum Creek Trails. There is a trail camp near the junction and at every trail junction along the way. Most hikers turn back here, especially late-spring and early-summer hikers who come to stretch their legs and see the wildflowers.

*Bunchberry*

**Options:** From Chiwaukum Fork, you may hike up the south or north forks of Chiwaukum Creek. The South Fork Trail leads to Timothy Meadow and Lake Flora, connecting with Icicle Ridge Trail 1570 at Ladies Pass in about 8 miles. The north fork trail leads to Glacier Basin Trail (1573) junction and beyond to Chiwaukum and Larch Lakes in 7 miles. These are popular multiday backpacks.

# Lake Ethel

**Overview:** *A hike to Lake Ethel, a small alpine lake in the Chiwaukum Mountains.*

**Distance:** 9.0 miles round-trip.
**Difficulty:** Strenuous.
**Best season:** Summer through fall.
**Traffic:** Foot traffic only; light use.
**High point:** About 5,600 feet.

**Maps:** USGS Chiwaukum Mountains, Mount Howard, Lake Wenatchee; Green Trails No. 177 (Chiwaukum Mountains).
**For more information:** USDA Forest Service, Lake Wenatchee Ranger District Office.

**Finding the trailhead:** Lake Ethel Trail 1585 begins just off U.S. Highway 2 between Stevens Pass and Coles Corner. Drive US 2 to Gill Creek Road (Forest Service Road 6940), about 15.2 miles east of Stevens Pass and 5.3 miles west of Coles Corner, on the south side of the highway. If approaching from Stevens Pass, the turnoff is just 1.2 miles past the White Pine turnoff; it is easily passed, if you aren't paying attention. Follow FS 6940 across the railroad tracks to the power lines. The road forks; stay left and follow the main road as it skirts around and under the power lines, then curves up to the Lake Ethel trailhead in 0.8 mile. The road is a little rough in places but not too bad. Low-clearance passenger cars might bottom out here and there, but most manage to reach the trailhead just fine. A Northwest Forest Pass is required.

### Key points:
**1.5** First logging road crossing.
**2.5** Fourth logging road crossing.
**4.0** Meadow basin.
**4.5** Lake Ethel.

**The hike:** Lake Ethel is a lovely lake nestled in a craggy, talus-lined basin on the northern edge of the Chiwaukum Mountains. A 4.5-mile trail leads up to the lake, climbing pretty much straight up from Nason Creek canyon, through old-growth

# Lake Ethel

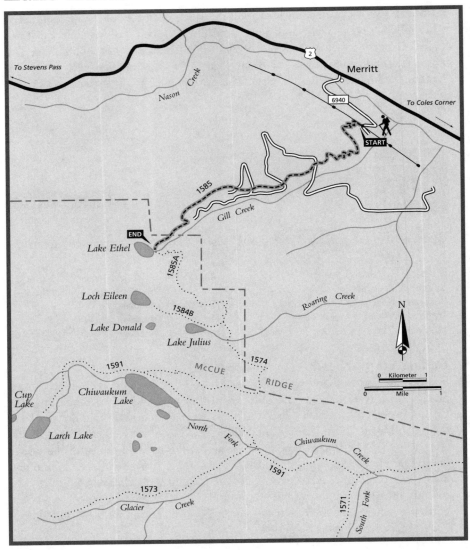

forest and clearcuts. It is a steep, dry hike and not exceedingly popular. Even so, it provides direct access to Lake Ethel and other nearby lakes and high ridges and deserves more popularity.

Assuming you managed the drive to the trailhead, get your permit at the trailhead register and start hiking. (If the road proves too rough, park lower down and hike up the road to the trailhead.) The trail begins in fir and pine forest, climbing gradually at first but soon switching back steadily up a dry, grassy slope. At one point, the trail comes close to a noisy creek, then switches back a few times and

*Lake Ethel*

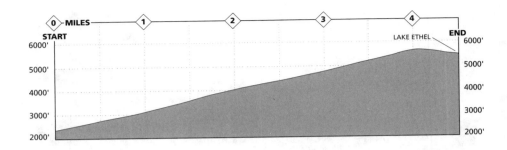

contours the slope to the edge of Gill Creek. In clearings below mature pines you get views down Nason Creek canyon and across to Nason Ridge. About 1.5 miles up the trail, the slope begins to level out as it rounds the crest of a sparsely wooded ridge, then breaks into the first of several clearcuts, with views to Mount Howard and the other high peaks of Nason Ridge.

Shortly above the clearcut, the trail climbs up to the first of four logging road crossings. Once across the road, the trail leads up a wooded rib, which is soon paralleled by logging debris. Not far above is the second logging road crossing, and soon above that is the third logging road crossing, with a stone bench and fire pit. The trail continues up the ridge crest, a narrow island of fir and pine forest between an ocean of clearcuts, and in 0.3 mile makes its fourth and final logging road crossing. Once past the logging roads and clearcuts, the trail leads up through silver-fir and pine forest laced with lupine, still on the ridge, but not as steeply as before, then leaves the ridge and descends eastward, traversing steep, open slopes into a narrow meadow basin. After crossing a little creek, the trail climbs over a ridge and drops into a deeply wooded basin and curves leftward, seemingly the wrong direction, but it soon doubles back up the basin, passing lovely meadows, to the Alpine Lakes Wilderness boundary at a trail junction just a few hundred feet from Lake Ethel. Take a right at the junction and hike to the lakeshore. There is a large campsite here and others nearby.

**Options:** Lake Ethel is only the first of several lovely alpine lakes in this area of the Chiwaukum Mountains. About 3 miles beyond are the Scottish Lakes and a connection with McCue Ridge Trail 1574 that links to Chiwaukum and Larch Lakes. There are several multiday backpack options in this area.

Although the purist will prefer to hike in the long way, there is a shortcut to Lake Ethel and the Scottish Lakes via Scottish Lakes High Camp, a private lodge that has an access road to a trailhead just 1.3 miles from Lake Julius and 3.5 miles from Lake Ethel. Access via the High Camp is not only shorter but much more scenic, although it isn't free.

# 48

# Merritt Lake

**Overview:** *A hike to Merritt Lake.*

**Distance:** 6.6 miles round-trip.
**Difficulty:** Moderate.
**Best season:** Summer through fall.
**Traffic:** Moderate.
**High point:** About 5,000 feet.

**Maps:** USGS Mount Howard; Green Trails No. 145 (Wenatchee Lake).
**For more information:** USDA Forest Service, Lake Wenatchee Ranger District Office.

**Finding the trailhead:** Merritt Lake Trail 1588 begins just off U.S. Highway 2 between Stevens Pass and Leavenworth. Drive US 2 to the Merritt Lake Trail turnoff, about 11.7 miles east of Stevens Pass and 8.8 miles west of Coles Corner. An unpaved, 1.4-mile road leads to the trailhead. Parking is limited. A Northwest Forest Pass is required.

## Key points:
**2.9** Nason Ridge Trail junction.
**3.3** Merritt Lake.

**The hike:** Merritt Lake is a pretty lake set in a talus basin near the crest of Nason Ridge. A popular hiking trail leads 3.3 miles to the lake from US 2. The hike is renowned for its beautiful fall colors, making it often visited in late season. It is a popular lake with anglers as well. Expect crowds.

Get your permit at the trailhead register and start hiking. The trail climbs switchbacks up the dusty slope, through fir and pine forest, always gaining elevation but not nearly as steeply as nearby Rock Mountain Trail (Hike 49). In about 2.5 miles, the trail ascends along the base of a talus field, with views out over Nason Creek valley and beyond. A short 0.5 mile beyond the boulders is the Nason Ridge Trail junction. Turn right and follow Nason Ridge Trail 1583 another 0.4 mile,

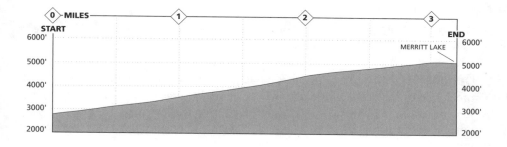

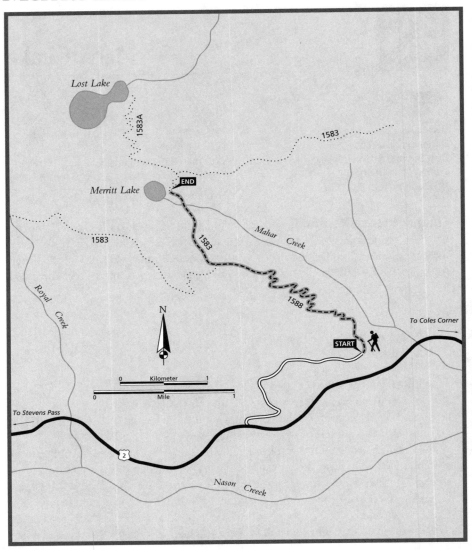

crossing Mahar Creek and climbing a final short rise to Merritt Lake. There are campsites at the lake and a privy with a view.

**Options:** If you want more private camping, Lost Lake is hidden in a basin on the other side of the ridge and is reached via a rough, unmaintained trail. The trail junction is just 0.4 mile up Nason Ridge Trail from the lake. The 1.3-mile trail is not a pleasant prospect, reviled by many hikers, although anglers don't seem to mind.

A better option is to hike up to the 6,237-foot Alpine Peak lookout, which is 2.5 miles east of Merritt Lake via Nason Ridge Trail 1583. The lookout offers excellent views of the surrounding peaks and valleys and down to Lake Wenatchee, and if you're lucky you might see mountain goats here.

# Rock Mountain

**Overview:** *A strenuous hike to an old lookout site atop Rock Mountain.*

**Distance:** 9.6 miles round-trip.
**Difficulty:** Very strenuous.
**Best season:** Summer through fall.
**Traffic:** Moderate.
**High point:** 6,852 feet.

**Maps:** USGS Mount Howard; Green Trails No. 145 (Wenatchee Lake).
**For more information:** USDA Forest Service, Lake Wenatchee Ranger District Office.

**Finding the trailhead:** Rock Mountain Trail 1587 begins from U.S. Highway 2 between Stevens Pass and Leavenworth. Drive US 2 to the Rock Mountain Trail turnoff, about 8.8 miles east of Stevens Pass and 11.7 miles west of Coles Corner. A short road leads to the trailhead. Parking is limited. A Northwest Forest Pass is required.

## Key points:
**4.3** Nason Ridge Trail junction.
**4.5** Ridge crest and junction with summit trail.
**4.8** Rock Mountain summit.

**The hike:** Rock Mountain is the westernmost peak of Nason Ridge, a high ridge dividing Nason Creek and the Wenatchee River. A hiking trail leads 4.8 miles from US (Stevens Pass Highway) to its 6,852-foot summit. The trail is steep—really steep!—gaining an average of 1,000 feet per mile, always climbing up and up, sometimes gradually but mostly steeply. Like other Nason Ridge trails, there are wildflowers galore in early season, as soon as the snow melts. The price of admission to these flower gardens is steep but worth it.

From the trailhead, the trail traverses eastward, crossing under power lines to the foot of a prominent ridge. Once you reach the ridge, the only way is up, via a series of unrelenting switchbacks. The trail climbs and climbs the rocky, dusty fir and pine slopes, with increasingly better views of Nason Creek canyon and across to the Chiwaukum Mountains. Eventually, after about 3 miles, the trail's steepness

# Rock Mountain

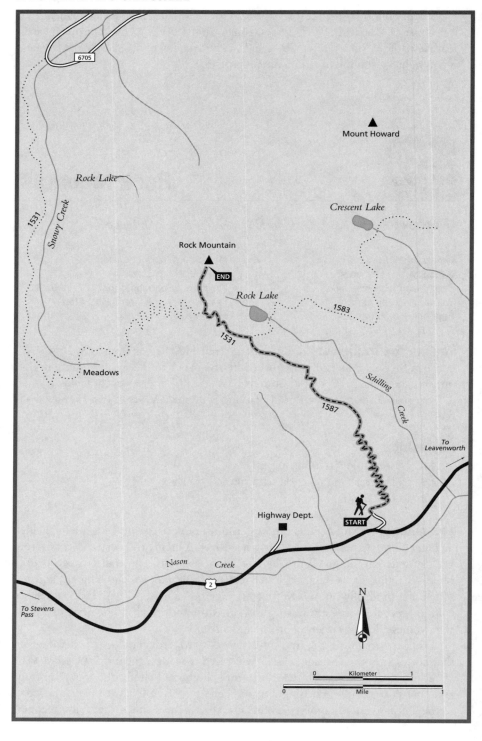

Mount Howard

6705

Rock Lake

1531

Snowy Creek

Crescent Lake

Rock Mountain

END

Rock Lake

1583

1531

Meadows

Schilling Creek

1587

To Leavenworth

Highway Dept.

START

Nason Creek

2

To Stevens Pass

N

| 0 | Kilometer | 1 |
| 0 | Mile | 1 |

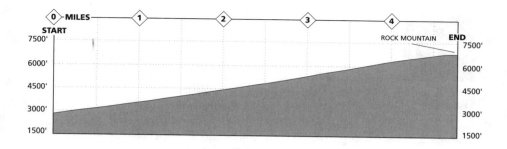

abates. The hot, dusty switchbacks are soon forgotten as the trail traverses sub-alpine forest and meadows, still climbing but not as steeply as before. Finally, after a last steep climb to the head of the meadow basin, the trail meets Nason Ridge Trail 1583, where Rock Mountain finally comes into view. You might be tempted to take a quick right turn and follow Nason Ridge Trail a short and mercifully downhill way to Rock Lake, elevation 5,850 feet; it's a good place to take a break, eat lunch, or take a dip. The lake is fed by a perennial snowfield, so it's cold. My preference, though, has always been to save the lake for later, after continuing to the summit of Rock Mountain; once you've rested at the lake, you might change your mind about the summit hike and miss out on the views. From Rock Mountain Trail take a left at the trail junction and climb Snowy Creek Trail 1531 to the ridge crest. From here a short trail leads to the summit of Rock Mountain. The climb is via an easy ridge trail, which wades through lupine, lousewort, and paintbrush, to the 6,852-foot summit, the second-highest point of Nason Ridge. This former fire lookout site features wide views of the surrounding mountains, including Glacier Peak to the north and Mount Stuart to the south.

You'll want to bring plenty of water to drink on this hike, especially if you come on a hot summer day. Come early in the day to avoid unnecessary suffering or heat-stroke. Take it easy on the way down or your knees will suffer. Be careful not to dis-place rocks on the trail; they can really get rolling down the ridge and could hit an unsuspecting hiker on the trail or a passing car on the highway.

**Options:** Rock Mountain is a popular spring snow hike, best done in May or early June, when avalanche danger is lower and the snow line is higher. You can hike pretty much directly up the snowfield from the trail junction to the summit ridge. If you are willing to lug skis up to the summit, an enjoyable 1,000-foot descent to Rock Lake awaits you. Slab avalanche danger is high here, so proceed with caution if you come early in the season. Beware of cornices and seracs on the ridge crest as well. Many hikers glissade down the snowfield all the way to Rock Lake. This can be great fun, but watch out for rocks on the snow and for crevasses, which some-times appear in late summer near the edge of the snowfield.

# 50

# Lanham Lake

**Overview:** *A short hike to Lanham Lake, just east of Stevens Pass.*

**Distance:** 3.2 miles round-trip.
**Difficulty:** Moderate.
**Best season:** Summer through fall.
**Traffic:** Foot and mountain bike traffic only; heavy use.

**High point:** About 4,150 feet.
**Maps:** USGS Labyrynth Mountain; Green Trails No. 176 (Stevens Pass).
**For more information:** USDA Forest Service, Wenatchee Ranger District Office.

**Finding the trailhead:** Lanham Lake Trail 1589 begins just east of Stevens Pass. Drive U.S. Highway 2 to the upper Mill Creek Road turnoff, about 5.9 miles east of Stevens Pass and 14.6 miles west of Coles Corner. Drive a short distance up Mill Creek Road (Forest Service Road 6960) to the trailhead, on the left. A Northwest Forest Pass is required.

## Key points:
**0.3** Power lines.
**1.6** Lanham Lake.

**The hike:** Lanham Lake is a small lake set in a deep basin below the north face of Jim Hill Mountain, just outside the Alpine Lakes Wilderness boundary. A short trail leads up to the lake. The hiking guides say the trail is 2 miles long. They must be rounding up to the nearest mile; the trail isn't that long. It is a popular hike, not only because of its brevity and accessibility, but for its fall colors, which are spectacular. The trail is multiuse; mountain bikers may come whizzing by, so keep the kids close and alert.

From the trailhead, the trail climbs along the western bank of Lanham Creek, well above the creek at first. In 0.3 mile the trail passes a brushy area beneath power lines, then reenters forest and contours for over 0.5 mile to reach the creek's edge.

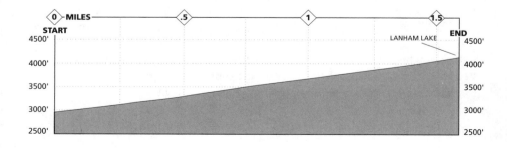

# Lanham Lake

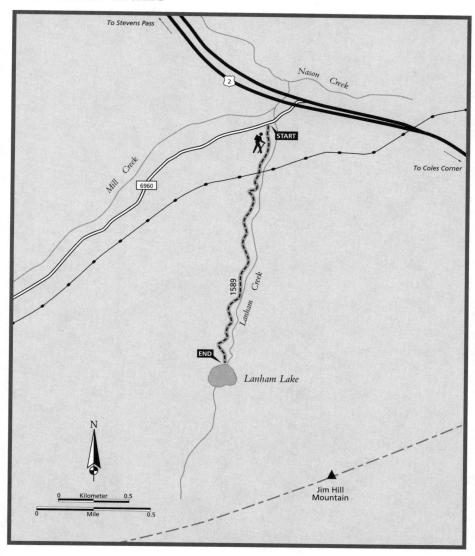

Continue along the creek for some distance, following an old roadbed, watching out for frogs hopping underfoot. The final 0.5 mile of trail climbs 300 feet to Lanham Lake, elevation 4,143 feet. In 1987, the lake completely drained through a sinkhole, which must have been a surprise to hikers. The lake has since refilled.

**Options:** This is a popular winter and spring snowshoe hike and ski trek. A Sno-Park Pass is required. Beware of avalanche hazard on the slopes above the lake.

# Stevens Pass
## AREA

# 51

# Pacific Crest Trail to Josephine Lake

**Overview:** *Hike a segment of the Pacific Crest Trail south from Stevens Pass to Josephine Lake.*

**Distance:** 9.2 miles round-trip.
**Difficulty:** Moderate.
**Best season:** Midsummer to fall.
**Traffic:** Foot and stock traffic only; heavy use.
**High point:** About 5,000 feet.

**Maps:** USGS Stevens Pass; Green Trails No. 176 (Stevens Pass).
**For more information:** USDA Forest Service, Skykomish Ranger District Office.

**Finding the trailhead:** This hike follows a segment of the Pacific Crest Trail (PCT) 2000 south from Stevens Pass. Drive U.S. Highway 2 to Stevens Pass and park in the south parking lot. Hike up a service road about 0.1 mile to the trailhead. A Northwest Forest Pass is required at the trailhead, but if you park in the Stevens Pass parking area beside the highway and walk up the road to the trailhead, no pass is needed.

## Key points:
**1.0**  Top of ski lifts.
**1.7**  The high point of the hike at a divide.
**2.0**  Power lines.
**3.1**  Lake Susan Jane.
**3.6**  Alpine Lakes Wilderness boundary.
**3.8**  PCT junction above Josephine Lake.
**4.6**  Josephine Lake.

**The hike:** Josephine Lake is a round lake set in a talus basin just below the PCT south of Stevens Pass. This segment of the PCT is heavily traveled, as it should be; once past the ugliness of the ski lifts and power lines, the trail traverses lovely sub-alpine meadow and forest along the Cascade Crest, passing lakes and ponds.

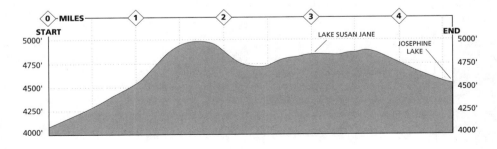

196

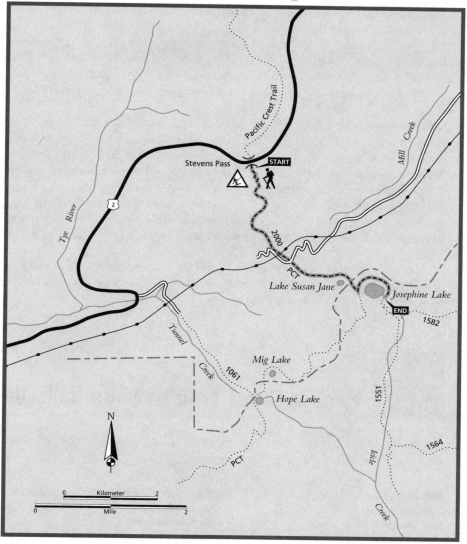

Josephine Lake makes for a convenient destination, a place to turn back for those who need to hike to a lake, a summit, somewhere.

Begin via the PCT from Stevens Pass. From the south parking area, hike up a service road briefly to the trailhead, then hike south up the edge of the ski area, climbing steep, bare slopes beyond the top of the ski lifts and up into a surprisingly nice talus basin to a 5,100-foot divide, the high point of the hike. Descend briefly to an access road beside the power lines, then hike east briefly and rejoin the trail, which crosses beneath the crackling power lines and contours the upper basin of

Mill Creek another 1.1 miles to tiny Lake Susan Jane, elevation 4,595 feet. There are campsites here, heavily used.

The trail crosses the wilderness boundary shortly beyond the lake, then climbs briefly to a pond-dotted shelf at a divide overlooking Josephine Lake. The trail forks here; take the left fork, which descends in a semicircle to Josephine Lake, the source of Icicle Creek, elevation 4,681 feet. There are campsites here as well.

**Options:** Josephine Lake is not a destination unto itself, but a starting point for many other hikes. Chain Lakes, only 5.2 miles away from Josephine Lake, are a recommended destination for hardy day hikers and overnighters. Excellent one-way hikes can be made starting from or ending at Josephine Lake, including Whitepine Creek, Icicle Creek, or a tremendous 27-mile loop connecting Whitepine Creek and Wildhorse Creek, over Frosty Pass and up Icicle Creek and back to Lake Josephine, or viceversa. This loop makes an excellent backpacking trip of three to five days' duration, especially if combined with an overnight detour to Chain Lakes.

You may also hike farther south along the PCT, to Swimming Deer and Mig and Hope Lakes, or down over Thunder Pass to Surprise Lake. With arranged transportation, many options are possible.

# 52 Pacific Crest Trail to Lake Valhalla

**Overview:** *Hike a segment of the Pacific Crest Trail north from Stevens Pass to Lake Valhalla.*

**Distance:** 11.2 miles round-trip.
**Difficulty:** Moderate.
**Best season:** Summer to fall.
**Traffic:** Foot and stock traffic; moderate use.
**High point:** About 5,000 feet.

**Maps:** USGS Labyrynth Mountain; Green Trails No. 144 (Benchmark Mountain).
**For more information:** USDA Forest Service, Wenatchee Ranger District Office.

**Finding the trailhead:** This hike follows a segment of the Pacific Crest Trail (PCT) 2000 north from Stevens Pass. Drive U.S. Highway 2 to Stevens Pass and park in the north parking lot. A Northwest Forest Pass is not required in the main parking area, but it should be displayed if you park at the trailhead.

## Key points:
**1.9** The trail turns west around a ridge and enters Nason Creek basin.
**2.7** A creek crossing.

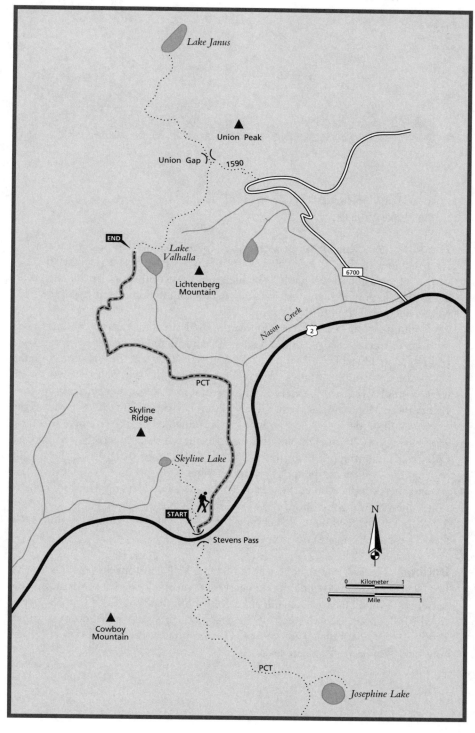

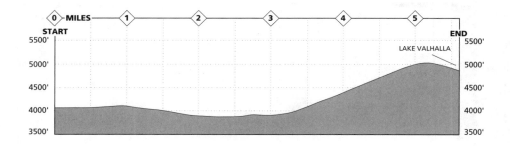

**3.3** Henry M. Jackson Wilderness boundary.
**5.6** Lake Valhalla.

**The hike:** Lake Valhalla is not within the Alpine Lakes Wilderness but is reached via a segment of the PCT beginning from Stevens Pass; it is a popular lake hike worthy of inclusion in this guide. The hike is not especially popular this way; there is a shorter path to the lake. Usually only hikers completing a segment of the PCT will be encountered until the lake.

Beginning from Stevens Pass, follow the PCT north. The trail contours along the foot of Skyline Ridge, through silver fir and mountain-hemlock forest, open and rocky, within sight and sound of the highway. The trail loses elevation gradually in the first couple of miles. After almost 2 miles, the trail quickly curves westward around a ridge and enters the upper basin of Nason Creek, with views of Lichtenberg Mountain, a craggy ridge with a rocky peak. The trail continues contouring, still gradually losing elevation, to an unnamed creek. The hike this far is easy, having lost 200 feet of elevation in 2.7 miles on this "superhighway" of Cascades trails. Continuing from the creek, the trail climbs briefly, then levels out, passing the wilderness boundary marker (Henry M. Jackson Wilderness, that is), and then climbs a bit to the head of a high basin, switching back a couple of times, then climbs some more across the head of Nason Creek before crossing a 5,000-foot-high divide and descending briefly to Lake Valhalla, elevation 4,830 feet. There are campsites near the lake, all overused.

**Options:** The sad thing about hiking to Lake Valhalla from Stevens Pass is that once you get there, you find out that nearly everybody else took a shortcut. If you'd prefer a 2.7-mile hike to a 5.6-mile hike, follow Smith Brook Road (Forest Service Road 6700, about 4.2 miles east of Stevens Pass) about 3.5 miles north to Smith Brook Trail 1590, which joins the PCT in only 0.9 mile, then follow the PCT another 1.8 miles south to the lake.

# 53

# Tunnel Creek–Hope Lake

**Overview:** *A short, steep hike up Tunnel Creek to Hope Lake.*

**Distance:** 3.0 miles round-trip.
**Difficulty:** Moderate.
**Best season:** Summer through fall.
**Traffic:** Foot traffic only; moderate use.
**High point:** About 4,400 feet.

**Maps:** USGS Stevens Pass; Green Trails No. 176 (Stevens Pass).
**For more information:** USDA Forest Service, Skykomish Ranger District Office.

**Finding the trailhead:** Tunnel Creek Trail 1061 begins just west of Stevens Pass. Drive U.S. Highway 2 to Tunnel Creek Road (Forest Service Road 6095) 4.2 miles west of the pass and 3.8 miles east of Deception Falls. The turnoff is near the apex of the sharp curve in the highway, so be sure to slow down and put on your turn signal early. You can only access the turnoff from the eastbound lanes of the highway; if you are coming down from Stevens Pass, you must continue down the road a bit to a turnout, turn around, and drive back up to the turnoff. Once on FS 6095, follow briefly to a fork, then take a right on spur road 110, cross a bridge, and continue 1.5 miles, ignoring two spur roads on the right, to the Tunnel Creek trailhead. A Northwest Forest Pass is required.

## Key points:
**1.5** Hope Lake and the Pacific Crest Trail (PCT) junction.

**The hike:** Hope Lake is a small lake located in a meadow basin on the Cascade Crest just south of Stevens Pass. The lake is most easily accessed via the Tunnel Creek Trail, a fairly steep 2-mile trail. Officially, the trail is 2 miles, but that's an overly generous estimate; even 1.5 miles might be an exaggeration. Perhaps it is the steepness that makes the hike seem longer than it really is. Tunnel Creek has some of the best fall berry picking around, and the fall colors are spectacular. Hope Lake,

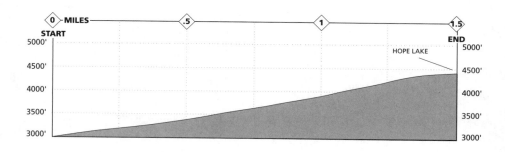

# Tunnel Creek–Hope Lake

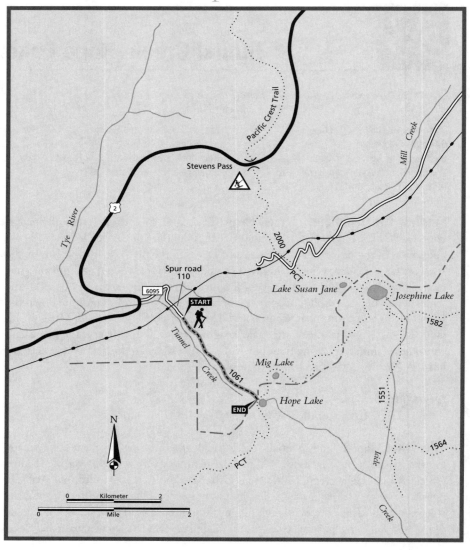

alas, is overused and not what one would call pristine. If you are looking for a short hike, this will do, but there are other, better hikes nearby.

The trail leads steeply up through forest, well above Tunnel Creek. As the trail nears the crest, it comes close to the creek; the angle abates, and subalpine meadows supplant forest. The trail reaches the PCT at a divide just above Hope Lake.

**Options:** Most hikers continue 0.5 mile "east" (really north) on the PCT to Mig Lake, another small lake set in a subalpine meadow basin. This is lovely meadow hiking, although hardly private; crest trail hikers come plodding by with regularity in late summer and early fall. There are campsites at both lakes, all heavily used. From Hope Lake, you can follow the PCT southward 3.3 miles to Trap Lake, a larger lake tucked into a basin below the shoulder of Thunder Mountain. Trap Lake is the better destination if you want more solitude, although you aren't likely to find much at any lake along the PCT, at least not during the late-summer hiking season.

# Surprise Lake–Glacier Lake

**Overview:** *A hike to Surprise and Glacier Lakes.*

**Distance:** 10.0 miles round-trip to Glacier Lake.
**Difficulty:** Moderate.
**Best season:** Summer through fall.
**Traffic:** Foot traffic only; heavy use.
**High point:** About 4,800 feet.

**Maps:** USGS Scenic; Green Trails No. 176 (Stevens Pass).
**For more information:** USDA Forest Service, Skykomish Ranger District Office.

**Finding the trailhead:** Surprise Lake Trail 1060 begins just off U.S. Highway 2 (Stevens Pass Highway) about 6 miles west of Stevens Pass. Drive US 2 to the small railroad stop called Scenic, about 6 miles west of Stevens Pass and 2 miles east of Deception Falls. The turnoff is not well marked at present. It is the road directly across the highway from the old Stevens Pass Highway. Turn off and follow the road across the tracks and rightward to the trailhead. Signs point the way. A Northwest Forest Pass is required.

## Key points:

**0.5** Alpine Lakes Wilderness boundary.
**1.1** Footlog crossing.
**4.0** Surprise Lake.
**5.0** Glacier Lake.

**The hike:** Surprise Lake is a pretty lake set in a rocky basin just northeast of Deception Pass. It is reached via a 4-mile trail leading up Surprise Creek, an ebullient stream that cascades down an old-growth forest valley. Because it is accessible and not too long, Surprise Lake Trail is a popular day hike. Surprise Lake is

# Surprise Lake–Glacier Lake

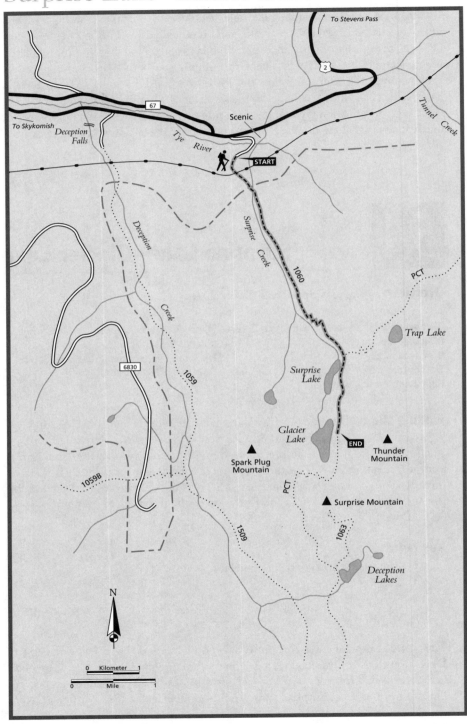

*Maidenhair fern*

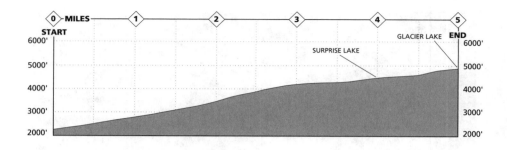

only one of many lakes in this area, making the trail a favorite of backpackers and anglers as well.

From the trailhead, hike up a road grade up to and under the power lines, then enter fir and hemlock forest. The trail climbs gradually through the shady woods past the Alpine Lakes Wilderness boundary marker, then contours above the creek. In just over a mile, the trail crosses the creek via a footlog and continues up the other side of the creek for another mile. All along the way, the creek cascades over rocks and logs, little falls plunging into quiet pools. The forest is lush, growing thick with ferns and devil's club, thimbleberry, and salmonberry. Just past the 2-mile mark, the trail suddenly turns away from the creek and starts climbing the eastern canyon wall, switching back abruptly for a short distance, then climbing beyond through increasingly open forest trending to subalpine. When the climbing is done, the trail contours alongside the creek once again and soon reaches a junction with the old PCT. Cross the creek and crest a small rise and—surprise!— there is the lake, a long, narrow lake set in a talus-lined basin. Areas of the lakeshore are being restored, but there is a good spot near the outlet stream where you can sit on big boulders. Camp in designated sites only.

Although Surprise Lake is lovely, and a suitable stopping point if you are short of time, the best part of the hike lies above and beyond. Another mile up the trail, soon joining the PCT, is Glacier Lake, a larger lake nestled in a cirque at the foot of Surprise Mountain. The trail doesn't reach the lake, but side trails lead down to the lakeshore.

**Options:** The trail climbs another 2.5 miles or so above Glacier Lake to 5,920-foot Pieper Pass and tremendous views across Deception Creek valley to Mount Daniel. In 3.3 miles from Glacier Lake are Deception Lakes. A spur trail leads to the summit of Surprise Mountain, a supreme viewpoint. This is an 18.6-mile round-trip, more if you summit Surprise Mountain (a must), too far for a day hike but a good two- or three-day backpack.

206

# 55

# Iron Goat Trail

**Overview:** *A hike along a historic railroad grade near Stevens Pass.*

**Distance:** 6.0 miles round-trip to Windy Point.
**Difficulty:** Easy.
**Best season:** Early summer through fall.
**Traffic:** Foot traffic only; heavy use.
**High point:** 2,800 feet.

**Maps:** USGS Scenic; Green Trails No. 176 (Stevens Pass).
**For more information:** USDA Forest Service, Skykomish Ranger District Office.

**Finding the trailhead:** Iron Goat Trail 1074 begins just north of U.S. Highway 2, about 6 miles west of Stevens Pass. Drive US 2 to the old Stevens Pass Highway turnoff, now Forest Service Road 67, a windy, narrow paved road on the north side of the highway that sometimes serves as a detour during highway construction. You can access the old highway by turning north off US 2 at milepost 55 or 58.4; signs point the way to Iron Goat Trail. Whichever access you use, follow the old highway to a well-marked junction with Forest Service Road 6710. Turn north up FS 6710 and follow 1.4 miles to the Martin Creek trailhead, on the right. A Northwest Forest Pass is required.

## Key points:

**0.1** Lower Martin Creek Connect junction.
**0.2** Upper Martin Creek Connect junction.
**0.5** Tunnel #14.
**0.6** Corea Connect junction.
**1.6** Spillway junction.
**1.8** Embro Tunnel.
**2.8** Windy Point Tunnel west portal.
**3.0** Windy Point viewpoint.

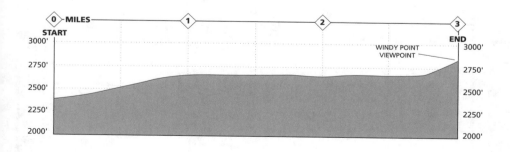

# Iron Goat Trail

**The hike:** Iron Goat Trail follows a segment of the old Great Northern Railroad line just west of Stevens Pass. Built in the early 1900s, this section of railroad traversed the slopes of Windy Mountain to reach the Cascade Tunnel but was abandoned after the new Cascade Tunnel was completed in 1926. I hiked some of the old rail line back before the trail project was begun in the late 1980s. Back then, we scrambled up steep, brushy scree slopes to get to the railroad grade, but it was worth it to hike along the old grade, marveling at the railroad ruins and hiking far into the Windy Point Tunnel, a dark, foreboding cavern that now marks the midway point of the restored trail. In the late 1980s, Iron Goat Trail was proposed as a historic trail that should be restored for recreation use, and Volunteers for Outdoor Washington adopted the project. Trail work has continued since 1992, and hikers should not be surprised to find work crews on the trail.

From Martin Creek trailhead, hike along a boardwalk, then a flat, wide path 0.1 mile to the Martin Creek Connect trail, which climbs briefly to the upper trail, the only steep section of the hike. Continue east along the wide, flat grade through alder, Douglas maple, fir, and hemlock forest, past remains of shelters built to protect trains from avalanches and rockfall. At 0.5 mile is Tunnel #14; a side trail leads close to the west portal. Hike around the tunnel and continue along the trail to milepost 1716, just before the Corea Connect trail, a 0.5 mile switchback down to the lower trail. If the kids are getting bored already, or you don't have much time, this is a good place to head back to the trailhead, a neat 2-mile loop. Otherwise, continue along the grade, crossing Stream #1 in another 0.5 mile and Stream #2 another 0.3 mile along. Here you pass the first of several old retaining walls. At the east end of Wall #1 is milepost 1715 and a junction with a short side trail leading up to a retaining pond and spillway built to divert water around the wall. The Embro Tunnel is the next feature you come to. Like all tunnels along the trail, signs warn of severe danger of falling rock, and Embro Tunnel is a perfect example, with tons of rock and timber debris littering the tunnel floor. The trail continues around the tunnel and follows the grade past several more retaining walls and milepost 1714, then comes to the west portal of Windy Point Tunnel. You can walk a short distance into the west portal of the tunnel without fear of imminent collapse but are cautioned not to hike through the tunnel because the east portal has a lot of loose rock poised and ready. For safety reasons, the trail skirts around the tunnel, following the pre-tunnel railroad grade around a sharp corner to a rocky viewpoint overlooking the upper Skykomish River valley.

**Options:** Most will hike to Windy Point viewpoint and return, but the trail continues another 4.8 miles along the slopes of Windy Mountain to the old Wellington townsite. This section of trail crosses several avalanche gullies and passes remains of the several snowsheds built to protect trains from avalanches. One of the nation's worst railroad disasters occurred here during the winter of 1910, when two trains delayed by a winter storm were swept off the tracks to the valley floor by a huge avalanche. Sections of the trail are still swept by winter and spring avalanches.

Although hikers hike the trail year-round, winter hikers must check avalanche conditions ahead of time. If you stash a bike at the upper end of the trail, you can hike the trail one way from Martin Creek to Wellington and ride back to Martin Creek, mostly downhill, for a fun loop.

The lower portion of the Iron Goat Trail is barrier-free for about 1 mile, a nice, flat, easy hike for all ages. The lower trail will eventually extend 3 miles farther, all the way to US 2.

The old Cascade Tunnel may someday be reopened, making for a 2.4-mile one-way hike similar to the Snoqualmie Tunnel (Hike 17).

# Skykomish
# RIVER AREA

# 56

# Tonga Ridge

**Overview:** *A high ridge and meadow hike with grand mountain views.*

**Distance:** 6.4 miles round-trip to Sawyer Pass; 7.4 miles round-trip if you also hike to Mount Sawyer.
**Difficulty:** Easy to Sawyer Pass, moderate to Mount Sawyer.
**Best season:** Late spring through fall.
**Traffic:** Foot traffic only; heavy use.

**High point:** About 4,800 feet; 5,495 feet if Mount Sawyer is included.
**Maps:** USGS Skykomish, Scenic; Green Trails No. 175 (Skykomish), 176 (Stevens Pass).
**For more information:** USDA Forest Service, Skykomish Ranger District Office.

**Finding the trailhead:** Tonga Ridge Trail 1058 is located above the Skykomish River valley just east of Skykomish. Drive U.S. Highway 2 to Foss River Road (Forest Service Road 68), about 2 miles east of Skykomish (just 0.6 mile east of the Skykomish Ranger District Office). Follow Foss River Road 1.1 paved miles to a fork, where a sign points the way to various trailheads, including Tonga Ridge Trail. Take the right fork, continuing 2.4 gravel miles on FS 68 to a well-signed fork. Take the left fork and follow Forest Service Road 6830 up the mountainside another 6.7 miles to a fork with Forest Service Road 310. Take the right fork and follow FS 310 another 1.3 miles to the trailhead at road's end. Parking space is limited; try not to block other cars. A Northwest Forest Pass is required.

## Key points:

**0.7** Alpine Lakes Wilderness boundary.
**2.0** Meadows below Mount Sawyer.
**2.3** Mount Sawyer trail junction.
**2.8** Mount Sawyer.
**4.2** Sawyer Pass.

**The hike:** Tonga Ridge Trail is one of the most popular hikes in the Skykomish Ranger District, and for good reason. The trail leads along a high ridge, through

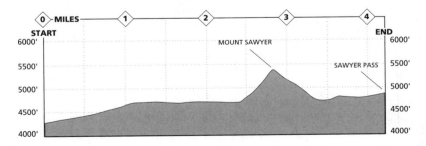

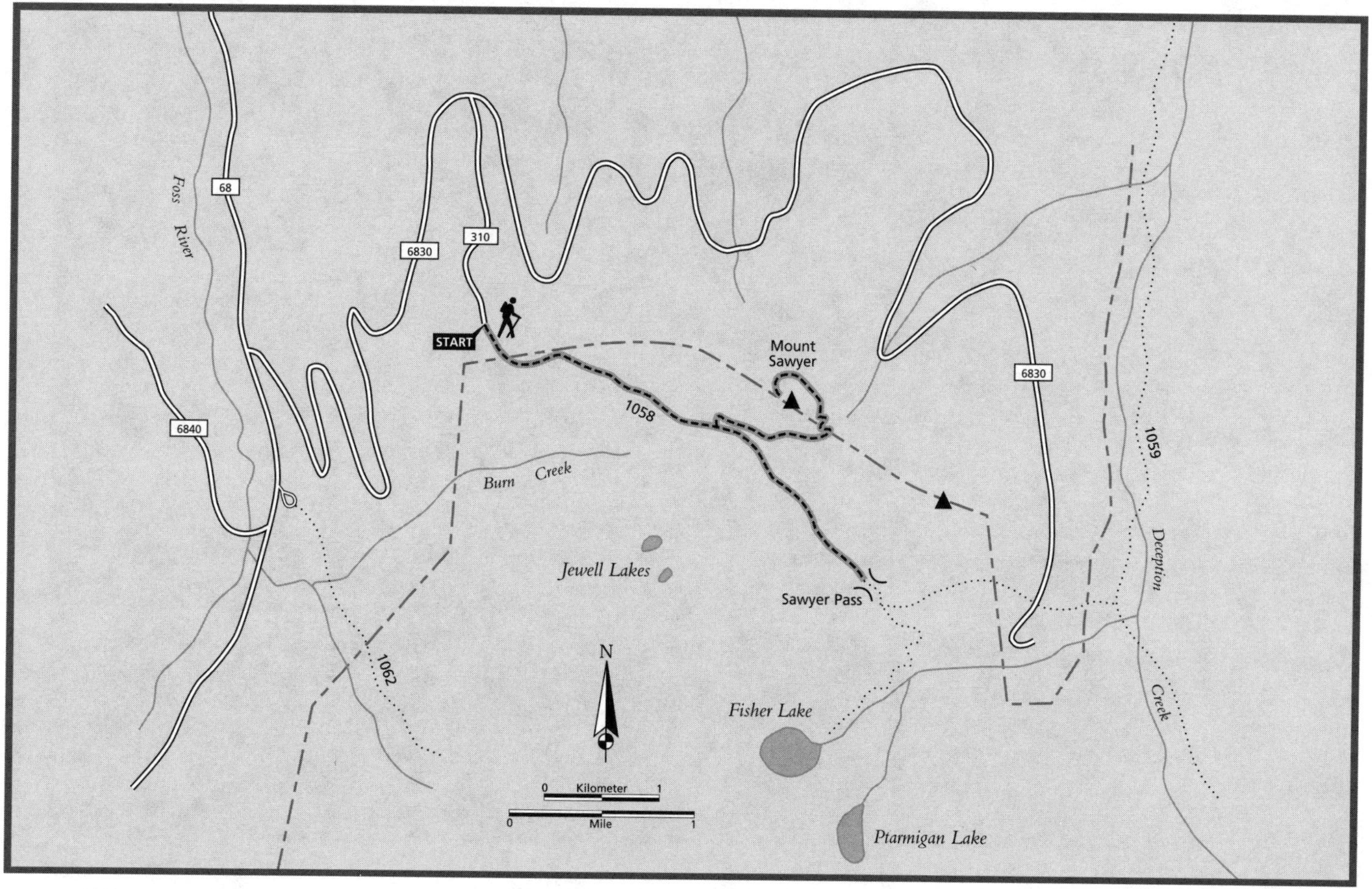

Tonga Ridge

1059    Deception    Creek
6830
Mount Sawyer
Sawyer Pass
Ptarmigan Lake
Fisher Lake
Jewell Lakes
Burn    Creek
1058
310
6830
START
68
Foss    River
6840
1062

N

Kilometer    1
0
Mile
0

*Mount Sawyer Trail*

subalpine meadows, and to the summit of a mountain, with very little elevation gain and panoramic views. This is an excellent autumn hike, when fall colors and huckleberries are at their peak.

The trail climbs briefly from the trailhead through silver fir, mountain-hemlock, and mountain-ash forest, then meanders through open forest along the ridge, dropping and climbing again to the wilderness boundary marker. The trail continues a bit on the ridge crest, then traverses increasingly open meadow slopes, descending then climbing steeply at one point, with views of Mounts Hinman and Daniel and other peaks to the south. Subalpine firs, mountain-hemlocks, and western white pines line the trail as it traverses the meadows; wildflowers include lupine, aster, pearly everlasting, and bead lily. Soon the trail crosses a broad, flat meadow area just below Mount Sawyer. There are confusing trails leading off in all directions; most lead to campsites in and around the meadows.

The trail soon passes the Mount Sawyer spur trail, on the left. The spur trail is unmarked, but unmistakable. The trail begins steeply at first but soon starts traversing across the open meadow slopes of Mount Sawyer, then switches back a few times on the mountain's huckleberry-laden east slopes, just below the summit rocks, then circles around to the north side, wading through bristling subalpine firs and mountain-hemlocks, and finally reaches the 5,495-foot summit via the rocky west ridge. Mount Sawyer provides a commanding, panoramic view of the surrounding mountains, including Mounts Daniel and Hinman, Chimney Rock and Overcoat Peak, Mount Thompson, Malachite Peak, Mounts Index and Baring, Sloan and Glacier Peaks, and Mount Stuart, to name only the most prominent. Golden eagles, Cooper's hawks, and other birds of prey are often seen soaring here.

Back at the Mount Sawyer trail junction, Tonga Ridge Trail traverses eastward along the lower slopes of Mount Sawyer, descending gradually into deeper, rocky forest with diminishing views. The trail soon arrives at Sawyer Pass and enters a broad, flat heather meadow. A proliferation of trails becomes confusing. At one point, an intersection of trails is passed. If you're not hiking through to the trailhead at the upper end of FS 6830, this is a good turnaround point. Stop, eat lunch, explore the meadows, then head back the way you came. There are several campsites here, a few near the trail, others hidden off at the edge of the meadows.

**Options:** One of the side trails leads off from the upper meadows to Fisher Lake. It is the path that seems to go "straight ahead" through the intersection of trails. It leads gradually down through the marshy meadows, then curves up into brushy forest, becoming hard to follow in places. Fisher Lake is 1.5 miles along this path, up and over a wooded ridge.

You can also scramble to the true summit of Mount Sawyer (the slightly higher, tree-covered ridge just east of the official Mount Sawyer), but it's brushy going and not popular. Those willing to leave the trail and hike cross-country can find a lot to explore in this area. Most seem content to stay on the trail.

# 57 West Fork Foss River–Trout Lake

**Overview:** *A popular trail linking a group of alpine lakes above the West Fork Foss River.*

**Distance:** 3.2 miles round-trip to Trout Lake.
**Difficulty:** Moderate.
**Best season:** Summer through fall.
**Traffic:** Foot traffic only; heavy use.
**High point:** About 2,100 feet.

**Maps:** USGS Big Snow Mountain; Green Trails No. 175 (Skykomish).
**For more information:** USDA Forest Service, Skykomish Ranger District Office.

**Finding the trailhead:** West Fork Foss River Trail 1064 begins via Foss River Road from U.S. Highway 2 near Skykomish. Drive US 2 to Foss River Road (Forest Service Road 68), about 2 miles east of Skykomish (0.6 mile east of the Skykomish Ranger District Office). Follow Foss River Road 1.1 paved miles to a fork, where a sign points the way to various trailheads, including West Fork Foss River Trail 1064. Take the right fork, continuing 3.5 gravel miles on FS 68 to another fork, and take a hard left onto Forest Service Road 6835, which curves and crosses two recently repaired bridges over the East Fork Foss River, then straightens out and continues to the trailhead at road's end, 5.5 miles from pavement's end. A Northwest Forest Pass is required.

### Key points:
**0.6** West Fork Foss River crossing.
**0.8** A huge Douglas fir tree.
**1.6** Trout Lake.

**The hike:** West Fork Foss River Trail is popularly known as Foss Lakes Trail, since it leads to five alpine lakes set among the granite ridges and peaks above West Fork Foss River. Whatever you call it, this is a popular hike, at least as far as Trout

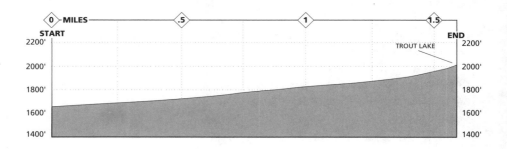

# West Fork Foss River–Trout Lake

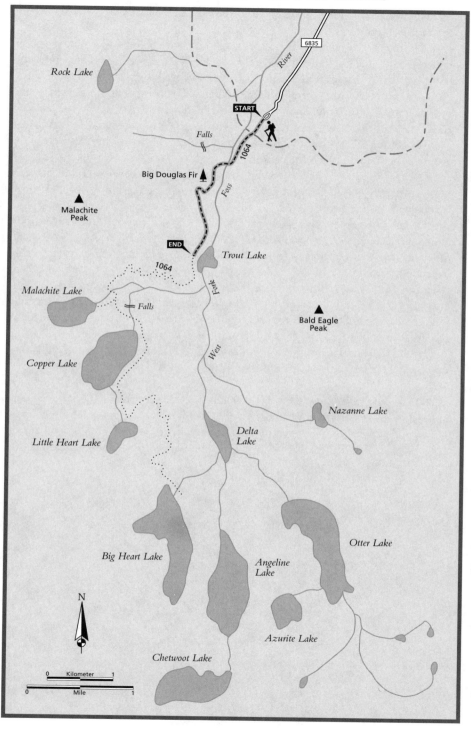

Rock Lake

6835

River

START

Falls

1064

Big Douglas Fir

Foss

Malachite
Peak

END

1064

Trout Lake

Malachite Lake

Falls

Fork

Bald Eagle
Peak

Copper Lake

West

Little Heart Lake

Nazanne Lake

Delta
Lake

Big Heart Lake

Angeline
Lake

Otter Lake

Azurite Lake

N

Chetwoot Lake

Kilometer

0        1

Mile

0        1

and Copper Lakes. The crowds seem to thin as exponentially as the views expand the farther up the trail you go.

Get your permit at the trailhead register and start hiking. The trail starts out flat and rocky, like a streambed, for a few hundred yards as you cross the wilderness boundary amid maples and hemlocks. Soon the trail climbs up a few feet and becomes more trail-like, through hemlock and alder forest, gaining very little elevation in the first 0.5 mile. Soon the trail nears and then crosses the West Fork Foss River via footbridges and rock hopping. If the river is running high, footlogs bridge the gap. A slender, 150-foot ribbon waterfall drops over a cliff directly across the river just before you reach the crossing.

The trail climbs a bit beyond the river crossing, then levels out and passes a huge specimen of Douglas fir before resuming its gradual climb through open hemlock and silver fir forest. At 1.5 miles, the trail crosses a wide rocky wash and drops a bit to a gravel bank dropping into the now-still river. A few steps beyond and you realize you are at Trout Lake, 2,020 feet elevation. Trout Lake is calm and quiet but eerie, mysteriously ringed by dead trees. This phenomenon is readily explained. Recall the rockslide you crossed just before the lake; a decade or so ago it dammed the river, raising the water level, which killed the trees and sent the hikers camped at Trout Lake scurrying for higher ground. Anglers flock to Trout Lake but are often disappointed; there are trout here, sure, but the lake is overfished, so the usual catch is small fry. If it's fish you're after, keep going.

Trout Lake has five designated campsites and a pit toilet. Restoration efforts are underway here, so please stay on the trail and use only designated campsites.

**Options:** The trail ascends from Trout Lake another 1.5 miles to Copper Lake, about a 6-mile round-trip with nearly 2,400 feet in elevation gain, definitely feasible as a day hike although much more strenuous than the lower trail. Past Copper Lake are Little and Big Heart Lakes, less often visited but good destinations for overnight hikers and anglers.

# 58

# Lake Dorothy

**Overview:** *A short hike to Lake Dorothy, the first of a chain of alpine lakes.*

**Distance:** 7.4 miles round-trip to the south end of Lake Dorothy.
**Difficulty:** Easy.
**Best season:** Late spring through fall.
**Traffic:** Foot traffic only; heavy use.

**High point:** About 3,100 feet.
**Maps:** USGS Grotto, Snoqualmie Lake; Green Trails No. 175 (Skykomish).
**For more information:** USDA Forest Service, Skykomish Ranger District Office.

**Finding the trailhead:** Lake Dorothy Trail 1072 begins from Miller River Road near Skykomish off U.S. Highway 2. Drive US 2 about 18 miles east from Gold Bar or 2.9 miles west from Skykomish to the Money Creek Campground turnoff. If you're coming from Skykomish, the turnoff is on the left, immediately after you drive through a tunnel. Turn off and follow the Old Cascade Highway past Money Creek Campground, continuing 1 mile to the Miller River Road fork. Follow Miller River Road (the left fork, Forest Service Road 6410) 9.1 miles to the trailhead at road's end. A Northwest Forest Pass is required.

## Key points:
- **0.3** Alpine Lakes Wilderness boundary.
- **0.5** Bridge crossing Camp Robber Creek.
- **1.6** Side trail to Lake Dorothy.
- **3.7** Inlet stream crossing at south end of Lake Dorothy.

**The hike:** Lake Dorothy is one of the largest lakes in the Alpine Lakes Wilderness and one of the most accessible, reached via a 1.6-mile trail that is among the most popular in the Skykomish Ranger District. Day hikers tend to stop at Lake Dorothy, but the trail continues on around the lake and up to a chain of lakes including Bear, Deer, and Snoqualmie Lakes.

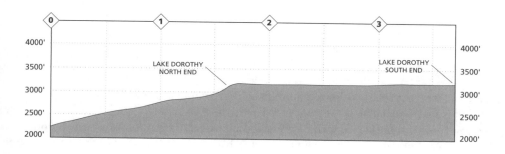

# Lake Dorothy

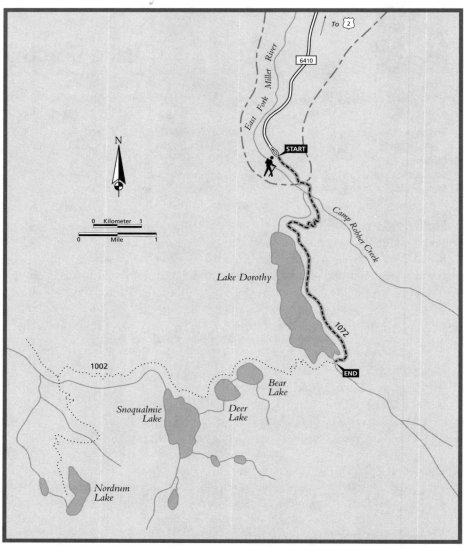

Register at the trailhead, then hike up through hemlock and silver fir forest, contouring well above the river. Deer ferns, vanilla leaf, and bunchberry line the trail. After passing the wilderness boundary marker, the trail leads closer above the river, where it splashes down granite slabs. The trail this far has its ups and downs but is mostly flat and easy going. At 0.5 mile the trail crosses Camp Robber Creek just above its confluence with East Fork Miller River, then climbs some away from the river but curves back soon, up staircase-like roots and rocks, switching back a

*Lake Dorothy*

few times, and at 1.6 miles reaches a fork. The trail on the right leads briefly to the brushy lakeshore, with limited views.

To appreciate the full size and splendor of Lake Dorothy, don't stop at the outlet stream, but continue on the main trail another 2.1 miles to the upper end of the lake. The trail climbs briefly to a wooded ridge, then contours some distance above the lakeshore for about a mile, crossing talus slopes and below slabby cliffs, leading through quiet hemlock and silver fir forest before dropping to the shoreline and continuing another mile to the inlet stream at the south end of the lake. Huckleberry, rhododendron, bead lily, trillium, and bunchberry line the trail; ducks paddle by, fish leap and splash.

Most make a day hike to Lake Dorothy, but there are many designated campsites along the trail, mostly above the lake's northeast shore, for those making an overnight trip. On summer weekends, the campsites fill up fast.

The first 1.5 miles of the trail to Lake Dorothy is scheduled for restoration work during 2002 and 2003, to repair erosion and hopefully fix the sagging footbridge.

**Options:** If you want to distance yourself from the crowds at Lake Dorothy, continue to Bear and Deer Lakes and Snoqualmie Lake. The round-trip to Snoqualmie Lake is about 15 miles, a good overnight trip. A 15-mile, one-way hike can be done from Lake Dorothy to the Taylor River trailhead with arranged transportation.

# Barclay Creek

**Overview:** *A muddy hike along Barclay Creek to Barclay Lake, below the towering cliffs of Baring Mountain.*

**Distance:** 4.4 miles round-trip.
**Difficulty:** Easy.
**Best season:** Late spring through early winter.
**Traffic:** Foot traffic only; heavy use.
**High point:** About 2,400 feet.

**Maps:** USGS Baring; Green Trails No. 143 (Monte Cristo).
**For more information:** USDA Forest Service, Skykomish Ranger District Office.

**Finding the trailhead:** Barclay Creek Trail 1055 is approached from Baring via Barclay Creek Road. Drive U.S. Highway 2 to the tiny "town" of Baring, about 5.6 miles east of the Index turnoff and 8 miles west of Skykomish. Turn north onto Barclay Creek Road (Forest Service Road 6024), just across the highway from Der Baring Store. Cross the railroad tracks and continue 4.2 miles to the trailhead at road's end. A Northwest Forest Pass is required.

# Barclay Creek

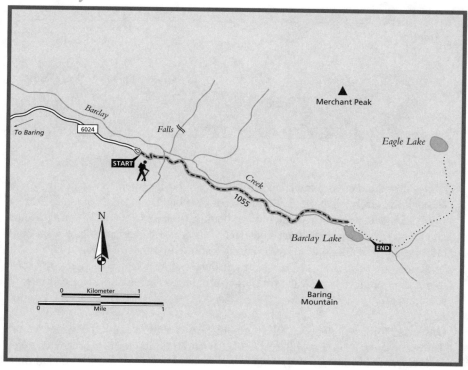

## Key points:
**1.6** The trail crosses Barclay Creek.
**2.2** Barclay Lake.

**The hike:** Barclay Creek Trail is not in the Alpine Lakes Wilderness, but it is one of the short, popular, easy lake hikes bordering the wilderness on the north, just across the highway, and deserves inclusion in this guide. The trail is often muddy and buggy, and leaves something to be desired in places, but is worthwhile, especially for views of the imposing 3,000-foot-high north face of Baring Mountain. Fortunately, the muddiest parts have been bridged over with puncheon boardwalk, making the trail more user-friendly. This hike suffers from its own popularity but is a good hike with little elevation gain and makes a memorable outing.

The trail descends briefly from the trailhead to the bottoms of Barclay Creek, then meanders up the canyon, through second-growth fir and hemlock forest, over and around roots and old stumps, through mud here and over sometimes slippery boardwalks there. Douglas maple and alder grow here and there, with salmonberry and devil's club in abundance. As the trail enters deeper forest, the brush gives way to bleeding heart, trillium, and a variety of ferns and mosses. At 1.6 miles, the trail

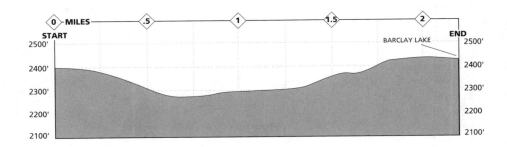

swings down and crosses the creek via a funky log bridge, then climbs briefly up the far bank and levels out again. In another 0.5 mile is Barclay Lake, elevation 2,422 feet. If the lake seems strangely quiet and foreboding, look up to see why. Baring Mountain seems to hang over the lake; 3,000 feet of vertical and overhanging rock shoot up into the sky. It's enough to make you dizzy just standing there looking at it.

There are several abused campsites at Barclay Lake. Come early if you expect to get one; the lake is crowded on sunny summer weekends. Bugs are bad in early season.

**Options:** Other guidebooks tell of a boot-beaten trail to Eagle Lake and Mount Townsend, just northeast of Barclay Lake. It's no trail; it's a rocky, brushy route up talus and over a wooded ridge, hard to find and follow if you haven't been led there before. You have to be willing to bushwhack through devil's club, slide alder, and maple to get to the lake. It's a chore but on the plus side you are nearly certain to escape the crowds (if not the bugs) and find solitude in the high country beyond Barclay Lake. There is a shorter way into Eagle Lake, via logging roads, but purists decry their use, preferring the miserable bushwhack from Barclay Lake.

# 60

# Heybrook Lookout

**Overview:** *A hike to a ridgetop lookout with impressive views of Mount Index and Gunn Peak.*

**Distance:** 2.0 miles round-trip.
**Difficulty:** Strenuous but short.
**Best season:** All year, except midwinter.
**Traffic:** Foot traffic only; moderate use.
**High point:** About 1,700 feet.

**Maps:** USGS Mount Index; Green Trails No. 142 (Index).
**For more information:** USDA Forest Service, Skykomish Ranger District Office.

**Finding the trailhead:** Heybrook Lookout Trail 1070 begins directly from U.S. Highway 2, just east of Index. Drive US 2 about 9.5 miles east from Gold Bar or 11.4 miles west from Skykomish. The trailhead is on the north side of the highway, almost directly across the highway from a sign that marks the Mount Baker–Snoqualmie National Forest boundary. There is a large parking area, usually uncrowded. This is a high car-prowl trailhead, so leave nothing of value in your car. A Northwest Forest Pass is required.

## Key points:
**0.8** Radio transmission tower.
**1.0** Heybrook Lookout.

**The hike:** Heybrook Lookout is an old fire lookout perched atop a forested ridge dividing the north and south forks of the Skykomish River. Small wonder a lookout tower was built here in the early 1930s, as it provides a panoramic view of the Skykomish River valleys and surrounding peaks, including the local giants, Index, Persis, Gunn, and Baring. The lookout was abandoned in the 1970s, but a new cabin was recently installed atop the lookout tower. Renovation work continues, and the lookout cabin may someday be available for overnight rental.

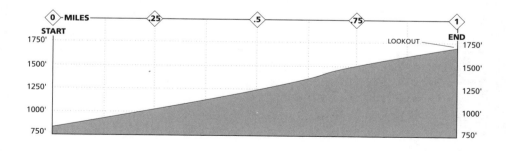

225

# Heybrook Lookout

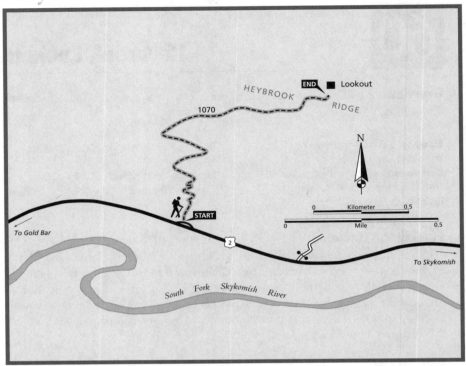

Heybrook Lookout Trail is all uphill from the first step, switching back gradually but persistently up second-growth forest slopes to the crest of Heybrook Ridge, then following the ridge past a radio transmission tower and up an old road grade to the tall lookout tower. This is a popular early- and late-season hike; its low elevation and easy accessibility from the highway make it possible to hike all year except midwinter or after heavy snowfall. It's a great hike to do on a clear winter day when snow has dusted the nearby peaks.

# 61

# Lake Serene

**Overview:** *A steep hike to a small alpine lake beneath the north face of Mount Index.*

**Distance:** 7.0 miles round-trip.
**Difficulty:** Strenuous.
**Best season:** Late spring through early winter.
**Traffic:** Foot traffic only; heavy use.
**High point:** About 2,500 feet.

**Maps:** USGS Mount Index; Green Trails No. 142 (Index).

**For more information:** USDA Forest Service, Skykomish Ranger District Office.

**Finding the trailhead:** Lake Serene Trail 1068 is located just off U.S. Highway 2, near Index. From the west, drive east through Sultan, Startup, and Gold Bar and continue just over 4 miles east from Zeke's Drive-In to Mount Index Road, on the right just before the bridge crossing the South Fork Skykomish River. From the east, follow US 2 about 0.4 mile west from Mount Index Cafe and take the first left turn past the bridge. This is a blind corner, so cross the oncoming lane with care. Follow Mount Index Road just over 0.2 mile and take the first right turn, which leads a hundred yards or so to the trailhead parking lot. A Northwest Forest Pass is required.

## Key points:
**1.5** Trail forks off from road.
**1.6** Bridal Veil Falls fork.
**1.8** Slabby waterfall.
**3.5** Lake Serene.

**The hike:** Lake Serene is a quiet lake nestled in a cirque beneath the north face of Mount Index. In the old days, the hike to Lake Serene was up a rugged trail beaten out by the boots of miners, climbers, and anglers, who knew the shortest distance between two points was a straight line. Hence, the old trail went pretty much

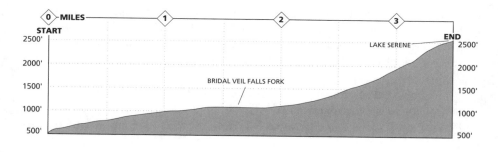

# Lake Serene

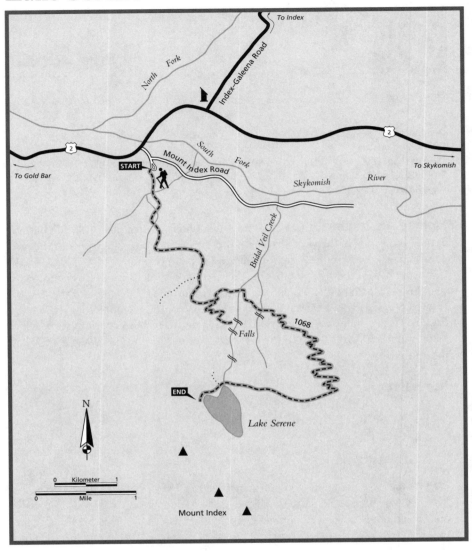

straight up, over roots and rocks, requiring a mix of route-finding and rock scrambling skills. But after several accidents on the "trail" (mostly unwise folks trying to get a closer look at Bridal Veil Falls), the Forest Service rerouted the trail, which still gets you to the lake and the falls but without the same sense of adventure as way back when.

The new Lake Serene Trail is longer than the old trail and takes longer to hike, but otherwise is a big improvement. The 3.5-mile trail follows an old road grade for the first 1.5 miles, gaining about 500 feet elevation. Some of the land bordering the road is private property, so please stay on the road. As you near "road's end," you can see and hear Bridal Veil Falls through the trees. Leave the road and follow the trail, which descends briefly into hemlock and maple forest, then climbs to a fork. Here you can venture a brief 0.5 mile up to Bridal Veil Falls, one of the scenic highlights of the Skykomish River valley, for an up-close look and feel of the falls. There are mining relics in the woods here, including several abandoned copper, gold, and silver mines and what's left of an old miner's cabin. However, steep cliffs make it unwise to wander off the trail here, especially to "get a better look at the falls," as several deceased hikers have found out the hard way. Foolish thrill seekers still leap or dash across the falls to prove their derring-do; wise hikers will stay back, mindful of the fact that most hikers killed on the old trail died right here. If you turn around at the falls, your hike will be 4.0 miles round-trip, but keep going, the best is yet to come.

Once down from the falls, continue on the main trail, which crosses a footbridge over Bridal Veil Creek just below the lower falls. Another waterfall, this one a smaller cascade over granite slabs and overhangs, is passed shortly along the trail. Pause here and gather yourself; the rest of the way is up. The trail starts climbing and seemingly never stops. The next 1.8 miles to the lake gains almost 1,500 feet elevation, switching back nearly all the way. The Forest Service put in stairs at the steepest sections; one source counted 700 steps on the trail. With all the switchbacks, the temptation exists to cut one or two. Please don't. Erosion is already apparent in a few places and will only get worse if hikers won't stay on the trail.

The trail climbs through fir and hemlock forest, passing several old-growth firs and Sitka spruces. The understory plants here are typical western Cascades—ferns, mosses, maples, devil's club—and a spectrum of wild berries—salmonberry, Cascades blueberry, red huckleberry, thimbleberry, and elderberry, to name a few. After the final switchback, the trail climbs more gradually, traversing up to and over the final ridge, with the first good views of Mount Index and great views down to the Skykomish River valley, then descending quickly to Lake Serene. It's a pretty lake, tucked in beneath the towering cliffs of Mount Index. A long footbridge leads across the outlet stream, where the trail forks a final time. The left fork leads along the lake shore, then up a talus slope and down to a polished rock slab at lake's edge, a popular spot to sit, rest, eat lunch, and snap photos. The right fork leads to a rocky viewpoint overlooking the Skykomish River valley, with views of Heybrook Lookout, Gunn Peak, the Monte Cristo peaks, and Glacier Peak, if you are fortunate enough to come on a clear day.

There are benches here and there along the lakeshore and a semiprivate pit toilet up a side trail just before you get to the lake. No camping or campfires are allowed within 0.3 mile of the lake; that pretty much means no camping, because there is hardly any level ground anywhere but near the lake's north shore, where camping is not allowed. The majority of hikers come and go; if you stay overnight, you could very well have the lake to yourself—except for the bugs, of course.

*New footbridge at Lake Serene*

**Options:** This is a good late fall and early winter hike, best done before snow gets too deep and avalanche danger climbs too high. The upper portion of the new trail crosses several avalanche slopes, so once the snow comes, it is not a good choice. In spring, visitors to Lake Serene often get to watch snow avalanches streaming off the north face of Mount Index. It's quite a spectacular show, until a big one cuts loose; then it's kind of scary. Rockfall off the cliffs is not uncommon, and rocks have been reported whizzing down the old trail. Although such occurrences are rare, hikers should be aware of these risks.

Many lake hikers like to make a loop around a lake, but the risk of avalanches, rockfall, and hidden cliffs make a loop around Lake Serene a bad idea. Likewise, hikers are advised to stay off the lake when snowed in or ice covered, as it is in winter and spring.

The old trail is still an option for those who remember where it goes. The Forest Service built the new trail to keep hikers off the old one and discourages use of the old trail. It is steep, rocky, slippery, brushy, and very difficult to follow these days.

# Wallace Falls

**Overview:** *A popular forest hike along the Wallace River to a series of waterfalls, including 265-foot Wallace Falls.*

**Distance:** 6.0 miles round-trip.
**Difficulty:** Mostly easy, strenuous near the falls.
**Best season:** All year.
**Traffic:** Foot and bicycle traffic; very heavy use.

**High point:** About 1,600 feet.
**Maps:** Green Trails No. 142 (Index).
**For more information:** Washington State Parks.

**Finding the trailhead:** Wallace Falls Trail is located just north of the town of Gold Bar. From whichever direction you come, follow U.S. Highway 2 to Gold Bar, about 14 miles east of Sultan and 37 miles west of Stevens Pass. Turn off the highway where the signs point the way to Wallace Falls Trail and follow First Street north 0.3 mile to an intersection just past the May Creek bridge. Turn right and follow May Creek Road 0.7 mile to a fork in the road. Take the left fork onto Ley Road, which leads 0.4 mile to the entrance to Wallace Falls State Park. Turn left and continue 0.3 mile past the gate to the trailhead. The parking lot is much too small for the many weekend hikers who visit, and parking is prohibited on the shoulders of the entry road and Ley Road, so if there's no parking, either wait patiently or find another hike. Tent camping is permitted in the small campground

# Wallace Falls

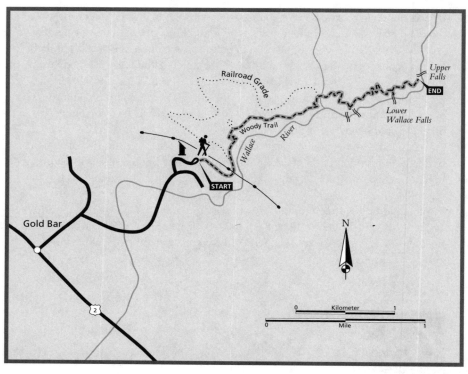

next to the parking lot; self-register and pay at the station. A Washington State Parks parking permit ($5.00 a day) is required.

## Key points:

- **0.4** Woody Trail junction.
- **0.5** Small Falls interpretive trail junction.
- **1.0** Railroad Grade cutoff trail junction.
- **1.1** Upper Woody Trail junction.
- **1.6** North Fork Wallace River bridge.
- **1.9** Lower Wallace Falls viewpoint and shelter.
- **2.3** Middle Wallace Falls viewpoint.
- **2.4** Middle Wallace Falls overlook.
- **3.0** Upper Wallace Falls viewpoint.

**The hike:** Wallace Falls is not within the Alpine Lakes Wilderness but is one of the landmarks of the Skykomish River valley. It is actually a series of falls, and the 265-foot lower waterfall is visible as you drive east on US 2 near Gold Bar. The falls are easily reached via a very popular, usually crowded, 2.4-mile trail. The trail is

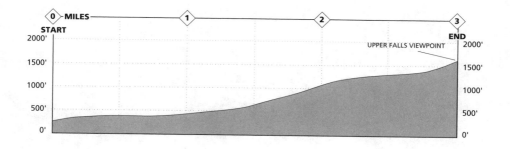

accessible year-round, whenever it isn't snow covered. It's a moderate hike, mostly flat and easy but occasionally steep and strenuous. This is a day-use area only; no overnight camping. Everybody and their dog hike to Wallace Falls and will probably choose the same day as you to hike to the falls. Join the crowds!

Sign in at the register and start hiking, or take a few minutes first to read the history of the park and look at a map and photos of the trail and falls. The hike begins along an old service road beneath noisy power lines but soon leaves the brushy clearcut and enters second-growth cedar and hemlock forest via an old railroad grade. The trail is flat and wide at first, following the road grade curving through the power line towers and into the woods, with no elevation gain. There are brief views of Mounts Baring, Index, and Persis, then you enter shady woods and the sound of cascading water. About 0.4 mile along and just 100 yards from where the trail leaves the power line swath, the trail forks. The left fork stays on the railroad grade and is the longer option (about 1 extra mile), best left to the mountain bikers and those willing to dodge them. Woody Trail, named for Sen. Frank Woody, leads off to the right alongside the Wallace River. Pass through a narrow gate (designed to keep mountain bikes out) and descend briefly, with views down to the noisy river, and cross a footbridge over a creek to a junction with Short Falls Logging Trail, a 0.1-mile interpretive loop describing logging activity in the early 1900s. The best feature of this side trail is Short Falls, a small waterfall visible from the trail. Continue on Woody Trail, past the 0.5-mile post and along the edge of the river on a flat, mossy shelf, then climb a bit, level out, then ascend a series of switchbacks to the ridge above, and cross a small stream to reach a well-placed bench. The trail continues along a shelf well above the river, climbing and dropping a bit through mossy second-growth forest and past many rotten old stumps, to the 1-mile post and a cutoff trail leading 500 feet to the Railroad Grade Trail. From the junction, the trail descends some distance, then climbs in spurts back uphill to a trail fork, where the Railroad Grade Trail reconnects with the Woody Trail, about 1.6 miles from the trailhead.

From the junction, drop down and cross a long footbridge over the North Fork Wallace River, which cascades noisily through mossy boulders. From the bridge, the trail climbs moderately, curving up a steep ridge slope. You'll see many long, slender tree trunks and limbs festooned with bright green mosses here, especially

*Wallace Falls*

noticeable during the rainy season. Cross an intermittent stream, switch back up the ravine, then contour eastward around the ridge, where the trail levels out and the sound of the river grows suddenly more urgent. Soon ahead is a picnic shelter at the edge of the Wallace River canyon, from where you get your first look at thundering Wallace Falls close above. A fenced-in viewpoint just down from the shelter provides a better view of the big falls and two smaller falls. Stay inside the fenced area, as steep cliffs drop off directly below. As side trails attest, many curious and adventuresome hikers have left the fenced area and scrambled down to the river or across to a rocky point. The views aren't any better, but you do stand a better chance of slipping and falling if you try it.

The trail continues from the shelter, up the flat ridge crest through shady fir forest. Hike through slender, bare tree trunks, needle-bearing branches high in the trees forming a canopy, shading out everything but ferns and little hemlocks rising up amid the shadows. The flat hiking ends abruptly at the foot of a steep slope, where the trail begins switching back. After a couple of long switchbacks, the trail reaches a cliff-side viewpoint overlooking Wallace Falls. Again, intrepid hikers and photographers have obviously skirted or surmounted the fence here for the sake of a better view—a bad idea. The trail continues up the steep slope, via several more switchbacks, then levels off and contours around a corner to the very top of the falls. You used to be able to scramble down to the rocks at the top of the falls, but they've fenced it in, which is just as well, because enough hikers have slipped into the creek and taken a ride down the falls already. One lucky hiker miraculously survived the plunge without serious injury; others have not been so lucky. Definitely keep your children and pets back from the edge and away from the creek here. If you slip on a wet or loose rock and fall into the creek, you will likely be swept away.

Most hikers stop here and head back, thinking they've reached the top of the falls, but there's more. An unmarked sign points to a trail that continues higher. This is the upper falls trail, which leads 0.6 mile upstream to a viewpoint opposite upper Wallace Falls, a 120-foot double waterfall. The trail is muddy in places and steep, climbing up roots and steps, but worth the extra effort. The upper falls are lovely, not as spectacular as the big falls but well worthy of the extra effort to get there.

Some park regulations to keep in mind: The park is open from 8:00 A.M. to dusk. Cars not removed before closing are impounded or at least locked in overnight. From the end of October to the beginning of April, the park is closed on Mondays and Tuesdays. Cutting switchbacks has led to serious erosion problems, so please stay on the trail. Pets must be leashed. Several dogs have fallen off cliffs and been swept over the falls, so it's for their own good to keep them on a leash. For that matter, many hikers have slipped on rocks and loose soil and have fallen down slopes and cliffs, so hikers, too, should stay on the trail and not climb over or around viewpoint railings. Also be sure to start back early enough to be off the trail by dusk. Several hikers have been injured falling off the trail while trying to hike out in the dark.

**Options:** Several old and new logging and mining roads crisscross the slopes above the falls. You can continue hiking from the upper falls viewpoint another 0.3 mile to reach a logging road, then turn left and hike 4 miles down to Wallace Lake. Logging activity was underway as this book was being researched, so hikers should avoid the lake for now.

Another option is to hike the railroad grade about 1.5 miles to a cutoff trail that leads 0.3 mile to an old road that climbs another 4.5 miles to Wallace Lake. This makes for a 12-mile round-trip, which is popular with mountain bikers and less so with hikers. There is a map at the trailhead showing all trails in the vicinity; many options are available.

# Appendix A: Passes and Permits

## Enchantment Lakes Wilderness Permit

Because of the overwhelming popularity of these areas, overnight hikers visiting the Enchantments, Nada and Snow Lakes (Hike 38), Colchuck and Stuart Lakes (Hike 39), and Eightmile Lakes and Lake Caroline (Hike 40) are required to obtain a Wilderness Permit prior to entry. The permit season is from June 15 to October 15, the prime season for visiting this area. Permits are available only from the Leavenworth Ranger Station, by mail or in person. Mail-in applications may be submitted on March 1; you may put them in the mail no sooner than February 21. In-person applications may be submitted after March 31. In-person reservations do not get priority, and reservations are filled at random starting on March 1, so you should mail in your application to improve your chances of getting a permit. The application process requires you to select three alternative entry dates and to choose the zone you want to camp in. If you get a permit, you may camp only in the designated zone. You may still day hike into another zone but may not camp anywhere except where your permit says you may camp. You must also submit an application fee equal to $3.00 per person, per day of your requested visit. So, if you are planning on taking a party of three into the Enchantments for four days, your fee would be $36.00. Permits must be picked up from the ranger station in person. Twenty-five percent of permits are given out in a daily lottery held at 7:45 A.M. each day at the Leavenworth Ranger Station.

Additional information is available from the Forest Service. Call the Leavenworth Ranger District Office for current permit information. If you ask nicely, they will mail you a permit application and informational brochure. Wilderness Permit information is also available on-line at www.fs.fed.us/r6/wenatchee.

## Northwest Forest Pass

Ostensibly to provide a "simpler, easier way to support recreation" in the national forests, the USDA Forest Service implemented its Northwest Forest Pass program in May 2000. This program, like its predecessor, the Trail Park Pass, requires zhikers and climbers using hiking trails and other designated "fee sites" in Pacific Northwest forests and parks to purchase and display a trailhead parking pass. An annual pass is $30.00; a daily pass is $5.00. The Northwest Forest Pass is available from the USDA Forest Service and many outdoor retail stores throughout the Pacific Northwest region. For more information about ordering or purchasing a Northwest Forest Pass, contact your nearest ranger district office, or log on to the Forest Service's Web site at www.fs.fed.us/r6/mbs/nwpass/order.htm or www.fs.fed/us/mbs/nwpass/vendors.htm.

## Other Parking Passes and Permits

Washington State Parks implemented a parking pass program effective January 1, 2003. Currently no other parking passes are required for hiking in the Alpine Lakes Wilderness and vicinity. The Washington Department of Natural Resources (DNR) does not have a permit system yet, but don't rule out the need to have a parking pass for DNR trails, including Mount Si and Little Si, in the future.

## Sno-Park Passes

The fees collected from the Winter Sports Sno-Park Permits pay for clearing and maintaining access to ski and snowshoe trailheads. A one-day pass costs $8.00 and allows one-day parking at all nonmotorized winter sports Sno-Parks, including special groomed trails areas. A seasonal pass costs $20.00 for a basic pass. Parking at special groomed trails parks costs $40.00 per season. One-day, seasonal, and groomed site permits are available at several state park locations or may be purchased through the mail from the state parks' winter recreation program headquarters (P.O. Box 42650, Olympia, WA 98504). One-day Sno-Park permits may be purchased on-line from December 15 through April 30. Permits may also be purchased in person (for an extra dollar to cover handling fees) from more than 125 different retailers throughout the state. Log onto www.parks.wa.gov/winter/vender.asp for a list of vendors.

# Appendix B: Local Contacts

Cle Elum Ranger District Office
803 West Second Street
Cle Elum, WA 98922
(509) 674–4411

Lake Wenatchee Ranger District Office
22976 Highway 207
Leavenworth, WA 98826
(509) 763–3103

Leavenworth Ranger District Office
600 Sherbourne Street
Leavenworth, WA 98826
(509) 548–6977

Mount Baker–Snoqualmie National Forest
21905 Sixty-fourth Avenue West
Mountlake Terrace, WA 98043
(425) 775–9702
http://www.fs.fed.us/r6/

North Bend Ranger District Office
42404 Southeast North Bend Way
North Bend, WA 98045
(425) 888–1421

Northwest Avalanche Center
7600 Sand Point Way NE
P.O. Box 15700
Seattle, WA 98115
(206) 526–6164

Outdoor Recreation Information Center
222 Yale Avenue North
Seattle, WA 98109-5429
(206) 470–4060

Skykomish Ranger District Office
74920 Northeast Stevens Pass Highway
P.O. Box 305
Skykomish, WA 98288
(360) 677–2414

Snoqualmie Pass Visitor Center
P.O. Box 17
Snoqualmie Pass, WA 98068
(425) 434–6111

Washington Department of Natural Resources
North Bend Office: (425) 888–1566

Washington State Parks
7150 Cleanwater Lane
P.O. Box 42650
Olympia, WA 98504-2650
(800) 452–5687
http://www.parks.wa.gov
Wallace Falls State Park: (360) 793–0420
Iron Horse State Park: (509) 656–2230

# Appendix C: Maps

Alpine Lakes Protection Society: The Alpine Lakes Wilderness and surrounding management unit, Central Cascade Mountains of Washington State (1:100,000-scale topographic map with trail data). Available from many outdoor retailers; somewhat outdated, but still useful.

USGS and Green Trails maps listed in each chapter. USGS maps may be viewed on-line via the Microsoft TerraServer at http://terraserver.microsoft.com; Green Trails maps may be previewed and ordered on-line at www.greentrails.com/.

The North Central Cascades pictorial map, published by Richard A. Pargeter, P.O. Box 844, Kent, WA 98032.

TOPO! Interactive Maps on CD-ROM: North Cascades, Mount Baker, and Surrounding Wilderness Areas; Seattle, Mount Rainier, and Central Cascades; and Olympic Peninsula, San Juan Islands, and Puget Sound. Preview on-line at www.topo.com/.

USDA Forest Service: Recreation Opportunity Guides (Skykomish, North Bend, and Cle Elum Ranger Districts); Trail Guide (Lake Wenatchee, Leavenworth, North Bend Ranger Districts); Mount Baker–Snoqualmie National Forest 1:168,959-scale Forest Visitor Map, 1988; Leavenworth Ranger District and Cle Elum Ranger District topo maps. These and other maps available at all Forest Service offices.

Washington State Department of Natural Resources (1:100,000-scale planimetric maps): Snoqualmie Pass, Wenatchee, Chelan and Skykomish River. Available from DNR Photo & Map Sales, 1111 Washington Street SE, P.O. Box 47031, Olympia, WA 98504, (360) 902–1234.

# Appendix D: Weather Information

Cascades Avalanche Report: (206) 526–6677.

Cascades Weather Report: (206) 464–2000 (category 9904 and 9908).

Washington State Department of Transportation Real Time Road and Weather Traveler Information ("Weather Beta"): http://test.wsdot.wa.gov/rwis/.

Washington Weather Web site: http://iwin.nws.noaa.gov/iwin/wa/wa.html.

# Appendix E: Selected References

Beckey, Fred. *Cascade Alpine Guide, Climbing and High Routes, 1: Columbia River to Stevens Pass.* 2d ed. Mountaineers, 1997.

——. *Cascade Alpine Guide, Climbing and High Routes, 2: Stevens Pass to Rainy Pass.* 2d ed. Mountaineers, 1989.

DeGraw, Robert. *Secrets of Si—The Mount Si Guidebook.* Ro-De Publishing, 1995.

Manning, Harvey, Ira Spring and Vicky Spring. *100 Hikes in Washington's Alpine Lakes.* 3d ed. Mountaineers, 2000.

Matthews, Daniel. *Cascade-Olympic Natural History.* 2d ed. Raven Editions, 1999.

Meyer, Kathleen. *How to Shit in the Woods.* Ten Speed Press, 1994.

Smoot, Jeff. *Climbing Washington's Mountains.* The Globe Pequot Press, 2001.

# About the Author

Jeff Smoot is a hiker, climber, and author based in Seattle, Washington. His other books include *Adventure Guide to Mount Rainier, Rock Climbing Washington,* and *Climbing Washington's Mountains.*

# American Hiking Society (AHS)

is the only national nonprofit organization dedicated to establishing, protecting, and maintaining America's foot trails—the same trails that are detailed in this book and around the country.

## As a trail user, your support of AHS is important to ensure trails are forever protected and continually maintained.

Join American Hiking Society today and you will learn about trails to hike, their history, their importance, and how you can help protect them. American Hiking Society is:

**A strong voice.** With increasing threats to our treasured open space and wilderness, American Hiking Society exists to actively represent hikers' interests to safeguard these areas. To protect the hiking experience, AHS affects federal legislation, shapes public lands policy, collaborates with grassroots trail organizations, and partners with federal land managers. As a member of AHS, feel assured that while you are hiking, AHS is going *the extra mile* for you.

**A helping hand.** With more than 200,000 miles of trails in America, AHS steps in with needed maintenance for trail managers and hiking clubs. Through our Volunteer Vacations program, we provide more than 24,000 hours of trail work annually to help preserve some of the most scenic places in America. As an AHS Member, you can take advantage of this opportunity to give back to the trails that you use and love.

**A critical resource.** Each year, crucial trail funding continually falls behind trail maintenance demands. Your favorite trail will **not** be next, thanks to American Hiking Society! Our National Trails Fund annually awards financial grants to local and regional hiking clubs for land acquisition, volunteer recruitment, and trail maintenance. As you support AHS, you share in the satisfaction of helping grassroots trails clubs nationwide.

Join TODAY!

American Hiking Society

1422 Fenwick Lane · Silver Spring, MD 20910 · (301) 565-6704
www.AmericanHiking.org · info@AmericanHiking.org